Passing Through

Passing Through

The Grand Junction Canal in West Hertfordshire 1791–1841

Fabian Hiscock

HERTFORDSHIRE PUBLICATIONS
an imprint of
University of Hertfordshire Press

First published in Great Britain in 2019 by
Hertfordshire Publications
an imprint of
University of Hertfordshire Press
College Lane
Hatfield
Hertfordshire
AL10 9AB

© Fabian Hiscock 2019

The right of Fabian Hiscock to be identified as the author of this work has been asserted by him in accordance with the Copyright, Designs and Patents Act 1988.

All rights reserved. No part of this book may be reproduced or utilised in any form or by any means, electronic or mechanical, including photocopying, recording or by any information storage and retrieval system, without permission in writing from the publisher.

British Library Cataloguing in Publication Data
A catalogue record for this book is available from the British Library

ISBN 978-1-912260-15-7

Design by Arthouse Publishing Solutions Ltd
Printed in Great Britain by Hobbs The Printers Ltd

To Alan Faulkner, whose research, writing, knowledge and love of the waterways has been an inspiration

Contents

List of illustrations	viii
Abbreviations	x
Author's preface	xi

1	Setting the scene	1
2	Hertfordshire in the early 1790s	28
3	The promise of the canal	59
4	The coming of the canal	71
5	The Grand Junction Canal in operation	95
6	West Hertfordshire in 1841	135
7	In conclusion	165

Appendices

A	Market town analysis: west Hertfordshire towns 1790–1840	171
B	Hertfordshire boat owners and operators 1802–41	175
C	Canal-related property in Hertfordshire *c.*1840	183
D	Sparrows Herne turnpike: simple financial model, 1786–1806	191

Bibliography	195
Index	207

Figures

1.1	A covered goods waggon, 1808	13
1.2	Canal boats at Paddington in the early nineteenth century	14
2.1	Map of the parishes of western Hertfordshire covered by the study	29
2.2	Map of the turnpike roads of west Hertfordshire, *c.* 1810	30
2.3	Batchworth Mill, *c.*1807	53
3.1	Canal boats on the Grand Junction Canal	63
4.1	The Grand Junction Canal through west Hertfordshire, *c.*1810	76
4.2	The diverted route of the Grand Junction Canal through Kings Langley, 1794	78
4.3	Section of the Grand Junction Canal as planned through its Tring summit	82
4.4	A typical canal labouring gang, *c.*1800	86
5.1	Pickfords route map, *c.*1832	96
5.2	A typical wharf complex, *c.*1828	100
5.3	A typical covered loading dock and horse boat, *c.*1828	101
5.4	Map showing Watford and its wharfs, *c.*1838	102
5.5	Map showing Rickmansworth and its wharfs, *c.*1830	104
5.6	The Grand Junction Canal at Two Waters and Boxmoor, *c.*1810	109
5.7	Batchworth Mills and the canal, *c.*1807	114
5.8	Paddington Basin, the terminus of the Grand Junction Canal, 1801	118
5.9	Gauging register entry – barge 'Fair Trader', 1802	120
5.10	Common Moor Lock, Croxley Green, 1824	123
5.11	Grand Junction Canal route variation at Apsley and Nash Mills, 1818	130
6.1	Map showing Tring and its wharfs, *c.*1839	144
6.2	Berkhamsted Town Lock, 1842	146
6.3	Map showing Berkhamsted and its wharfs, *c.*1840	148
6.4	Map showing Boxmoor (Hemel Hempstead) and its wharfs, *c.*1840	150
6.5	Railway bridge over the canal at Nash Mills, *c.* 1850	153
D-1	Sparrows Herne turnpike, individual toll gate takings, 1786–94	194
D-2	Sparrows Herne turnpike, individual toll gate takings, 1795–1805	194

Tables

2.1	Parish population data from 1801 census	44
4.1	Sample of land purchases and valuations in Hertfordshire, 1796/97	74
6.1	Population of Hertfordshire, 1801–41, compared to that of England	138
6.2	Populations and Growth Rates of west Herts parishes, 1801–41	138
6.3	Populations of parishes, 1801–41, compared with the population of Hertfordshire	139
A-1	Attributes of west Hertfordshire towns in the 1790s	173
A-2	Attributes of west Hertfordshire towns in 1841	174
B-1	West Hertfordshire boat owners, 1802–41	176
C-1	Canal-related property in Hertfordshire, c.1840	183
D-1	Sparrows Herne turnpike revenues, 1786–94	193
D-2	Sparrows Herne turnpike revenues, 1794–99	193
D-3	Sparrows Herne turnpike revenues, 1800–06	193
D-4	Sparrows Herne turnpike individual toll gate takings, 1786–94	194
D-5	Sparrows Herne turnpike individual toll gate takings, 1795–1805	194

Abbreviations

BL   British Library
CBS   Centre for Buckinghamshire Studies
DHT   Dacorum Heritage Trust
GJC   Grand Junction Canal
GJCCo   Grand Junction Canal Company
HALS   Hertfordshire Archives and Local Studies
LMA   London Metropolitan Archives
NWA   National Waterways Archives
TNA   The National Archives
UBD   *Universal British Directory*

Author's preface

This book has its roots in the history of the English canals, a central personal interest since I started boating in the early 1980s. The Grand Union Canal, as it has been named since 1929, has been my 'home waters' all that time, and Hertfordshire therefore part of the scenery. But it was not until I moved to the county in the late 1990s that the disparity between the economic importance of the canal from its earliest days and the extent to which it featured in accounts of Hertfordshire became clear. How, I wondered, could the canal have had over twenty-five of its original ninety-two miles in the county and yet have had so little apparent effect? If it really did have so little effect, why was that? And what effect did it really have?

I was able to examine these questions as a post-graduate research student at the University of Hertfordshire, work of which this book is a result. It started as an enquiry into the canal itself, but rapidly became at least as much a local history project covering social and economic life in the western part of the county. It draws on much of the work of the historians of the area and its towns as well as on those of the canal: they are listed in the bibliography and acknowledged with gratitude. It has been necessary to set boundaries around the task, so the chronological span is limited to the first fifty years of the canal's existence, and the geographical area to the western part of Hertfordshire. The study considers only the ten historic parishes through which the canal passes as well as, for comparison, the important town of St Albans. The centrepiece remains, however, the Grand Junction Canal.

The end date of 1841 was chosen because it brings together three important events. One was the coming of the London and Birmingham Railway, conceived in 1831, operational from 1837 and completed during 1838: by 1841 it was starting to have real economic effects. Another was the preparation of tithe maps and the granting of apportionments across most of the county, including the western parishes, between 1838 and 1844, which gave the opportunity to look at the canal's effect on land ownership and usage across the area. And the 1841 census, the first to record in detail the occupations of the population, has allowed some measure of understanding of the ways in which the industrial make-up of the area had changed during the period. By no means all those changes are attributable to the coming of the canal, however, and so it was appropriate to look first at what was happening elsewhere in England at this remarkably dynamic time – in economic, industrial and social development, in both towns and agriculture – as described in a vast body of work on the eighteenth century, the industrial revolution and the overall development of England during that time. I have hardly scratched the surface, but I hope it is enough to present something of the context.

This is not in any way a history of Hertfordshire, nor of any of its towns, nor of the Grand Junction Canal, and it should not be read as such. Rather, I have tried to describe what *sort* of place Hertfordshire was in the 1790s and again in the 1830s, and to present what happened – one set of circumstances relating to the social and economic conditions of the people of one small part of the country – in between. I hope that the information presented here will provide something new.

In doing this I have been supported and helped by many. The staff of the History Department of the University of Hertfordshire have been most generous in their help and advice, and I am greatly indebted to my unfailingly good-humoured supervisors, Dr Katrina Navickas and Dr Julie Moore, without whose forbearance, prompting and guidance this project would have run into the sand on several occasions. My colleague researchers were, and remain, very important for both their friendship and their academic example and advice. I have also been inspired by the work of my several friends working in both waterways and local history, whose work is acknowledged in the text; the members of the Rickmansworth Historical Society, St Albans and Hertfordshire Archaeological and Architectural Society ('the Arc and Arc'), Abbots Langley Local Historical Society, Tring Local History and Museums Society and the Railway and Canal Historical Society have been unstintingly helpful. I am grateful, too, to the staff and volunteers of Hertfordshire Archives and Local Studies, the National Waterways Archive, Watford Museum and Dacorum Heritage Trust, as well as the National Archive and the British Library: all have made me welcome and have guided my footsteps. Michael Stanyon, in his roles at both Frogmore Paper Mill and with the Hemel Hempstead Local History and Museum Society, and Mary Forsyth at Watford Museum have been especially generous with time and advice, while the work of Sarah Wroot on interpreting the physical space with her careful cartography has been very important.

The support of Dr Heather Falvey, chair of Rickmansworth Historical Society, has been exceptional. Her careful and probing reading of my drafts has allowed me to correct many errors, and I am deeply grateful for her time and her advice. My other readers, Jenny Barzilay and (again) Dr Julie Moore, have given generously of their time, and have caught several residual issues. I hope I have corrected them – the errors and omissions that remain, however, are wholly my own.

I owe a particular debt to Jane Housham, Sarah Elvins and Chris Dunkley of Hertfordshire Publications, who have guided me through the process with wonderful patience and care. But my special thanks go to my wife Pat, without whose prompting and encouragement little (not least the boating) would have been started, let alone finished.

Chapter 1
Setting the scene

In the 1790s Georgian Britain was changing at a great pace. War went hand in hand with technological and economic change to affect great swathes of the growing population, and the impact was profound across the whole country and in every aspect of life. This book is concerned, however, with one small area of England over one short period, and looks at the effect of just one of the many economic innovations of the time: the area is western Hertfordshire, the period is from 1791 to 1841, and the innovation is the Grand Junction Canal.

But, having set those limits, the broader picture, the context in which the detail is set, should first be considered. The area being studied here was neither unique nor detached: it was an integral part of the country, and what was happening elsewhere had an impact here that needs to be understood. Hertfordshire has been famously characterised as 'a county of small towns'; but it was also an agrarian county. It had some industry – and it was close to, and much affected by, the great metropolis of London.[1] Like the rest of the country, it changed during the fifty years of this study, and we will try to chart how it changed: but by no means all of the changes are due to the coming of the canal, and we should look first at what was happening elsewhere in England at this remarkably dynamic time – in economic, industrial and social development, and in both towns and the countryside around them.

Agriculture in late eighteenth-century England
At the end of the eighteenth century notable features of English agriculture included strong tenant–landlord relationships, an easy exchange of influences between town and countryside that provided both capital and a commercial

---

1   T. Slater and N. Goose (eds), *A county of small towns* (Hatfield, 2008); Nigel Agar, *Behind the plough* (Hatfield, 2005); William Branch Johnson, *The industrial archaeology of Hertfordshire* (Newton Abbot, 1970).

outlook to farming, and a technologically innovative group of farmers and landowners. It was also relatively difficult to break up family estates but easy to invest in them, so they tended to remain commercially viable; and the owners of the land generally recognised that it should be used for production and not simply to demonstrate their wealth and prestige. The result was that English farming was able to respond to its market in terms of both farm size and the use of farming techniques best suited to the area. The market was highly volatile and under increasing pressure from a growing population, and farming became particularly flexible and productive in response.[2]

Until about 1775 England had been self-sufficient in the products required to feed the nation, and indeed was exporting in most years to mainland Europe. The Corn Laws had been in place for many years, controlling the flow of grain exports and ensuring that the home market had preference. They worked, particularly after 1773, by paying a bounty to exporters when stocks were high and prices low, and by reducing the import duty when stocks were low, especially after a poor harvest, and prices high. The aspiration was to balance the interests of consumer and farmer by keeping prices relatively stable, and while the overall effect was probably to raise prices somewhat, they did ensure that the home market was supplied with (principally) wheat in most years – a vital consideration, since bread formed the staple diet to a remarkable degree.[3]

Until the early eighteenth century local requirements had to be met locally, with a mixed system of farming in most areas and consumption limited to what was available. Little could be done to change the conditions for farming: naturally poor soils, heavy clays and rich loams remained so, with the types of farming practised on them changing little and serving a largely local market.[4] But as techniques improved there was an increasing degree of regional specialisation of product and a widening of markets, helped by transport improvements that allowed produce to be moved more easily from source to market and thus production to concentrate on what best suited the conditions. Thus, in very broad terms, arable crops came to be found south and east of a line roughly between Peterborough and Worcester, with pastoral farming to the north and west and sheep very important in, for example, Yorkshire: in the sandy and dry East Anglian conditions, the fens having been drained from the seventeenth century, wheat was a major crop.[5] Over time, light-soil farming in the south and east came to have

---

2   J.D. Chambers and G.E. Mingay, *The agricultural revolution* (London, 1978), pp. 200–2. Note that the situation in Scotland and Ireland was different, and is not included in this analysis.
3   M.J. Daunton, *Progress and poverty* (Oxford, 1995), pp. 546, 547.
4   Daunton, *Progress and poverty*, pp. 26, 27.
5   G.M. Trevelyan, *English social history volume three: the eighteenth century* (Cambridge,

distinct advantages over that on the wet and heavy soils of the Midlands and north. The addition of sheep dung to the thin soils made them more suitable for arable farming, with wheat for bread, oats for horse feed and barley for malting becoming important crops. The heavy soils further north supported a different mix, but all types of farming were able to increase their output and so meet the growing demand. Techniques were improving and organisation, not least in marketing and trading, developing quickly: farming was becoming steadily more efficient, more so in some regions than others, but nonetheless measurably so everywhere.

There was, however, a steadily emerging problem in most parts of the country. The population was increasing in both countryside and towns, but the amount of agricultural work available to the rural inhabitants was not keeping pace: more efficient farming was producing more but needed relatively fewer people to do so. The overall number employed increased, certainly, but the population as a whole was growing more quickly. The resulting surplus population responded in quite different ways in different parts of the country, and the interaction of industry and agriculture is important for this study. But it was inevitable that those dependent on agricultural work, especially in the south, would have their incomes severely restricted, and rural poverty became both widespread and endemic.[6]

The development of industry
Historians do not agree over the nature of the relationship between the rise of industry and the movement of people. It is, however, undeniable that industrial growth had already started in the Midlands and north in the early eighteenth century, before the discovery of coal in large quantities, the development of the factory or 'mill' and the introduction of machinery for mass production. Much early manufacturing, such as spinning thread, weaving cloth, knitting garments or making nails, was done in the home of the artisan. This domestic or proto-industry was based on the family, but its practitioners worked in mutually supportive groups from an early stage, so that they could be serviced easily by both suppliers and purchasers. Growth in this 'domestic system of manufactures' was rapid, and a high proportion of those engaged in manufacturing worked in this way.[7] Next to them, and sometimes emerging from them, were people engaged in new and differently organised industries based on and making real the scientific and technological

---

    1950), pp. 82, 83.
6 Pamela Horn, *The rural world* (London, 1980), pp. 32–4.
7 Daunton, *Progress and poverty*, pp. 127, 150.

development emerging across Europe.⁸ But even then traditional and new industries co-existed for many years; they were to an extent interdependent, with traditional hand-crafts filling in the gaps where mechanised production was unable to provide what was required or where it needed intermediate materials for its process. Productivity might be improved by small manufacturers changing their materials, for example, or by having women or children use simple hand tools by rote, or by responding particularly quickly to the demands of their customer. This was 'flexible specialisation' rather than 'mass production', and its selection depended partly on the nature of the target market: mass production produced standardised goods for a large market driven by a range of incomes (as, even at this time, in the USA), while flexible production produced high-value goods for a sizeable wealthy class (as in France). Eighteenth-century Britain had some of each of these population groups, but also a growing middle class of professionals in the towns and a large population of agricultural and industrial workers in countryside and town respectively.⁹ But many of the traditional industries, usually hand-crafts, were unable to increase their productivity either by specialisation or by the application of power, especially when serving only a local market, and they made, in the end, a very limited contribution to economic growth during the century. We will see later how Hertfordshire's proto-industry, mainly in straw plait and hat-making, developed and held its own at this time: but no other industry did so in the county.

Some English 'cottage industries' nonetheless produced goods for a truly national and international market: an example is Pennine cloth, centred on Leeds, where travelling merchants, London-facing buyers for both export and the London market and internationally commissioned merchants for overseas markets all came to buy. The spinning of yarn, weaving of fabrics and making of hosiery could be and were done in homes with hand-powered machinery: so was even the forging of metal goods in the West Midlands and Sheffield, and much of the population of these places was engaged in this way. Some historians have suggested that 'urban merchants' consciously promoted such industry in areas, often the northern uplands, with surplus low-wage populations and low agricultural productivity, although that does not fully explain why some areas of this sort – Hertfordshire was arguably one – failed to attract manufacturing industry at all.¹⁰ But it does seem that the skilled artisan 'domestic' producer in these areas came under the control

---

8   A.E. Musson and Eric Robinson, *Science and technology in the Industrial Revolution* (Manchester, 1969), pp. 60–4.
9   Daunton, *Progress and poverty*, pp. 133, 134.
10 Daunton, *Progress and poverty*, p. 150.

of the merchant buying his goods, who was able to control output by limiting the raw materials he provided ('put out') to match the production for which he was willing to pay. The artisan producing for his own customers became a wage labourer working for others, and the logistical problems of managing the putting-out process began to be solved by collecting the workers together into one building (a manufactory, or 'factory') rather than taking the work to them piecemeal.[11] There were, of course, several lowland areas with manufacturing industries, and there is reason to think that the type of agriculture was more relevant to the process of industrialisation than its location: the rhythms of pastoral work, daily rather than seasonal, were more amenable to part-time industry than those of arable, and part-time or by-employment of farmers and their workers became important in the development of manufacturing.[12] The extent of agricultural enclosure, the limitations imposed by the community on movement and settlement and the extent of domination by one landowner were also relevant, and we will see in more detail the extent to which Hertfordshire was affected by these factors.

There was, of course, a great deal of purely local industry in the most rural of settlements. Even in the late eighteenth century the chief 'makers' of implements and tools were still the village blacksmith and the carpenter. Most village blacksmiths were primarily 'shoeing smiths', but they also made a great range of tools. Ploughwrights were specialists to some degree, but they too made other items – and plough-making required contributions from carpenter and wheelwright, although not all villages had all three. A good wooden plough was probably preferred to a poor iron-tipped one, although in flinty Hertfordshire this may not have been the case – with good reason. Iron could be expensive and difficult to get in the late eighteenth century: it was in shortage nationally, and most iron for agriculture was wanted in areas remote from its production, so there was a great deal of reuse and recycling.[13] But by 1800 supplies had begun to improve and cheapen – and, as we shall see, the canals had a role in this.

New technology was not as important to the agrarian economy as new ideas and institutions – the role of iron we have seen, but steam power and factories were almost irrelevant to farming, although coal or coke were becoming the standard heating fuel in most malthouses, breweries and forges in the early nineteenth century as canals helped to distribute it to them. In any case, steam power was not introduced quickly where water or

---

11   Daunton, *Progress and poverty*, p. 151.
12   Daunton, *Progress and poverty*, p. 163.
13   E.J.T Collins, 'The agricultural servicing and processing industries', in Mingay (ed.), *Agrarian history vol. VI*, p. 523.

horse power were adequate, and both remained important in many areas, including Hertfordshire. Water power was much more important, nationally, for much longer than is often recognised. Steam power gained in the long run, but it *was* a long run, and the need for water mills in many industries continued well into the nineteenth century.[14] The arrival of the large 'county iron foundry' in the first quarter of the nineteenth century formed the basis of agricultural engineering in several areas, notably East Anglia, but that never took off in Hertfordshire, although later the businesses of Cranstone in Hemel Hempstead and Tidcombe in Watford emerged in quite different industries.[15] Elsewhere, smaller iron foundries and ironmongers emerged about this time, using pig iron from major industrial centres to make castings of many sorts, and it was these small market town foundries, not village blacksmiths, that were the starting point of most engineering concerns – blacksmiths became agents and repairers rather than producers. Agricultural machinery, initially from 1794 the threshing machine and then broadening rapidly, was developed to replace labour that had already been removed, largely by war with France. Such machines were initially static, multi-purpose and built by millwrights, although portable threshing machines became popular in the south. Many but not all of the wartime makers of threshing machines disappeared after the war, however, and the drive for agricultural investment faded quickly with the return of surplus labour: blacksmith and foundry continued without necessarily becoming machine builders, moving later into industries other than agriculture, such as casting railway track chairs. Thus it was that manufacturing industry did not appear on any great scale in agricultural areas such as Hertfordshire.

Ownership of the land

There were a few hundred great landowners scattered across the country, and these men controlled parliament and dominated government. About half the land in the country was owned by a much larger group of country gentlemen, a few of whom came to hold high office: but power still lay with the 'landed interest' of the aristocracy.[16] There developed during the eighteenth century, especially but not only near London, a very strong urge, and the means, for the growing middle classes to cement their place

---

14 Richard Byrom, *William Fairbairn: the experimental engineer* (Market Drayton, 2016), pp. 70–4; Musson and Robinson, *Science and technology*, pp. 67–71; Peter Mathias, *The brewing industry in England 1760–1830* (Cambridge, 1959), p. 81.

15 Collins, 'Agricultural servicing and processing industries', p. 523; Barrie Trinder, '18th- and 19th-century market town industry: an analytical model', *Industrial Archaeology Review*, 24.2 (2002), pp. 81–3.

16 Chambers and Mingay, *The agricultural revolution*, p. 17.

in society by owning a reasonable estate – even Admiral Nelson, at the height of his national fame and already holding a peerage, felt obliged to buy over 150 acres at Merton between 1801 and 1803 in his quest for the full recognition that only 'property' bestowed[17] – and some of this land was taken out of agricultural use to lay out a park or garden.[18] But more often farmers were able to share the costs and risks of farming with a progressive and considerate landowner: the system at its best – not, of course, working in every case – saw the landlord providing the infrastructure of the farm buildings and land, the farmer the stock and working capital as well as expertise and skill, and the two working together.

Some land was still held by 'copyhold' – 'owned' for practical purposes, but with links, usually largely ceremonial, to the historic manorial court.[19] Most, however, was 'freehold', or was simply rented on long or short leases from a landowner. Locally, county landowners looked after their own estates and became justices of the peace, maintaining law and order and the local regulatory framework, including dealing with the Poor Law, markets and fairs, weights and measures, and roads and bridges – matters that affected the daily lives of people much more than most acts of parliament. Many landowners took a keen interest in the farming activities on their land: while the 'great' were more inclined to take their rent and the proceeds of the sale of timber and mining rights and then pursue other interests, plenty of others were much more engaged. Some, tending to the lower end of the social scale, actively farmed their own land, often renting additional space from one or more neighbouring estates.[20] Most farmers were tenants, although some also owned part of the land they farmed, while there was a very large number of owners of small holdings, sometimes single plots or houses, which they occupied on their own account or rented out. As we will see, a large number of Hertfordshire's estates were medium-sized, which had implications for the engagement of their owners in their parishes.[21] We will return briefly in Chapter 2 to the role of the East India Company's 'nabobs', who bought estates across the country but especially near London and the Company's Leadenhall Street headquarters.[22]

---

17 John Sugden, *Nelson: the sword of Albion* (London, 2014), p. 525; Chambers and Mingay, *The agricultural revolution*, pp. 19, 21.

18 Tom Williamson, 'Gardens and industry: the landscape of the Gade Valley in the 19th century', in Deborah Spring (ed.), *Hertfordshire garden history* (Hatfield, 2012), pp. 127, 128.

19 Chambers's *Encyclopaedia vol. III* (London, 1868), pp. 228, 229.

20 Chambers and Mingay, *The agricultural revolution*, p. 18.

21 Anne Rowe and Tom Williamson, *Hertfordshire: a landscape history* (Hatfield, 2013), pp. 232, 233.

22 Margot Finn and Kate Smith, *The East India Company at home, 1757–1857* (London,

In many parts of the country the land was worked in large 'open' fields, with tenants renting strips, sometimes widely separated, sometimes alongside each other.[23] As the eighteenth century wore on it was increasingly accepted that this was not an efficient way of farming, and these open fields were often 'enclosed' into blocks by the exchange of strips between owners. This might be done informally by agreement between the parties, but on many occasions it was formalised by act of parliament, dealing with whole parishes and worked out by appointed Commissioners. This caused problems for some, notably the poor, as we will see: but it was a factor in the increasing efficiency of farming. Enclosure, unsurprisingly, increased the value of the land. In 1804 Arthur Young estimated that the rent, typically then about 15s per acre before enclosure, could be about 5s greater if enclosed, while it has been estimated that the rental return on the investment in enclosure was over 15 per cent, well above that from the available investment funds or stocks (3 per cent), private lending (5 to 6 per cent) or land purchase (5 to 6 per cent), although it will have been accompanied by liability for higher poor rates.[24] Higher rents did, however, encourage landowners to treat enclosure as a financial investment – it has been observed that 'land is an illiquid asset', and opportunities to capitalise on it will have been keenly sought by some.[25] Bearing in mind that there was no true national 'land market', a typical sale value of land after enclosure was about £25 to £30 per acre, and we will see how canal companies dealt with those valuations.[26]

The 'parish' was not only an ecclesiastical entity – from the sixteenth century it was, next to the borough, also the unit of local government across much of England. The number of landowners in a parish made a difference to the way in which the parish administration worked. In an 'open' parish with several landowners no one had exclusive control over the daily lives of the parishioners and the presence or absence of individual landowners was less important – when they were resident elsewhere the dominant influence might lie with the vicar or rector, or even the various farmers, but that

---

2018), pp. 1–12. The term 'nabob' described an East India Company official who had lived in India, amassing a large fortune and a taste for Asian luxuries, practices and indeed women. They were increasingly caricatured as corrupt on the basis of their use of their Company fortunes to acquire both country estates and parliamentary seats (pp. 7, 8).

23   Agar, *Behind the plough*, p. 18; Chambers and Mingay, *The agricultural revolution*, p. 78.
24   Chambers and Mingay, *The agricultural revolution*, p. 84; Arthur Young, *General view of the agriculture of Hertfordshire* (London, 1804; reprinted Newton Abbot, 1971), p. 44.
25   J.R. Ward, *The finance of canal building in eighteenth century England* (Oxford, 1974), pp. 143, 153, 156.
26   Chambers and Mingay, *The agricultural revolution*, p. 89; F.M.L Thompson, 'The land market in the nineteenth century', in Mingay, *Agrarian history vol. VI*, pp. 31–4.

influence was weaker. There was a greater propensity for migration both in and out of the parish, and often a more sympathetic approach to poor relief and the provision of housing than in 'closed' parishes, where the land was owned by a single person who often completely dominated the life of the inhabitants. All the parishes considered in this study, and most of those of Hertfordshire, were 'open', with a significant number of property owners – Tring, for example, had 160 when it was enclosed in 1799.

The financial importance of transport
A crucial feature of developing industry and commerce in the eighteenth century was the control of costs. The cost of production, embracing raw materials, premises, processes and labour, was important: but so was the cost of transporting both materials and products, and of selling the products. It can be argued that reducing the cost of transport and increasing its capacity released more potential for economic growth than did controlling the costs of production. Increased transport capacity allowed both agricultural and industrial goods to be exchanged more cheaply and quickly, so encouraging areas to specialise in those goods to which they were best suited: what they could not grow or make could come from elsewhere. Low transport costs allowed low-cost producers to serve a larger area, threatening the competing but local high-cost producer and potentially providing goods to communities otherwise unable to afford them. This was to have a significant effect on some elements of Hertfordshire's economy, but, as we shall see, it did not itself generate economic resources. Technological innovation affected the volume of production and made the headlines, but was far from the only factor in industrial success – transport was an essential element.[27]

While the manufacturing industry that developed in the last quarter of the eighteenth century needed relatively little capital – a mill owner could often borrow what he needed – transport systems needed a great deal, especially when constructed on a national scale, such as a canal or a dock in a sea port or, later, a railway. These therefore needed and had to attract major investment, which added greatly to the overall costs of national industrialisation.[28] In England much of this investment was by the 'landed' or the professional classes, albeit often in only small amounts. As the canals developed, the bringing together of investors in a joint-stock company released a considerable amount of capital, although still not usually enough

---

27 Philip Bagwell and Peter Lyth, *Transport in Britain* (London, 2002), pp. xi, xii; Daunton, *Progress and poverty*, pp. 2, 285–317; Charles Hadfield, *British canals* (Newton Abbot, 1974), p. 20.
28 Daunton, *Progress and poverty*, p. 286.

to complete a project in the face of escalating costs, and allowed a return to both the investors in and the users of the waterway, which typically connected or served centres of population and therefore of wealth.[29] But relatively few industrialists invested in them after the initial surge of the 1760s and 1770s, preferring to keep their capital to invest in their own business while the public or the wealthy invested in canals – landowners could in any case mortgage their estates to raise much more money than industrialists could, as demonstrated by the duke of Bridgewater at the start of the Canal Age. Nevertheless, the range of private investors was considerable.[30] Investors wanted their own profits: but the 'social savings', the indirect benefits to the population at large, were often higher, coming from the lower cost of transport and the reduced need for merchants to hold large stocks of goods, so that what there was went further – it was more available and more affordable. Rural canals rarely produced either individual or social savings – they carried insufficient value as opposed to volume of trade to justify the investment, and we see the same effect in ports, with prosperous industrial Liverpool contrasting strongly with less responsive Bristol – but the industry-facing canals serving cities and larger towns did much better.[31] This was to be relevant later in the economic history of Hertfordshire.

The importance of roads should not be overlooked, and they can be seen as a significant complement to water transport; indeed, road transport made a very important contribution to the development of the economy from at least the start of the eighteenth century and probably before, with the long-distance specialist carrier a key figure in the commerce of the time.[32] Goods, materials and products, including grain, were routinely collected and taken by road to their market or customer, or perhaps to a port or river (later a canal) wharf to be moved on by water. But until turnpikes were developed road transport attracted no investment and carriers incurred little direct cost, as there were few, if any, improvements and users did not pay to maintain or use the road – the indirect cost to them was in delay and vehicle damage caused

---

29 Bagwell and Lyth, *Transport in Britain*, pp. 7, 8; Hadfield, *The canal age* (Newton Abbot, 1968), pp. 34–9.
30 Daunton, *Progress and poverty*, p. 290; Hadfield, *Canal age*, pp. 27–36; Ward, *Finance*, pp. 126–42.
31 Hadfield, *The canals of south and southeast England* (Newton Abbot, 1969), pp. 19, 20, 28; Daunton, *Progress and poverty*, p. 291.
32 Daunton, *Progress and poverty*, p. 297; Philip Bagwell, *The transport revolution from 1770* (London, 1974), pp. 55–9; Hadfield, *British canals*, p. 118; Anthony Burton, *The canal builders* (Cleobury Mortimer, 1993), pp. 61–3; Dorian Gerhold, *Road transport before the railways* (Cambridge, 1993), pp. 1–20.

by the poor roads.[33] By far the greatest cost of road transport was feed for the draught animals, with their purchase and that of the vehicles some way behind.[34] So the unit cost of road transport might have been much less than of water, especially if items being transported were small and valuable, and the cost would have been even less important if speed over a short distance was required. In any case some cargoes survived road transport better than they did water, especially perishables that otherwise would have had to go by sea.[35] Agriculture itself was better suited to wheeled vehicles, which could cover a wide area even without roads, than to boats, which were constrained to the linear waterway. This was important in places such as Hertfordshire, where producers were close to their urban market: if a farmer had to load a cart or waggon to get his produce from fields covering several hundred acres to a canal or river wharf he might as well take it straight to market, while a factory or mill covering even twenty acres would be perfectly well served by a single canal arm, wharf or basin with boats loaded by cart and crane.[36] For all these reasons road transport was, and remained, important, and investment in it could have a considerable impact on a local economy.

How was this done? Few roads were initially long-distance. Maintenance from the late sixteenth century had been carried out by parishes, with two unpaid surveyors of highways elected each year to supervise 'statute labour' supplied by the parishioners according to successive acts of parliament.[37] Quarter sessions magistrates were empowered to compel the work, and money was raised by the introduction of commutation payments in place of labour, and from 1662 by the addition of a dedicated rate.[38] This was satisfactory only as long as the roads connected local farms and villages to market towns: but as long-distance freight traffic built up in the late seventeenth century, and as the roads became more heavily used by coal mines or iron works in the eighteenth, it became harder to justify local people bearing the whole burden of road maintenance from which they took little benefit but strangers a great deal.[39] Nor did the system generate new, or even improved, roads.

---

33 Bagwell and Lyth, *Transport in Britain*, p. 45.
34 Gerhold, *Road transport*, pp. 127–48.
35 Daunton, *Progress and poverty*, pp. 297–8.
36 E.A. Wrigley, *The path to sustained growth* (Cambridge, 2016), p. 136; Daunton, *Progress and poverty*, p. 298.
37 Highways Acts 1555 (2 & 3 Ph. & Mary c.8) and 1562 (5 Eliz.I c.13); Bagwell, *Transport revolution*, p. 36.
38 Highways Act 1662 (14 Car.2 c.6).
39 Daunton, *Progress and poverty*, p. 299.

The introduction of turnpikes from 1663, initially on the main routes out of London, began to address this. These roads, which reached a peak between 1751 and 1772, were authorised by acts of parliament to be maintained by trusts from tolls charged for their use.[40] Funded initially by borrowing and so encumbered by debt, turnpike trusts were sometimes criticised for being unaccountable and for being more interested in raising tolls than with improving the road. This may well have been due to the need to deal with debt, but many of the criticisms were unjustified, at least as far as personal gain was concerned, it being limited by the legislation.[41] The real problem was a lack of overall or centralised control, certainly until the London roads were brought together in 1826. An attempt to do this nationally during the 1830s failed, but administration had already become steadily more professional, and improvers such as the McAdams were heavily and widely engaged. In the period 1834–38 70 per cent of the national turnpike revenue went on repairs.[42] But trusts still had to raise a great deal of capital, by borrowing – again, more from local landowners than from the industrialists who might have benefited, but with small investors involved as well – or by mortgage of the tolls.[43] Strong factors in the initial funding of a turnpike therefore included the prosperity of the local economy, which generated some of the need for it and the toll income to pay for it, and the willingness of local people to invest in it. But turnpikes were steady performers as investments returning about 5 per cent, and much less vulnerable than canals and later railways to speculative mania and unrealistic expectations.

This investment in roads allowed pack horses to be replaced by carts and waggons, and for these to get bigger and, along with coaches, faster, so giving considerable savings to industry. Passenger transport, which is not further addressed in this work, evolved through stage coach and mail coach development from the seventeenth century, with a very sophisticated network of contractors, coachbuilders, inns and horse suppliers that reduced the time between, for example, London and Bristol from forty hours in 1750 to twelve hours in 1811.[44] More importantly for this study, freight charges fell during

---

40 For full accounts of the history of English turnpike roads see in particular W. Albert, *The turnpike road system in England 1663–1840* (Cambridge, 1972); Dan Bogard, 'The turnpike trusts of England and Wales', in L. Shaw-Taylor, D. Bogart and M. Satchell (eds), *The online historical atlas of transport, urbanization and economic development in England and Wales c.1680–1911* <https://www.campop.geog.cam.ac.uk/research/projects/transport/onlineatlas/>, accessed 1 February 2019.

41 Daunton, *Progress and poverty*, p. 300.

42 Daunton, *Progress and poverty*, p. 304; Albert, *Turnpike road system*, p. 238.

43 Daunton, *Progress and poverty*, pp. 304–5.

44 Daunton, *Progress and poverty*, p. 306.

Figure 1.1. This 1808 engraving of a broad-wheeled waggon and its team is plate 38 in W.H. Pyne's *Costume of Great Britain* (Guildhall Library, City of London). The great size of these waggons, with the waggoner driving the team from his pony and the goods stacked to the very top of the vehicle, can be clearly seen. Each might have a payload as great as five tons, and passengers as well as goods could sometimes be carried.

the eighteenth century, with better roads enabling fewer horses to haul more goods more quickly. Local services were provided by 'private' carriers – usually farmers with spare capacity – who could charge whatever they could get for the casual jobs they took on. It was the 'common' carriers, required by statute to take any job they were offered at a reasonable charge that could be set by the justices, who provided the regular, long-distance services. They might be large concerns, or might have but a single waggon; but all had to follow the rules, and they provided a 'dense network' of carrier services.[45]

But the biggest problem on the roads was capacity. In the eighteenth century all long-distance haulage was by waggon carrying perhaps six tons but often less (Figure 1.1). The number of services listed from London – one waggon at a time drawn by at least four horses and driven usually, but not always, by one man – increased steadily from 348 a week in 1690 to 565 in 1798.[46] This number was to further increase greatly between 1790 and 1838, when about a thousand waggons entered and left London weekly,[47] and the overall volume actually carried grew considerably, largely because it became

---

45 Albert, *Turnpike road system*, pp. 169–83.
46 Bagwell, *Transport revolution*, p. 57; Daunton, *Progress and poverty*, p. 307.
47 Gerhold, *Road transport*, p. 1.

Figure 1.2. Canal boats at Paddington, the London terminus of the Grand Junction Canal (LMA, City of London Collage: 304138). Although showing a scene of about 1828, these boats had not changed since the 1790s, and their carrying capacity (about twenty-five tons) compared with that of the road waggon, is clear. A three-man crew seems to have been the standard.

increasingly diverse as the industrial towns grew. The capacity – the space theoretically available – despite growing by over 250 per cent between 1690 and 1798, was still restricted, however: the working day was lengthened, waggons ran through the night, and smaller vans were introduced from about 1814, especially by Pickfords on the Manchester route, to improve the speed of service, but the loads that could be carried were limited.[48] By 1800, by contrast, canal boats with a capacity of about twenty-five tons and barges carrying up to sixty tons, moving at about three miles per hour overall and manned by two or three men, had taken much of the heavy long-distance traffic in heavy, bulky and low-value goods, with roads catering increasingly for high-value and short-haul traffic and with local services often radiating from a canal wharf (Figure 1.2).[49]

Nonetheless, waterways could not serve every city and town. There were considerable developments in road freight transport during the rise of the canals, and it was to remain important until the coming of the railways.[50]

---

48 Gerhold, *Road transport*, pp. 189–93; Gerard Turnbull, *Traffic and transport: an economic history of Pickfords* (London, 1979), pp. 24, 27; Bagwell and Lyth, *Transport in Britain*, p. 44.
49 Daunton, *Progress and poverty*, p. 308; Bagwell and Lyth, *Transport in Britain*, pp. 13–16.
50 Bagwell and Lyth, *Transport in Britain*, p. 42.

Hertfordshire lay across most of the road routes north out of London, and the roads were important to the development of the county's economy. How that development progressed will be considered later.

The Georgian town

By the end of the eighteenth century a growing proportion of the English population lived in towns, with both existing and new settlements expanding especially where water power, mineral ores, coal and other resources were found.[51] Although patterns of migration varied from area to area, the need for many people to move was universal. Towns, particularly the newer industrial centres but also the older towns that industrialised, attracted migrants especially from areas where labour was in surplus: in the south-east of England most migration was to London, but movement from countryside to town was seen across England.[52] The excess of labour in agriculture caused women especially, with their role in agriculture largely limited to working, unrecognised, next to the men and to family support, to move into towns nearby.[53] They seem to have moved more often, but less far, than men; migrants typically fulfilled the most arduous and menial jobs, and many young women moving to London entered domestic service, although women both married and single might find roles in trades growing out of increasing 'consumerism'. There was often a predominance of women in urban populations: in 1801 across south-east England the sex ratio in 931 rural parishes was 107 men to 100 women, but in 143 towns it was 97 to 100, falling to 79 to 100 in sixty-six city parishes.[54] Migrants, whatever their gender, tended to be influenced by a range of social factors. Although all towns were growing at this time the expansion of London in particular was at the expense of smaller towns, and we will see later the effect on Hertfordshire.[55]

The emergence of an identifiable working class was matched by the rise of a differentiated middle class that was an essentially 'urban phenomenon with its roots in the countryside'.[56] We have seen how the London merchants and other professionals, their numbers growing greatly to include officers of

---

51 John Langton, 'Urban growth and economic change', in Clark (ed.), *Cambridge urban history of Britain II*, p. 465.

52 Pamela Sharpe, 'Population and society', in Clark (ed.), *Cambridge urban history of Britain II*, p. 493; Peter Clark, 'Small towns 1700–1840', in Clark (ed.), *Cambridge urban history of Britain II*, p. 746.

53 Sharpe, 'Population and Society', p. 498.

54 Nigel Goose, *Population, economy and structure in Hertfordshire in 1851: St Albans and its region* (Hatfield, 2000), p. 38.

55 Sharpe, 'Population and Society', p. 522.

56 Sharpe, 'Population and Society', p. 523.

the army and navy, administrators of the East India Company, West Indies plantation owners, practitioners of the law, medicine and the Church, and highly skilled and accomplished manufacturers, invested in land close to London; and their provincial colleagues did the same around other cities. These people, typically self-made men used to hard work and respectful of order and property, often provided a greater degree of social investment than the aristocratic landowner had previously done, and so became at least as prominent and influential in their towns, appearing as churchwardens and overseers of the poor in towns and parishes alongside their local and farmer neighbours. But there were others levels, including the artisans, the shopkeepers, the innkeepers, the clerks and many others. While these people often had local status they were rarely wealthy, but they made up the rich tapestry of the typical Georgian town.

Towns needed to develop and change in response to their population growth, and the building industry burgeoned during the eighteenth century.[57] Houses were subdivided to make tenements, open spaces were built over and those who could moved out into the expanding suburbs while workers' cottages were built near places of work. Purpose-built industrial buildings and warehouses had been commonplace since early in the century, although dedicated commercial (office) buildings were not provided until later.[58] In bigger towns during the eighteenth century assembly rooms[59] were provided, but in smaller towns their function was usually provided by inns, frequently already large by this time. The streets, however, were often unimproved even if turnpiked, and they came under increasing pressure from growing populations and businesses, and from passing road traffic where they lay on main roads.[60] The infrastructure of towns changed little until Improvement Commissioners intervened from the middle of the century, and even that was by no means universal or quick. As a consequence towns and cities were unhealthy and disease-ridden, but they were also social and business centres where people of all ranks made lives for themselves.[61]

---

57 Michael Reed, 'The transformation of urban space', in Clark (ed.), *Cambridge urban history of Britain II*, p. 616.

58 Reed, 'The transformation of urban space', pp. 620–7.

59 The Assembly Room was a social space for 'assemblies' or balls, and attracted visitors from within and outside the town. Rosemary Sweet, *The English town* (Harlow, 1999), p. 234.

60 In October 1811 the Watford surveyors of the highways, one of whom was the canal carrier and wharfinger John Holladay, were particularly thanked by vestry for their diligence in improving the roads of the town in the preceding five years. This seems not to have been commonplace. HALS DP/117/8/2 Watford vestry minutes 1785–1812.

61 Sharpe, 'Population and society', p. 527.

The towns of west Hertfordshire were small, and the small towns of England at this time deserve special consideration. They 'bridged the urban and rural worlds', which is particularly apposite to this study.[62] Ninety per cent of towns in the 1790s were 'small', with populations of less than 5,000, and with commercial competition between them increasing some were reduced to the status of villages – others grew quickly, but only where industry had been established, and thus not in areas such as Hertfordshire, where towns were and remained 'minor centres'.[63] In the seventeenth century market towns had flourished in the south and east, with the 'mean towns', dirty and impoverished, in the north, but during the eighteenth century the position reversed. The provision of a turnpike service to a town did not itself generate prosperity, although it was important: more important was the development of a unique specialisation, and a town that failed to specialise was often eclipsed by one which did.

Often, and especially in west Hertfordshire, small towns continued to depend heavily on the surrounding countryside. It has already been noted that improving agricultural productivity, declining craft manufactures (where they had existed) and growing population caused considerable rural poverty and the migration of the rural poor to towns. Towns without a non-agricultural industrial base were poorly placed to deal with these influxes, especially if their marketplaces also declined. Manufacturing for a 'hinterland' was a basic function of any eighteenth-century town, and shoemakers, blacksmiths, carpenters, tailors and bakers were commonplace 'makers'.[64] But in small towns their output was limited, producing locally most of what was consumed locally, except for goods sold by mercers (fabrics, hosiery, paper, dry groceries), chemicals and medicines, and iron for iron founders. Consumer goods went no further than the local carter's round, and at least up to 1840 this sector experienced no real industrialisation, with low levels of productivity and growth. A mix of functions – marketing, service and manufacture – was the key to preserving the balance between agriculture and the independent prosperity of a town, and where that balance was skewed prosperity could be problematic. It has been suggested that the early emergence of a true 'middle class' occurred mainly in manufacturing centres, and we will see how far that was true in west Hertfordshire: but

---

62 Clark, 'Small towns', p. 733.
63 Clark, 'Small towns', pp. 739, 740; Sweet, *English town*, pp. 8, 9. A range of population from 1,000 to 5,000 has been used in this work to define a small town in the 1790s, increasing to 2,000–7,000 by 1840. No Hertfordshire town exceeded either upper limit.
64 Barrie Trinder, 'Industrialising towns', in Clark (ed.), *Cambridge urban history of Britain II*, pp. 806, 807.

the general pattern was that the well-to-do lived in town on the High Street, with the poor in the courts, alleys and tenements behind and the wealthy in mansions outside.[65] A town's size dictated the range of its social facilities – its meeting places, clubs, societies, sporting gatherings and indeed high-class shops – and these in turn determined whether that town was attractive to the better-off: where the facilities were lacking, decline generally followed a downward spiral.

A further point to be considered is the local government of a town in the late eighteenth century. In general it was still by the parish vestry, often with the support of local landowners and the dwindling influence of the manor; some older and larger towns or boroughs had a parliamentary seat as part of the picture, but most did not. But as the economic pressures increased traditional government by vestry and manor became less effective, and there was an increasing contrast between the quality and vigour of government in small towns and that in larger, often newer, places that were able to 'start from scratch' to some extent. This was matched by increasing concern over the fragility of the social order in an urbanising, industrialising society.[66] Small towns with reducing or non-existent industry were at an increasing disadvantage against the development of industrial towns and all the facilities they attracted, and the economic condition of their inhabitants often did not improve much more than those of their neighbours in the fields.

The market for manufactured goods
Despite the opportunities offered by the colonies, the home market for industrial goods was much greater than the export market.[67] As we have seen, domestic industry was strongly encouraged in the Midlands and north, where agriculture was at a relative disadvantage, and it was here that industry tended to grow – helped, not coincidentally, by the location of coalfields nearby. Thus the north–south economic divide began to form early in the eighteenth century. It became financially worthwhile to make an effort to link these two quite different markets, each consuming the produce of the other. By the time food prices began to increase in the later eighteenth century midland and northern manufacturing industry was well enough developed, with coal-based technology of increasing significance, to sustain itself by importing the food required for its workers rather than by returning to agriculture.

It has been argued that until about 1750 in agrarian areas cheap grain

---

65 Clark, 'Small towns', pp. 767, 768.
66 Daunton, *Progress and poverty*, p. 491.
67 E.L. Jones, *Agriculture and the Industrial Revolution* (Oxford, 1974), p. 110.

raised the real incomes of those, mainly the poor, whose staple diet was bread, and may have released enough cash for them to start to buy manufactured goods for the first time, although at least some of any spare cash would have been spent on other foodstuffs.[68] The market formed by agricultural labourers is unlikely to have been sufficiently large to account on its own for much of the increase in manufacture, however, which is more likely to have resulted from both the growth in the middle classes, who were economically relatively insensitive to changes in food prices, and consumption in the Midlands and north, where wages at this time were much higher than in the south.[69] Although farm labourers' incomes were generally comparatively high during the boom years of the eighteenth century, parish poor rates were high in slump periods, as in 1795/6 and 1799/1801. In either case it was farmers, especially in rural counties such as Hertfordshire, who paid most of them, and the money available to the poor from agriculture will not have changed much whether they were working or not: their purchasing power will have been sharply reduced as inflation rose.

But price inflation in the 1790s encouraged efficiencies, including enclosing any land that was still unenclosed, and allowed farmers generally to be reasonably well off. Some of their purchases were manufactured consumer goods, but it does not appear that the available technology for farm implements and machinery was used widely for some time to come – the pioneering earl of Bridgewater in the early 1810s was to be alone in west Hertfordshire for some years.[70] During the Napoleonic Wars there was some demand for industrial goods – pottery, cutlery, fabrics, iron cooking ranges – among even the poorest farm hands: the removal of much vigorous labour to the army and navy and the emphasis on war industry kept real incomes up and allowed at least some demand for consumer goods.[71] We may accept, then, that across England the agriculture sector made some contribution to the home market for manufactured goods, but it does not appear that agricultural labourers, in Hertfordshire or elsewhere, had enough disposable income to buy much, if anything, in 'the shops' or from travelling peddlers.

The market for agricultural goods

By the 1790s the classic 'markets' for agricultural produce had already changed. Improved transport helped, by allowing agricultural produce to be

---

68   Jones, *Agriculture*, p. 111.
69   G.E. Mingay (ed.), *Arthur Young and his times* (London, 1975), pp. 141, 152; Horn, *Rural world*, pp. 32–5.
70   Jean Davis, *Aldbury* (Aldbury, 1987), p. 81; Agar, *Behind the plough*, p. 54.
71   Jones, *Agriculture*, p. 117.

moved more easily over longer distances, holding down retail prices and, by encouraging a national market, levelling out some of the fluctuations in farm-gate prices. The local market hall was often in decline, but the urban market was crucial, with London naturally dominant. Not all farmers were close to a large town, however, so those that were had privileged access. Transport was important to them; for grain producers, good roads were especially important because of the bulk of the load. A full waggon of grain might weigh about four tons, with thirty-five miles probably close to the maximum economical journey, even though such a load was relatively, and increasingly, easily moved – at least as grain rather than flour, the latter having a much shorter shelf-life and being easily spoiled.[72] Costs cancelled out benefits at about the thirty-five-mile point and water transport was used from there on where available. In any case, farmers did not have much choice of roads to market, but had to select the market that they could best access by road. Turnpikes were generally satisfactory, and tolls were in some places remitted for agricultural produce going to market, although this was not the case everywhere. In the 1770s Arthur Young, an inveterate critic of poor roads, noted that in Essex ten quarters of grain (approximately two tons) needed five horses and two men to haul it, at the high cost of £2 for a journey to London, although a back-load of some sort might recoup 18s. His figures for the bad roads of North Wales in about 1800 confirmed this, observing that two tons of payload required five strong horses.[73]

Nevertheless, the hauling of cart- or waggon-loads of grain or hay or the regular driving of herds of livestock to market towns in the centre of areas of population had reduced greatly during the eighteenth century. For centuries it had been expected that dealers, 'higglers' and other middlemen, and millers or perhaps factors from cities, would examine the produce on offer, and treat for it, in the public marketplace before taking it away in vehicles of their own to sell in the wider market in which they had experience and expertise. But by the late eighteenth century grain markets were of two sorts: the developing 'sample' market, operating on the basis that the whole crop was represented by a sample brought by farmers in lieu of their entire stock; and the much older 'stock' or 'pitched' market, to which loads of stock were brought, to be either sold or taken away again. Generally by the 1790s the sample market prevailed – it was much easier and cheaper for farmers, although there were still some pitched markets. Part of the incentive for a 'sample' market was avoiding unnecessary turnpike tolls, and the proprietors of some pitched

---

72   Richard Perren, 'Markets and marketing', in Mingay (ed.), *Agrarian history vol. VI*, pp. 219–23.
73   Quoted in Perren, 'Markets and marketing', p. 220.

markets complained that stocks being brought were deliberately small for this purpose, being effectively a rule-bending sample. The sample market – which, although tolerated, was technically unlawful, as it prevented open trading and public recognition of a fair price – saw farmers, especially of grain, which could be reliably judged on the basis of a sample, and their miller, corn factor or other large customer shifting to conducting their business in inns and in relative privacy, rather than in the market hall. The business of some older markets declined sharply as a consequence, especially where industrial development nearby shifted the economic balance, and these markets became irregular or simply ceased altogether.[74] But already, even in a pitched market, there was private dealing in inns – thus avoiding market tolls as well as turnpike tolls. And the dealing began to shift to the farm gate, thus avoiding the market and public scrutiny altogether. Although this made it difficult for farmers to know the details of the wider market conditions, it did allow them to know before moving any stock whether it had been sold. More direct marketing was probably beyond the resources of most farmers, who needed to maintain their cash flow with early sales but would not have been able to access the market opportunities open to the professional dealers to whom, realistically, they had to sell. But part of the problem for poorer inhabitants, often critically dependent on the price of bread, was that larger farmers had sufficient cash resources to distort the market by holding back their stocks until the price had risen and then accepting delayed, sometimes badly delayed, payment. This would explain the quest in Rickmansworth in mid-1795, before that year's harvest, to check who had stocks left from the previous year – some might have been hoarding it, which would have been seen as very anti-social. The Hertford resident Thomas Green was well aware of the practice in 1775:

> The Farmers, early in the morn,
> Come with their Teams and bring their Corn:
> Their Wheat, and Barley, Oats and Rye,
> But seldom bring a large supply;
> Tho' ne'er so good their crops appear,
> They keep it back, and sell it dear.[75]

We have a clear picture of the way in which the public, especially the poor in times of high prices, turned on farmers and millers to 'set the market'

---

74 Perren, 'Markets and marketing', p. 226; Daunton, *Progress and poverty*, p. 323.
75 HALS DP/85/8/9 Rickmansworth vestry minutes 1783–1796; Thomas Green, *On Hertford and its environs 1775*, eds Jean Purkis and Philip Sheail (Hertford, 2016), p. 40.

by force – or at least by threat.⁷⁶ Fair regulation of the market was a real concern of the public all over the country, especially when profiteering was suspected, and this was one of the duties of the magistrates. During the war pressure on smaller farmers to sell early to maintain cash flow combined with their rising overheads to make life very hard for many; but even they, as well as their wealthier colleagues, were sometimes subject to harsh public scrutiny.⁷⁷

This changed style of marketing, although much less relevant to livestock, reduced the vitality and prosperity of market towns and led to a rationalisation of the national market network, with some towns simply relinquishing their markets. The declining markets continued to attract itinerant traders and dealers, and in some the long-standing permanent stalls around a market hall persisted; but they tended to become 'pannier markets', visited more by higglers and peddlers catering for local retail customers than by large dealers in commodity produce.⁷⁸ We will see later the effect of this on Hertfordshire towns: generally, markets did not suddenly vanish here, but a smaller number of larger, more specialist centres emerged with more diverse economies and a more distinctive urban identity.⁷⁹

The agricultural labour market

In the 1790s English agriculture employed, overall, about seven labourers to four land-occupiers, and that number was to rise only to eleven to four by 1831.⁸⁰ Arthur Young's rule of thumb was that, at the end of the century, a farm of over 500 acres required only about one 'hired hand' (man, boy or milkmaid) to about forty acres of grass, either pasture or meadow, and about two men to fifty or sixty acres of arable.⁸¹ Most farms could be worked by the farmer's family only, with outside help at harvest time. The numbers required varied with region and farming system, but one of the key features of English rural society was the fine gradation in its tiers: there was no great gulf between the very wealthy and the proletariat – rather, there were very many people in between, generating 'consumption, activity and animation'.⁸²

---

76   Horn, *Rural world*, pp. 41, 42.
77   Perren, 'Markets and marketing', p. 242.
78   Daunton, *Progress and poverty*, p. 322.
79   Nigel Goose, 'Urban growth and economic development in early modern Hertfordshire', in Slater and Goose (eds), *County of small towns*, pp. 118, 119.
80   Jones, *Agriculture*, p. 212.
81   Chambers and Mingay, *The agricultural revolution*, p. 18.
82   Chambers and Mingay, *The agricultural revolution*, pp. 204, 205.

This illustrates the potential effect on the labour market of pastoral farming compared with arable, an effect enhanced by differences in the rhythms of the two. During the eighteenth century farmers in less productive (wetter/heavier) areas often took up or even started secondary employment in proto-industries, especially in the Midlands and north, and surplus labourers went to work in the industrial centres that grew up there. Arable districts, however, did not generate concentrations of rural industry, although straw plaiting was certainly significant in Hertfordshire by 1680.[83] What industry there was in those areas tended to be based on agriculture, especially corn milling: much of it was capital intensive, as was paper making, and generally it did not grow to become large-scale 'manufacturing'. Any capital available in arable areas tended to be put back into the land or into estate expansion, or was invested in industry elsewhere. As agriculture became more efficient and productive the dichotomy deepened: rural industry, helped by the growth of the rural population, grew and developed quickly in non-arable areas, but in arable areas it generally declined or moved away, with the effect intensified by the presence of coal in large quantities in, by and large, pastoral but not in arable areas. With business economics pushing industry to move to the coal fields but impeding coal moving to new industry elsewhere, the non-industrial nature of counties such as Hertfordshire was fixed from the start.[84]

There is little clear evidence for the state of the agricultural labour market from 1790, but many factors were in play. It is generally accepted that there was a reduction in the available workforce during the Napoleonic Wars and a glut of labour from their end, when men returned from the armed forces, until about 1850. Until 1815 the armed forces and the war industries took a large proportion of the fit young men of the country, even those already hired by farmers. It has also been suggested that the 'canal mania' of the 1790s created a drain on remaining resources, although the number of men involved in canal building at the end of the century was relatively small, at about 50,000, while the number in the army and navy and in their supporting industries was about ten times that.[85] As the engineer William

---

83 Jones, *Agriculture*, p. 132; Mark Freeman, *St Albans: a history* (Lancaster, 2008), p. 177. Jones also argues that this tendency for arable areas not to have a great deal of household manufacturing was international, but this is not explored further here.

84 Daunton, *Progress and poverty*, pp. 38–42, 142, 143.

85 Burton, *Canal builders*, p. 161; David Howarth, *Trafalgar* (London, 1969), p. 25. The war effort required men in the army and navy, but also in the merchant fleets, the home militia, the dockyards and the arsenals. In March 1794 parliament authorised the strength of the army at 60,244 and the royal navy at 85,000 (BL, *The Gentleman's Magazine*, vol. 64, p. 239). Both grew rapidly from those numbers.

Jessop observed, there was actually a shortage of canal labour as well.[86] In April 1793 the promoters of a bill intended to prevent canal builders from recruiting during the harvest period argued a severe adverse effect on arable farming, but were countered successfully by the point that many of the labourers employed, often Irish and Scottish, had no agricultural relevance at all, and that in any case 'the harvest' was not a consideration everywhere.[87] There were concerns at this time over the lack of available labour in many areas, but this was not only felt in agriculture – it was a problem for the canal companies as well.[88]

At this time farm prices were rising and the demand for labour generally increasing, not least to provide the roads, drainage, hedges and (not generally in Hertfordshire) fencing for enclosure, and to recover 'waste' land in order to increase the area under cultivation. Thus labourers' wages generally increased, reflecting William Jessop's concern about the escalation in canal labourers' wages that was doing so much damage to his cost estimates.[89] But this was not universal: much of the work, especially in arable areas, was seasonal, and, in any case, despite all the draws on labour, the number of people on the land continued to grow.[90] As we will see later, summer wages in Hertfordshire were fairly steady at about 9s a week throughout the 1790s.[91] The (limited) mechanisation available was widely used for winnowing and threshing, although there is little evidence of it in Hertfordshire, but many of the harvests in the 1790s were actually poor, so the available labour was sufficient to collect them. Even during the Peace of Amiens (March 1802 to May 1803) wages did not fall or rise appreciably – it seems that the returning servicemen were simply not taken on by farmers, and then went back to military service before the 1803 harvest.[92]

Industry and the relief of poverty
In parts of the country where industry was developing, able-bodied workers were encouraged, by better pay and opportunities, to move perhaps thirty miles from their agricultural village to an industrial town or village.

---

86 William Jessop to Lord Sheffield 1792, quoted by Charles Hadfield and A.W. Skempton, *William Jessop, engineer* (Newton Abbot, 1979), p. 37.
87 Jones, *Agriculture*, p. 212; Burton, *Canal builders*, p. 161.
88 Hadfield, *British canals*, p. 112.
89 Faulkner, *The Grand Junction Canal* (Newton Abbot, 1972), p. 106.
90 Horn, *Rural World*, p. 38; Jones, *Agriculture*, p. 211.
91 G.E. Mingay (ed.), *The agrarian history of England and Wales, vol. VI 1750–1850* (Cambridge, 1989), Appendix z, p. 1042.
92 Jones, *Agriculture*, p. 214.

Where industrial employment was not available, however, rural poverty and unemployment was much more marked, and this was generally true of Hertfordshire. It was not enclosure that caused the problems, but the unavailability of work outside farming. More money seems to have been spent on poor relief in heavily enclosed counties such as Hertfordshire that remained agricultural than in those that became industrialised.[93] Per capita expenditure on the poor grew steadily from 1750 to 1800, and continued to do so. The proportion of able-bodied men requiring relief also increased. Meanwhile, the parish and county Poor Law administrators produced a range of responses to the increasing poverty, especially in the 1790s.

Wage levels were generally higher in the north after 1750, especially where industry was strong, than in the south, where there was little alternative employment. Arable farming was lower-waged than pastoral, and the arable cycle forced many of its agricultural labourers onto parish relief for three or even four months a year. There was simply not enough alternative industrial employment to mop up the spare labour, and 'open' parishes, as in Hertfordshire, were more prone to immigration and thus to the creation of 'rural slums' and high poor-rate expenditure. Particular concern was felt at the increasing number of able-bodied men seeking relief. Nationally, most of those on parish relief (93 per cent) were relieved 'outdoors', as permitted by Gilbert's Act of 1782 and evidenced by the Poor Law returns of 1802/3, and the Old Poor Law was seen as providing relief very expensively to families of the distressed able-bodied, whose under-employment and unemployment had grown so considerably.[94]

In the 1790s the 'simple' problem of 'insufficient wages' had to be addressed. Several measures were taken: one, fairly universal, was to provide subsidised food to the poor, perhaps through voluntary funds or from the Poor Rates. Fuel might also be subsidised, and in the 'famine' of 1795–1801 the justices and indeed parliament even tried to encourage the reduction of the wheat content of bread, although this was unpopular even with the beneficiaries, at least in the south of England, who saw wheaten bread as a basic right.[95] In some places the food subsidies were linked to the size of the family. Of particular note is the scheme now known as 'Speenhamland', which was initiated by the magistrates in the Berkshire parish of that name

---

93 J.P. Huzel, 'The labourer and the Poor Law', in Mingay (ed.), *Agrarian history vol. VI*, pp. 761–70; Chambers and Mingay, *The agricultural revolution*, pp. 103–6.

94 W.A. Armstrong and Huzel, 'Food, shelter and self-help, the Poor Law and the position of the labourer in rural society', in Mingay (ed.), *Agrarian history vol. VI, Part VIII. Labour II*, p. 770.

95 Trevelyan, *English social history volume three*, p. 83; Horn, *Rural world*, pp. 38–41.

in 1795, when the very harsh weather caused particularly severe problems. They established a fixed scale of top-up allowances, to be paid only to families, which related the number of dependent children in the family up to a maximum of eight to the price of bread and the basic income of the family. It was adopted in a number of areas – although not in Hertfordshire, where other approaches were taken – and provided a monetary supplement to the insufficient or non-existent wages of able-bodied labourers.[96] The 1834 Poor Law report implied that it was a very widespread system, but this was not the case – one estimate has only a fifth of the southern counties' parishes using it, even fewer in the north.[97] But other 'child allowances' were more common: in various places labourers drew lots to be allotted to groups of ratepayers, or were sent to a farmer who provided some sort of work for some sort of wages and then sent the man back to the overseers for another top-up. This was known as the 'roundsman' system, and it was to continue in Hertfordshire until 1834.

In some cases, more so later after 1815, the parish itself provided employment, both indoor and outdoor, such as spinning silk in the poorhouse. But there was not very much parish work to do, and it was not easy for the overseers to supervise those who were working. But overall, although the Speenhamland system was widely attacked for causing huge increases in Poor Law expenditure, the administrative system used was probably just a minor part of the problem: the real causes were the poor wages, the farming system – arable vs. pastoral – and the inflexibility of the structure of employment, especially the lack of alternative work.[98] Agricultural labourers were very poorly paid before 1793, and remained so for the whole of our period; their position deteriorated with the inflation of the war, but at least there was generally some work for those able to do it. After 1815 and the end of the war there was less work but no more money, and we will see later how this affected the people of west Hertfordshire.

Conclusion

By 1791, when this study opens, England had become divided along north–south lines. In the north, the coming together of soils suiting pastoral rather than arable farming, inland coal in large quantities and the presence of iron and other minerals allowed manufacturing industry to grow apace. In the

---

96   Huzel, 'The labourer and the Poor Law', in Mingay (ed.), *Agrarian history vol. VI*, p. 773.
97   Huzel, 'The labourer and the Poor Law', in Mingay (ed.), *Agrarian history vol. VI*, p. 776; Mark Blaug, 'The myth of the Old Poor Law and the making of the New', *The Journal of Economic History*, 23/2 (1963), pp. 151–84.
98   Huzel, 'The labourer and the Poor Law', in Mingay (ed.), *Agrarian history vol. VI*, p. 782.

south, where conditions favoured arable farming but there were no minerals, industry was established on only a limited scale. Meanwhile, the population was growing and farming was becoming more efficient, although by the 1770s it was unable to feed everyone: some imports of grain were needed. In consequence, there was surplus labour: in Midland and northern areas this was available to developing industry and helped generate a market for manufactured goods, but in the south there was, except in London, little option to do this, so that wages were low, poverty extreme (especially away from London) and migration to towns, especially London, relatively high. Even the manpower extraction caused by the French wars and the cutting of the late-generation canals did not result in great improvements to the economic condition of the agricultural worker and his family, most of whom, markedly in the southern counties, were forced to seek parish relief for at least part of the year.

Transport improved considerably during the period, with longer-distance movement permitted by road and by water. This helped farmers to get their produce to markets further afield, industry to develop and manufactured goods to be available much more widely: but the capacity of the very large road component was limited by the size of the vehicles available and the cost of operating them, and only the centres of population really benefited. In any case, the market for many agricultural products, previously based in the market town, was itself changing: more dealing was done privately, and some small towns saw their vitality diminish and their populations fall.

The rise of a sizeable middle and professional class and a broadly based gentry provided a growing market for manufactured goods, and the large industrial working class contributed to both that and the market for agricultural produce. But although an increasing number and proportion of people lived in towns, urban infrastructure was still underdeveloped and towns had high mortality rates as well as social and economic dynamism. A disproportionate number of women moved into towns, largely into domestic service, leaving behind a serious imbalance in the sex ratio in some rural parishes.

The next chapter will consider how western Hertfordshire experienced, and responded to, these influences on its economy, before we go on to look in detail at the role of the Grand Junction Canal.

Chapter 2
Hertfordshire in the early 1790s

The first chapter sketched a general picture of England at the close of the eighteenth century, and introduced factors relevant to the development of Hertfordshire and of the Grand Junction Canal. We will now look much more closely at west Hertfordshire and its towns and rural parishes, covering the places through which the canal passed – Tring, Aldbury, Northchurch, Berkhamsted, Hemel Hempstead, Kings Langley, Abbots Langley, Watford and Rickmansworth (Figure 2.1) – and relate this area to the big picture described in the last chapter. The important town of St Albans, off the canal but intended from an early stage to be connected to it, will be compared with the towns directly affected by the waterway.

A feature of Hertfordshire at this time was the extent to which people with London or colonial wealth took up small and medium-sized estates. They often sought a 'rural retreat', and the county was able to provide that within easy reach of London. There were some larger and older estates – Ashridge (Berkhamsted), Gorhambury (St Albans), More Park (Rickmansworth) and Cashiobury (Watford), for example – but generally the incoming and often newly rich gentry took smaller estates, often with established tenant farms or even 'villas' with but a little land.[1] The country mansions were often built or rebuilt on an elevated prospect, and the large townhouses on the high streets, such as that of the distinguished 'old-money' Spencers in St Albans, were next to those of local merchants and professionals in a new wave of Georgian building.[2] Hertfordshire at this time was particularly attractive to the 'nabobs' of the East India Company, but they were relatively sparse on the west side of the county. While More Park was bought by Thomas Bates Rous in 1785 and then by Robert Williams on Rous's death in 1801, and George Thelluson took Wall Hall, a few miles north east of Watford in

1 Rowe and Williamson, *Hertfordshire*, p. 207.
2 Rowe and Williamson, *Hertfordshire*, p. 253; Goose, 'Urban growth and economic development', p. 120.

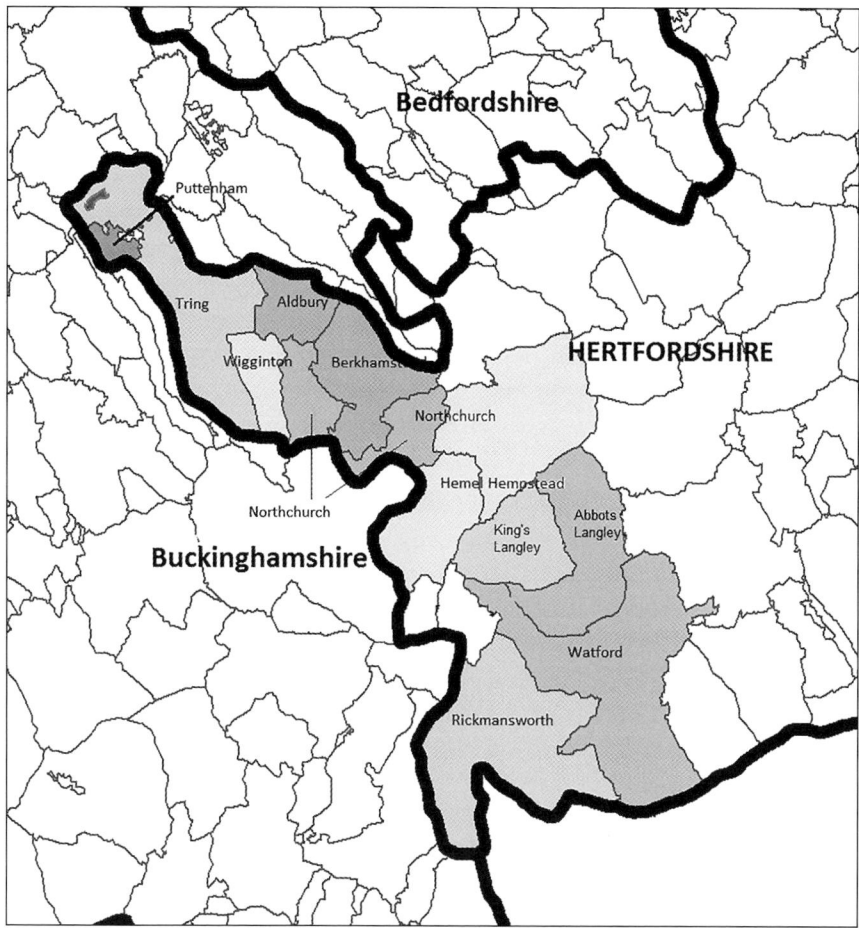

Figure 2.1. The parishes of west Hertfordshire through which the Grand Junction Canal passed as described in the text (R.J.P. Kain and R.R. Oliver, *Historic parishes of England and Wales: an electronic map of boundaries before 1850 with a gazetteer and metadata* (2001) [data collection] UK Data Service. SN: 4348, http://dx/doi.org/10.5255/UKDA-SN-4348-1).

Aldenham parish in 1799, few others are identifiable.[3] They do not seem to have used their wealth or influence significantly in the parishes or towns covered in this study, and they do not feature further, although deeper research might be rewarded.

---

3 Chris Jeppesen, 'Growing up in a company town: the East India Company presence in South Hertfordshire', in Margot Finn and Kate Smith, *The East India Company at home, 1757–1857* (London, 2018), pp. 257, 258.

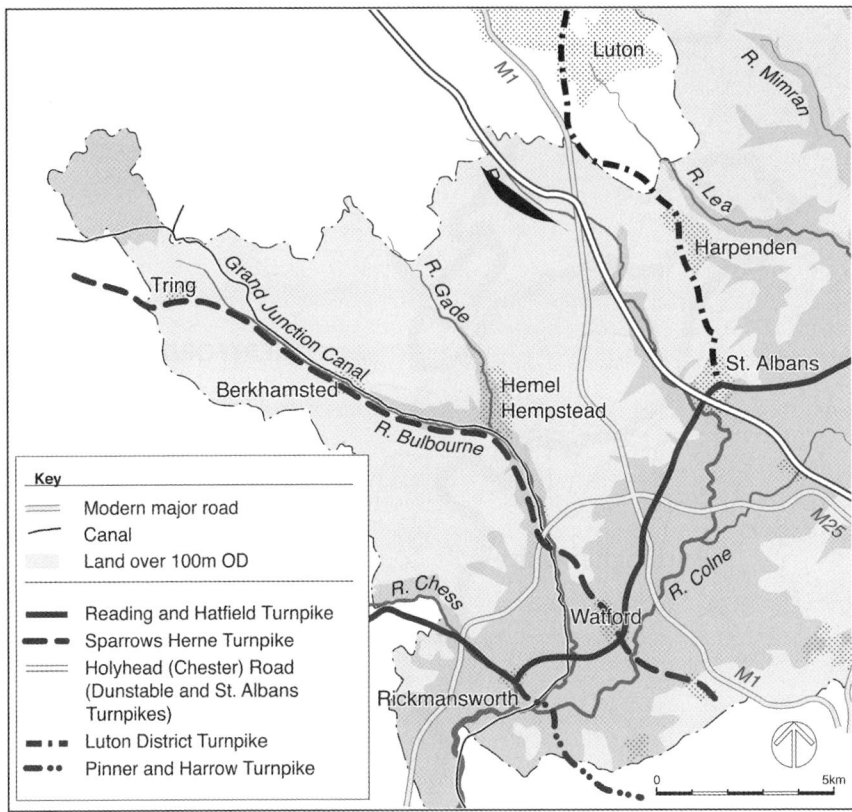

Figure 2.2. The turnpike roads of west Hertfordshire, c.1810 (after http://www.turnpikes.org.uk/map%20Hertfordshire%20turnpikes.jpg). The main modern roads are shown in addition, for comparison and orientation.

The extent to which the new owners really influenced the local economy is unclear. The incomers used their wealth to buy 'pleasant houses and grounds' along with their medium-sized tenanted estates, and did not interfere with the well-established agricultural activity that generated their rental income.[4] The fact that they moved here at all is some evidence of 'gentrification', but this was uneven: for various reasons St Albans probably attracted the highest number of gentlefolk, but they featured widely in west Hertfordshire, some with long-standing connections and others more recently arrived. There was, however, little industry for them to invest their money in, and we will see the degree to which they generated commerce or new urban building. Whether this resulted in wider economic benefit is therefore uncertain, but their

---

4   Rowe and Williamson, *Hertfordshire*, pp. 26–7, 207, 228–34.

residences certainly provided opportunities for employment as domestic servants, largely but not only for young women.

Hertfordshire lay, as it still does, across most of the main routes between London and the heart of England. By the 1790s all these roads had been turnpiked, and those relevant to this account are shown in Figure 2.2.[5] The parishes north of Watford were connected by the Sparrows Herne turnpike, which continued the Kilburn turnpike coming out of London and then passed through Tring and on to Aylesbury towards the south Midlands. Established by a parliamentary act of 1762, it followed the line of the rivers Gade and Bulbourne, preceding the canal which was to take the same course.[6] It was crossed at Watford by the Reading and Hatfield turnpike (1768), which connected the Great West Road to the Great North Road without going into London. The Reading and Hatfield also linked Watford and Rickmansworth to St Albans. But to what extent were these turnpike roads major trade routes?

Answering that question depends largely on the extant trade directories, including those relating to London, and the picture they present is neither clear nor complete.[7] It is nonetheless clear from the listings of waggon services to each town that neither the Reading and Hatfield nor the Sparrows Herne turnpikes were as important as the road through St Albans, authorised in 1715. This formed part of the strategic route connecting London and Ireland via Chester and Holyhead, and it received a great deal of government attention after the upheavals in Ireland of 1796. Even without that, however, its role in the Manchester traffic, for which it was the main artery, gave it great economic importance in the 1790s. Pickfords was probably the main carrier on this route, having started before 1756 and using waggons on a journey taking only five days by the mid-1780s, but there were many others.[8]

---

5   Based on <http://www.turnpikes.org.uk/mappercent20Hertfordshirepercent20turnpikes.jpg> (accessed 11 October 2018).

6   2 Geo.3 c.63 Sparrows Herne turnpike, 1762.

7   In addition to the *Universal British Directory of Trade, Commerce and Manufacture* (London, 1792–98) (*UBD*), the *London Directory for 1798* includes a 'Guide to Stagecoaches, mails, Diligences, Caravans, carts, coasting vessels, barges and boats'. Some of the services listed are the same as those in the *UBD*, but others differ. *Kent's Directory* for *1794* (London, 1794) has little information. While further detailed research might permit more detailed conclusions, this book draws a more general picture. The large national carriers advertise themselves as serving major towns at a distance (Manchester, Birmingham, Derby, Nottingham) without mentioning the Hertfordshire towns at all, and while each entry for Watford, St Albans, Rickmansworth, Berkhamsted, Hemel Hempstead and Tring details local waggon and cart services the inference is that they were just that – local services.

8   Turnbull, *Traffic and transport*, pp. 15, 19, 25. Dr Turnbull's earlier 'Pickfords 1750–1920: a study in the development of transportation', PhD thesis (University of Glasgow, 1972) has also been very helpful.

As we have seen in Chapter 1, road transport was always relevant for goods of high value, especially where speed was important, and the small amount (5 per cent) added to the price of Newcastle steel by moving it by road to London via Birmingham shows the limited effect of these costs. The increasing volume of, for example, cotton cloth sent from Manchester to London was carried partly by canal initially to Braunston, latterly to Coventry, by Pickfords and others such as Roper and Barnes, and then onwards by road to London until the opening of the Grand Junction Canal in 1800 (Chapter 4). Much of this traffic came through St Albans. The value of this is shown by the fact that the tolls on the St Albans and South Mimms turnpike were £164 13s 8d for the single month of July 1787 in a short hiatus between toll-collecting contractors, suggesting annual tolls of about £1,950. A little later the tolls were 'farmed' (collected by a contractor), with £1,923 a year paid by him to the trust from June 1793 and £2,205 from April 1796. The actual tolls taken will have been considerably more than that, as the contractor had already taken his fee and expenses. For comparison, the tolls on the Sparrows Herne turnpike – collected directly by the trust – were much less: £1,218 in 1786, £1,428 in 1793, and £1,550 in 1796.[9] There is no indication that the major carriers used the Sparrows Herne turnpike on their way north, but they certainly took the Holyhead/Chester road, and the level and growth of the tolls tend to confirm that the west Hertfordshire parishes were not served by a major trunk road as was St Albans. Changes in the toll takings on the Sparrow Herne turnpike later in the decade provide more evidence, to which we will return in Chapter 4.

In the west of the county, then, most of the road traffic of the 1790s was able to use reasonable local turnpike roads orientated north–south (the Sparrows Herne turnpike) or east–west (the Reading and Hatfield turnpike). But much still moved on 'parish' roads between the towns, villages and outlying hamlets, and it was arguably these that were of most importance to local people, businesses and farmers.

Agriculture

The core of Hertfordshire's economy was its arable farming. In broad terms, wheat was grown widely in the centre and north, barley in the east and hay in the south, although there were wide variations, especially to the west. Hertfordshire had neither major towns nor mineral resources, and had always

---

9   HALS, TP5/15 St Albans and South Mimms turnpike treasurer's accounts 1785–1822; TP4/28 Sparrows Herne turnpike treasurer's journal accounts 1786–1793.

been relatively sparsely populated.[10] But it was not a rural backwater: rather, it was undergoing changes as profound as those in industry at the same time. Before 1800 it could well be said that 'the farmer fed the nation', with the Hertfordshire farmer supplying wheat for the London market in particular and, from the east of the county, malting barley for the London brewers.[11] During the eighteenth century the developing sophistication of the national economy, increasingly urban and industrial, resulted in the growing specialisation of agriculture and increasing farm sizes. Proximity to London was a major factor in the development of arable agriculture in Hertfordshire, providing as it did both a market for produce and a source of essential soil-improving manures.[12] The process of enclosure, by which land was subdivided for purposes of ownership, occupation and cultivation, was also important, with landowners consolidating their holdings and letting them to tenant farmers who employed labour and worked on a relatively large scale. In 1804 Arthur Young was able to observe of Hertfordshire that while these developments were not yet complete their effect would clearly be 'very great'.[13] The increasing productivity of arable farmers was due partly to enclosure, but also to developing techniques and to the improvement of the land by draining and manuring. Wheat was the main crop, with the arable yield improved by the dung of sheep farmed on the uplands (largely for meat but also for a little wool).

The Hertfordshire farmer of the 1790s was generally a full-time professional with little scope for alternative employment. Plenty of advice was available from men such as Joseph Hodskinson (1735–1812) and Young, who made detailed observations about techniques being used in the county.[14] Although not usually owner-occupiers, Hertfordshire farmers were by no means poor: they had incomes of up to £300 a year (four times what the Grand Junction Canal Company was to pay its highly valued pay clerk), employed perhaps twenty people and often more, and knew their business,

---

10   Terry Slater and Nigel Goose, 'Panoramas and microcosms', in Slater and Goose (eds), *County of small towns*, p. 11; Rowe and Williamson, *Hertfordshire*, p. 252; Agar, *Behind the plough*, pp. 14, 15.

11   Agar, *Behind the plough*, p. 11; J.A. Chartres, *Market integration and agricultural output in seventeenth-, eighteenth-, and early nineteenth-century England* (Leeds, 1993), p. 20; Mathias, *The brewing industry*, pp. 396, 405; Agar, 'The Hertfordshire farmer in the age of Industrial Revolution', in Doris Jones-Baker (ed.), *Hertfordshire in history* (Hertford, 1991), p. 247.

12   'Manure' includes any material for addition to the soil in order to improve it. See Rowe and Williamson, *Hertfordshire*, p. 24, and Agar, 'The Hertfordshire farmer', p. 247.

13   Agar, *Behind the plough*, p. 18 *et seq* gives a full description of enclosure in Hertfordshire; HALS, DP/111/26/2, Tring enclosure map, 1799; Young, *General view*, p. 44.

14   Joseph Hodskinson, *Plain and useful instructions to farmers – or an improved method of management of arable land* (London, 1794); Young, *General view*, pp. 148–76.

markets and cost drivers.[15] Paying an annual rent that varied according to the usage and location of the land, but was typically around 18s an acre, they farmed largely as tenants of landowners interested in the business, and they had a key role in the community as employers, rate-payers and parishioners.[16] As noted earlier, however, agriculture all across the country was becoming more efficient, and although it was employing more people its take-up of the growing population was slower than the growth of that population. This was the case also in Hertfordshire, and without industry here to absorb the surplus population economic hardship was inevitable for many agricultural workers.

While there seems to be little doubt that enclosure was necessary for farming efficiency, it had an adverse social effect that caused concern to many observers, including Young.[17] And it was the agricultural labourer, arguably the main contributor to the rural economy, who was most affected, because he lost access to open land on which he had perhaps previously pastured an animal, or where he had gathered fuel, or had even grown a crop of vegetables. In general, in 1790s Hertfordshire he and his family were living in a cottage not tied to the farm but rented from a landlord, who might have been the owner of the land being farmed but was more usually a local person whose main asset it was.[18] Sometimes there was a garden for growing vegetables; indeed, Young noted a few labourers who themselves had small holdings of land or particular benefits from their employer.[19] But, generally, earnings of perhaps 9s per week meant that life was hard for families even in work, especially because wages remained fixed during the high inflation of the mid-1790s. Straw plaiting, done largely by women and one of very few 'proto-industries' in the area (and one not suited to factory industrialisation), was crucial in helping the Hertfordshire rural poor keep their heads above water, but not much more – in any case, it was at this time largely seasonal, between about December and May.[20] The farm labourer had real skills and

---

15 Young, *General view*, p. 17; Horn, *Rural world*, p. 24; Agar, *Behind the plough*, p. 1; TNA RAIL 830/37 GJC lower district committee minutes, 17 July 1793. Pamela Horn, *Life and labour in rural England* (Basingstoke, 1987), p. 34; Daunton, *Progress and poverty*, pp 37–41.

16 Horn, *Life and labour*, pp. 31–5; Young, *General view*, p. 28.

17 Agar, *Behind the plough*, p. 23, quoting Young, *General view*, p. 25; Mingay, *Arthur Young*, pp. 10, 112–38.

18 Agar, *Behind the plough*, pp. 150–2.

19 Young, *General view*, p. 222.

20 Plaited straw was sold to dealers either in markets or collected from the home, and made into hats in factories in, mainly, St Albans and Luton. Freeman, *St Albans*, pp. 177–80; Agar, *Behind the plough*, pp. 64, 71, 72; Johnson, *Industrial archaeology of Hertfordshire*, pp. 70–3; Eileen Wallace, *Children of the labouring poor* (Hatfield, 2010), p. 55.

great experience, but very limited scope to capitalise on them: he was, to a very large extent, stuck where he was in both location and status.[21]

Although Hertfordshire was an agricultural county, the 1801 census shows that only about 21 per cent of its inhabitants (the farmers themselves, their labourers and their specialist farm workers, such as ploughmen or shepherds) were directly employed in farming. Others were in trades, many – blacksmiths, wheelwrights, carters, grain merchants – supporting agricultural activity; the rest were 'not specified', although plenty, especially the women and children of farm workers' families, were no doubt labouring unnoticed, or in some quite different employment, such as domestic service.

But west Hertfordshire differed from the rest of the county, however, partly because of the topography. Enclosure here was already of long-standing, largely informal and by agreement – Tring, enclosed by an act of 1797, was an exception. The land was more undulating: small but important rivers flowed south from the Chilterns, with cattle pastured in these wet river valley bottoms, while the southern parishes, including Rickmansworth and Watford, were on the edge of the hay belt north of London.[22] Although Hertfordshire's reputation was, and is, as an arable, largely wheat-growing, county, the farms of the western river valleys were much more mixed, although Tring, on the high ground to the north, was different again.[23] In April 1789 in Rickmansworth parish the Loudwater farmer James Belch insured a granary, hog sties, a barley barn, a separate wheat barn, a cow house and a sheep house – a very mixed farm overlooking the Chess valley, and one that seems to have been pretty typical of the area.[24] The canal was to affect those river valleys in particular, and we will look briefly at the individual parishes below.

Hertfordshire industry

Agriculture and the estates of the wealthy were not the only economic activities in the west of Hertfordshire in the 1790s: the many water mills, producing paper, silk and cotton thread as well as flour, were important, and brewing, brick-making and iron-working were also widespread here,

---

21 Agar, *Behind the plough*, p. 62; *Victoria History of the County of Hertford*, vol. 4 (London, 1902–1914), pp. 228, 229.

22 Rowe and Williamson, *Hertfordshire*, pp. 25, 89–113; Agar, *Behind the plough*, pp. 24, 40–4; Agar, 'The Hertfordshire farmer', p. 248; Roger and Joan Hands and Eve Davis, *The book of Boxmoor* (Hemel Hempstead, 1994), p. 50.

23 Young, *General view*, pp. 182–4; G. Longman, *A corner of England's garden* (Bushey, 1977), vol. 1, pp. 54–67; Agar, *Behind the plough*, pp. 1–3.

24 LMA, MS11936/359 Sun Insurance policy 556297, April 1789.

as everywhere.²⁵ There had already been a general shift of economic development from the east of the county to the south, due in part to the turnpikes, which provided improving road links largely radiating from London, and to the west, as the paper mills became established. This shift may have been a factor in the influx of London money to buy Hertfordshire estates.²⁶

PAPER MAKING

In the 1790s the paper-making industry was already significant in west Hertfordshire. The requirements for a paper mill included plentiful and reliable clean running water for the preparation of the pulp and for driving the machinery; a centre of population nearby to secure labour; rags as a raw material; a ready market for the product; reasonable transport to that market; and, preferably and provided the other requirements were met, proximity to existing mills as a source of skilled workers.²⁷ In the late eighteenth century Hertfordshire had all these attributes, and of nineteen paper mills identified across the county thirteen were in the south-west, on the rivers Gade, Colne and Chess.²⁸ Six were directly relevant to the Grand Junction Canal: four (Two Waters, Frogmore, Apsley and Nash) near Hemel Hempstead and two (Batchworth²⁹ and Mill End) near Rickmansworth. Four more on the Chess near Rickmansworth and two on the Colne near Watford do not feature in the early history of the canal, while Bourne End's small role in paper making ended at about this time.³⁰

By its very nature paper making, using bulky machinery (by this time the Hollander beaters) to grind the rags into pulp, had to be carried out in dedicated premises: it could never have been a 'cottage industry'. But the actual making of the paper was by hand, and the processes required for true

---

25 Trinder, 'Market town industry', gives a strong basis for assessing the attributes of small towns.
26 Rowe and Williamson, *Hertfordshire*, p. 26; Agar, *Behind the plough*, pp. 4, 5; Terry Slater, 'Roads, commons and boundaries in the topography of Hertfordshire towns', in Slater and Goose, *County of Small Towns*, pp. 68, 69.
27 Eric Finerty, 'The history of paper mills in Hertfordshire', *The Papermaker and British Paper Trade Journal* (April 1957), pp. 308, 309.
28 Michael Stanyon, 'Papermaking', in Short (ed.), *Historical atlas*, pp. 80, 81; Finerty, 'Paper mills in Hertfordshire', April, p. 308.
29 Batchworth became a cotton mill sometime between 1774 and 1786 and remained so until 1811.
30 Austin Pilkington, 'Frogmore and the first Fourdrinier', in *A history of The British Paper Company, 1880–1890* (published privately by The British Paper Company Ltd, 1990), pp. 27–9; A.H. Shorter, *Paper mills and paper makers in England 1494–1800* (London, 1957), pp. 175–9; Richard L. Hills, *Papermaking in Britain 1488–1988* (London, 1988).

industrialisation had not yet been invented. As noted, there were several paper mills, but their local economic effect was limited: at the end of the eighteenth century the number of mills in England was between 450 and 500, with about 5,000 employees producing about 15,000 tons annually, and many of them, notably in Kent, were bigger than those of Hertfordshire. This suggests that in west Hertfordshire the thirteen mills mentioned above would together have employed only something over a hundred people, mostly rag-cutting labourers and often women, to produce by hand and distribute by road around 380 tons of paper each year.[31] But they did need infrastructure: linen rags had to be found and delivered, water-powered machinery delivered and maintained, watercourses designed and cared for, wire mesh frames ('deckles') made and alkaline solution and fuel provided for the preparation of the rags. The paper then had to be made, dried, cut, and taken off to the customer. All of this relied on horse-drawn road vehicles and, although the volume was not great and the workforce small, there were clearly benefits to be had from the co-location of the various mills, even though in competition. But the main observation to be made is that the paper industry, whose market was growing quickly with the increasing use of newspapers, banknotes and writing paper in administration, was ripe for mechanisation. In Chapter 5 we will examine how that developed – and the canal's role in it.

SILK AND COTTON

Silk throwing mills arrived in Watford from the 1760s and in St Albans and Rickmansworth between 1800 and 1810.[32] Spinning thread from raw silk imported mainly through London from Italy, India or China, these mills were a significant part of the local economy.[33] Like paper mills, they required a power source, transport links and labour: all three were available in Hertfordshire from the middle of the eighteenth century, and at least some production moved from the well-established London throwing centre at Spitalfields to Watford, where water power and skilled as well as unskilled labour were more readily available.[34] The importance of silk cloth, a luxury product, was already being rapidly eclipsed by cotton, but most of the Hertfordshire thread was used in the manufacture of ribbons

---

31 G.T. Mandl, 'The case for common sense', in Mandl (ed.), *300 years of paper*, p. 14.
32 Sheila Jennings, 'A ravelled skein: the silk industry in south west Hertfordshire 1790–1890', PhD thesis (University of Hertfordshire, 2002); Jennings, 'The silk industry', in Short (ed.), *Historical atlas*, pp. 96, 97.
33 Jennings, 'Ravelled skein', p. 54.
34 Jennings, 'Ravelled skein', pp. 38–9.

rather than fabrics, providing a measure of robustness in the market for it.[35] It is not possible to calculate with any confidence the numbers employed in the throwing mills in the 1790s, but several hundred seems a reasonable estimate: although not large, therefore, they were significant employers, not only of paid workers but also of pauper labour both in the mills and in the workhouse – evidence of the latter being found, for example, in the 1792 agreement between the master of the Ruislip workhouse and the Watford silk mill owner and merchant Thomas Watson.[36]

A side-note on the manning of the mills comes from the alarm in Watford vestry at Watson's death in 1802, which resulted in a number of children from outside the parish being admitted to the workhouse and then sent away (and not back to their homes) as 'apprentices'.[37] The silk mills certainly made a real contribution to the prosperity of the county, but they seem to have done it using labour largely under duress.[38] The only cotton spinners in this area, the brothers John and Joseph Strutt, had a large mill building at Batchworth (Rickmansworth) from at least 1785. Few records have survived for the Strutts' operation, but the skills required for cotton spinning are likely to have been similar to those for silk, and Batchworth Mill too would have had a local economic impact, as we will see shortly.[39]

BREWING

Brewing was arguably the most widespread industry of any from the Middle Ages onwards.[40] Every village had at least one pub or beer house, with beer (hopped ale) being brewed on the premises; the 'common brewer', selling wholesale and not themselves providing food or accommodation, was well established in many towns by the middle of the eighteenth century. This was as true of Hertfordshire as anywhere else, and although the county, especially the eastern side, had a particular role in supplying malted barley to the large London breweries, by no means all of Hertfordshire's production of barley went there. Hertfordshire beer houses and breweries were as prosperous as any outside London.

---

35 Jennings, 'Ravelled skein', p. 63; E.V. Parrott, 'A survey of the industrial archaeology of Rickmansworth (part 2)', *The Rickmansworth Historian*, 27 (1974), pp. 672–5.
36 HALS, DE/B1157 B11, Draft agreement between the Master of the Ruislip Workhouse and Thomas Watson of Watford to wind silk in the workhouse, 1792.
37 HALS, DP/117/8/2, Watford vestry minutes 1785–1812.
38 Jennings, 'Ravelled skein', p. 178; Wallace, *Children of the labouring poor*, pp. 69–89.
39 Jennings, 'The textile mills at Rickmansworth', *Rickmansworth Historical Society Newsletter*, 52 (2001), pp. 4–7.
40 Mathias, *The brewing industry*; Allan Whitaker, *Brewers in Hertfordshire* (Hatfield, 2006).

There is, however, the scale of operation to consider. The brewing industry had become focused on London at an early stage, if only because of its size, and, while porter was the main product there from the mid-eighteenth century, beer brewing continued, as it had done since the early sixteenth century, on a smaller scale.[41] At the start of the nineteenth century four of the London beer brewers were each producing between 16,000 and 27,000 barrels[42] a year, while the big porter brewers were producing around ten times as much. The production level at which a brewer could at this time make cost-effective use of steam machinery has been estimated at about 20,000 barrels a year, enough to sell to more distant markets.[43] At lower levels of production the mill horse provided enough power, and the market remained small and local.

Compare this with the Hertfordshire brewers. By the end of the eighteenth century there were many small breweries here, each serving a limited area – and, importantly, many of the inns and large beer houses brewed their own.[44] Beer was a low-value product that was also bulky to transport, and carrying it by horse and cart more than about five miles was difficult and uneconomic. By this time many of the common brewers had bought inns and public houses and tied them to the brewery. Some of these breweries were to become quite large businesses, several incorporating their own maltings, but most were still to be associated with relatively small areas well into the nineteenth century. In western Hertfordshire at the end of the eighteenth century common brewers of significant size were found only in Watford and Rickmansworth.[45] They had good access to malted barley from the east of the county, and some even of the smallest (in, for example, Berkhamsted and Kings Langley) bought their own grain before passing it to the maltster or malting it themselves. The grinding of the malt and other parts of the process then required power provided by mill horse.[46] Even then, a great deal of hot water was needed, and a busy brewery required a steady supply of fuel. But by the later eighteenth century timber had for practical purposes been exhausted, and what remained was reserved for ship and house building.[47] Although Hertfordshire commons were covered with a range of scrub, gorse (furze), broom, heather and bracken, much of which was useful for fuel, both

---

41 Mathias, *The brewing industry*, p. 14.
42 1 barrel = 36 gallons. A full barrel weighed around 400lb.
43 Mathias, *The brewing industry*, p. 81.
44 Whitaker, *Brewers in Hertfordshire*, p. 3.
45 Whitaker, *Brewers in Hertfordshire*, pp. 4–5.
46 Whitaker, *Brewers in Hertfordshire*, p. 15.
47 Bagwell, *The transport revolution*, p. 88.

domestic and commercial, it was becoming depleted. Various measures had to be taken to limit consumption, but the population was growing and, with it, demand for fuel for brewing, baking, brick-making and iron-working, as well as domestic heating.[48] So coal was becoming the only realistic option (even in the sixteenth century London common brewers were among the most voracious users of coal in the country),[49] but it will have been hard to get it by road transport. Many, but not all, of the brewers were in operation many years before the coming of the Grand Junction Canal, and the extent to which the canal influenced their businesses will be considered briefly below.

COMMERCE AND FINANCE

The extent of an area's banking and financial management sector has been taken here as a useful indicator of the strength of its business and commerce. Banks in a form recognisable today had been well established in London since the sixteenth century, and in 1694 the Bank of England had been set up as a Joint Stock company to manage the national debt.[50] Since the start of the eighteenth century provincial or 'country' banks had been appearing in all parts of Britain under conditions that required them to be licensed to issue bank notes.[51] These were often based on the existing businesses of local solicitors, and were responsible for a great deal of local financial management involving, for example, turnpike trusts and almshouses; investment in canals and other enterprises, including industry, where there was any; and the transfer of money from tradesmen's sales. Most country banks were connected to a larger London bank described as their 'agent', such as Dorrien's, in which the Berkhamsted resident Thomas Dorrien was a partner.[52]

Of those English towns that by 1790 had a 'country bank' 87 per cent were on a turnpike road and had facilities for 'staging', or changing horses for coaching: there may well be a connection between these early banks and road improvements.[53] Except for Hemel Hempstead, a mile north of the turnpike, all the west Hertfordshire towns in our study fit that pattern, and one might therefore expect to find 'country banking' established here

---

48 Bracken was found especially on Aldbury, Tring and Berkhamsted commons. Rowe and Williamson, *Hertfordshire*, p. 102.
49 Mathias, *The brewing industry*, p. 6.
50 David Sinclair, *The pound – a biography* (London, 2000), pp. 186, 187.
51 Daunton, *Progress and poverty*, pp. 346, 347.
52 Margaret Dawes and C.N. Ward Perkins, *Country banks of England and Wales* (London, 2000), pp. 15–19.
53 Dawes and Ward-Perkins, *Country banks*, pp. 2–5.

by this time. On the contrary, however, it came relatively late, and was in the hands of only a few individuals. None of the towns in the west of the county, including St Albans, had a bank (at least, one licensed to issue notes) before 1800, suggesting that the scope of their commerce was too small in the 1790s to require one.

This commercial banking should not be confused, however, with Savings Banks, which were completely different and related to the rise of Friendly Societies. By 1793 there was considerable interest in encouraging the poor (or at least those not wealthy) to fend financially for themselves, and Friendly Societies were becoming widespread, supported by parliament: the 'Poor Act' of that year 'for the Encouragement and Relief of Friendly Societies' held that

> the protection and encouragement of Friendly Societies in this Kingdom for securing by voluntary subscriptions of the members thereof separate Funds for the mutual relief and maintenance of the members in sickness, old age, and infirmity, is likely to be attended with very beneficial effects by promoting the happiness of individuals and at the same time diminishing the public burdens.[54]

The promoters of the act were trying to reduce the cost of maintaining the sick and aged poor under the Poor Law by encouraging the poor to support themselves, with the justices supervising the rules under which voluntary subscriptions were to be taken.[55] These early 'personal insurance' schemes aimed to raise money from members' subscriptions, along with fines for late payment and donations, for the mutual relief and maintenance of members in sickness and infirmity, and (usually) 'for no other purpose', although some provided for help with the funeral expenses of a spouse or child. They were often based in a public house or inn, the name of which often appeared in the title of the Society.[56] By 1803 there were only forty-four in Hertfordshire, and although they were to grow in number to 148 by 1831 even rural counties typically had many more: in 1801 industrial Lancashire, which dominated the movement, already had 820, Somerset 123 and Devon 156.[57] The friendly societies were strongest in the north-west of

---

54 33 Geo.3 c.35 An Act for the Encouragement and Relief of Friendly Societies – 'Poor Act', 1793.

55 'A History of Friendly Society Law in the British Islands', <http://www.isle-of-man.com/manxnotebook/history/socs/fslaw.htm>, accessed 15 October 2018.

56 R.J. Morris, 'Voluntary societies and British urban élites', in Borsay (ed.), *Eighteenth century town*, p. 350.

57 33 Geo.3 c.35 Poor Act, 1793; Horn, *Rural world*, p. 144; HALS, QS/Misc/2643 Return of Friendly Societies registered with the Clerk of the Peace, 1832.

England, and the presence in Hertfordshire of branches of the Manchester Unity of Oddfellows suggests that Hertfordshire's economic structure did not immediately trigger the widespread establishment of Friendly Societies by Hertfordshire people, although one was apparently set up at the Swan Inn in Rickmansworth in 1796.[58]

The role of the Hertfordshire Savings Bank, albeit in 1816 and so a little later than the focus of this opening review, merits consideration as part of the social structure of the county, not least because many of the Friendly Societies deposited their funds there. 'Sunday Banks', which seem to have been little more than formalised parish-based piggy banks for the poor, had been operating, certainly in the Hertford area, for some years. The Savings Bank, strongly rooted around Hertford, was different. It remained strong throughout our period, and its purpose was 'affording a secure investment of industrious persons of the lower orders, or others, for such money as they may be able to deposit therein'. Using the deposits made, which had to be more than a shilling collected weekly by parish clergy and passed to the deputy treasurers at Hertford on the first Saturday of each month, the treasurers bought 3 per cent Consols and paid interest to the savers once the individual holding, recorded in a deposit book, had reached £1. The 1793 act suggests that this was a local manifestation of wider high-level attempts at social engineering, meant for the benefit of the poor. The initial patron was the marquess of Salisbury, the initial trustees included the earls of Bridgwater, Essex, Clarendon, Verulam and Cowper, eight other titled men and ten MPs, while the managing committee included twelve clergymen, some identifiably local: and one of them was the Rev. Thomas Malthus, the political economist and demographer and a national figure.[59]

It is the remarks occupying much of the prospectus that attract our attention in this context, however. The scheme was based on the belief that, with few exceptions, all the poor could save if they tried, while many others not of the lowest rank would value an inducement to save. Examples are given of the benefits of doing so, featuring 'The Small Tradesman', whose profits might be stolen or squandered unless invested; 'Domestic Servants', who should 'preserve that money which they have hitherto frittered away in dress or dissipation'; 'Servants in lower situations, Bargemen on the navigable rivers, and the Journeymen and Artisans who live in the towns'; 'Apprentices'; and 'Agricultural Labourers', who 'form the great mass of the

---

58   Daunton, *Progress and poverty*, p. 281; HALS, DE/Hx/B25 Rules of Hertfordshire Friendly Societies, 1823–1852.
59   From the Clergy Database, <http://db.theclergydatabase.org.uk>, accessed 11 October 2018.

lower orders in Hertfordshire'. The essay on this last group is the longest, and allows the great and good promoting the scheme to justify their approach to dealing with the agricultural poor and to offer advice on how they should live: in particular, it observes that,

> Unhappily, by early and imprudent marriages, the poor too often plunge themselves into misery, from which no economy afterwards can rescue them ... . [Their] situation would be greatly improved if they were wise enough to live single, till they could afford to feed and clothe their children, and to provide for them an education suitable to their station in life.[60]

This point of view, in which we may detect the thoughts of Malthus himself, was already widespread in the 1790s and was to remain extant well into the middle of the century.

The towns in the 1790s

The aim of this book is to see how west Hertfordshire changed under the influence of the Grand Junction Canal, and the first part of this chapter has been a general review of the industries and agriculture here. Before we turn our attention to the canal itself we should look briefly but in some detail at the towns and parishes that make up the area and which were to be affected directly by the canal.

All the towns (Tring, Berkhamsted, Hemel Hempstead, Watford and Rickmansworth) were in some degree market towns, as described in Chapter 1. We have few descriptions of such markets, but Thomas Green's description of Hertford market in 1775 can perhaps give an impression:

> The market on a Saturday
> Makes all the town look brisk and gay.
> The Gentry come from different parts,
> The neighb'ring Squires, the Beaus and Smarts:
> Some only for an Airing come,
> And others take provisions home;
> A pig, or fowls, or Butcher's Meat;
> Or anything they choose to eat:
> For here in plenty they may find
> Provisions brought of ev'ry kind;
> With Eggs, and Butter, Fish and Fruit,

---

60   HALS, DP/37A/29/1 *Regulations and Prospectus of the Hertfordshire Savings Bank*, 20 March 1816.

Table 2.1. Parish data from the census of 1801.

Parish	Total pop.	No. in agriculture	No. in trade	Males	Females	Families	Inhab. dwellings
Tring	1621	137 (8%)	156 (9.5%)	722	899	327	323
Berkhamsted	1690	160 (9.4%)	167 (10%)	799	891	395	333
Hemel Hempstead	2722	391 (14%)	775 (28%)	1348	1374	527	418
Kings Langley	970	149 (15%)	114 (12%)	467	503	189	101
Abbots Langley	1205	357 (30%)	100 (8%)	601	604	224	222
Watford	3530	311 (9%)	711 (20%)	1736	1794	991	661
Rickmansworth	2975	513 (17%)	451 (15%)	1477	1498	553	490
St Albans	3038	96 (3%)	575 (19%)	1297	1741	625	515

The very large numbers whose occupation was 'not stated' includes the young, old and unemployed as well as those in service, and no attempt has been made to draw conclusions from that figure. St Albans includes the Town, St Peter's and St Michael's parishes.

> And all that may the Palate suit.
> The Higglers come from different parts,
> They buy them up and load their carts;
> And make it worth their while, no doubt,
> To serve the Gentry round about.[61]

Before we move to the particular we can look first at the numbers of people living here. The returns from the 1801 census (Table 2.1) allow an initial assessment of the populations of each of the canal-line parishes just three or four years after the canal was constructed and less than two years after it was opened through Hertfordshire. Some caution is needed: it is possible that the canal had already had an effect on the towns and parishes whose information was being reported. But it seems unlikely that this effect was so strong in so short a time as to change the nature of the towns, and I have assumed that it did not and that conclusions from the census data are valid for the 1790s.

While these figures are for the parishes, and thus over-state the populations of the towns themselves, they do allow a degree of comparison – in every case the parish is but a small extension of the town.[62] They confirm the

---

61 Green, *On Hertford*, p. 38.
62 The difference is clearly shown, although for a later census, by Goose, 'Urban growth and economic development', p. 100.

generally agrarian nature of the area at this time, even though it seems unlikely that the census recorded the full extent of agricultural employment, often seasonal, among women and children, so that many of the occupations noted as 'not detailed' were in fact agricultural.[63] An indicator of wealth and growth, derived from the ranking prepared by Nigel Goose of the twenty-three towns of Hertfordshire in 1801, is shown for each: although this was intended to make a different point about growth in the sixteenth, seventeenth and eighteenth centuries, it highlights the difference between historical development and this snapshot of 1800, and is relevant to the discussion of the towns here.[64] Another guide to the nature of a town is the number of families compared with the number of houses, a parameter reported in the 1801 census and included in the analysis that follows. We saw in Chapter 1 that a feature of an industrialised town or city was, by this time, an increased crowding into tenement buildings with multiple occupancy. Completion of the census was in the hands of unsupervised parish officers, so comparing returns from different parishes is not necessarily comparing like with like. We would nonetheless expect to find that in an agricultural area such as this the number of dwellings would match fairly closely the number of families, whereas in an industrial area there would be many more families than houses. This says nothing, of course, about the size of family or building, and we may be confident that some of the labourers' cottages were grossly over-filled by their family.[65] We will also consider the implications of gender imbalance: we saw in Chapter 1 the effect on the sex ratio in towns of the migration of young women, in particular, into 'service'. Further evidence is available from the 1803 Poor Returns: although made five or six years after the canal arrived, the impact of the war had already been felt for some years and little else had changed in the interval. The 'market town model' helps assess the degree to which these market towns were, in fact, typical (Appendix A), and the first comprehensive trade directory relevant to our area, the *Universal British Directory* (*UBD*), has been used where possible, although with caution: not all will have come forward to be listed, and the entries may be somewhat deficient.[66] We can now look at the particular.

TRING

Tring, a parish of about 1,600 inhabitants, was dominated by the small market town mentioned, but not detailed, in the Appendix (Vol V) to *UBD*.

---

63 E. Higgs, *Making sense of the census* (London, 1989), pp. 78–92.
64 Goose, 'Urban growth and economic development', pp. 114–19.
65 Wallace, *Children of the labouring poor*, pp. 12, 47.
66 *UBD*, vols II, IV, V (London, 1792–98); Trinder, 'Market town industry'.

Ranked thirteenth in Hertfordshire by Goose, it lay near the end of the Sparrows Herne turnpike with the toll gates at Veetches to the west and New Ground nearby to the east, although their small receipts (Appendix D) suggest that trade along it relating to the town was limited. There was little manufacturing except small-scale canvas weaving established as early as 1718, when the vestry bought looms for the use of paupers, and straw plait was an important female occupation, with the product sold in the weekly market. Brewing was on only a small scale at this time.[67] Tring was one of the few parishes in this area to seek parliamentary enclosure, and the 1797 act, which stopped the practice of 'allotting' common fields in strips, certainly caused hardship, as is captured in the vestry records: the compensation did not make up for the loss of opportunity, especially for grazing, that had previously existed.[68] This generally reflects Young's sentiment: enclosure was necessary for efficient farming but there was a serious disadvantage to the poor, and these effects were being felt in the years either side of 1800, especially as the weather damaged the harvest and required the better-off locals to make special provision for the support of the poor.[69] The enclosure award lists 161 owners of nearly 1,000 pieces of property, dominated by the London banker Drummond Smith, who had bought Tring Park in 1786, but with significant holdings also belonging to several other people and institutions. But alongside these wealthy people (there were three notable estates and several other sizeable landowners) there were about seventy who owned just one house or cottage, and a number of these would surely have been owner-occupiers.

The demographic make-up of Tring parish was unusual, however. The 1801 census recorded 722 males and 899 females, a sex ratio of 81:100, which suggests that there was a great deal of 'in-service' work for women – and perhaps also that men had migrated, which runs counter to the national trend outlined earlier. There were 327 families living in 323 occupied dwellings, showing little evidence of the sort of overcrowding seen in industrial settings. Agriculture was arguably the most prominent single occupation, with pasturing of cattle heading for London via the Vale of Aylesbury probably more important than arable farming; but at only 8 per cent agriculture did not employ as large a proportion of the inhabitants as in other parishes – and just 9.5 per cent were 'in trade', which tends to confirm that many were 'in service'. Comparison with the general attributes

---

67   Sheila Richards, *Tring* (Tring, 1974), p. 49.
68   HALS, CD CP111/26/2, Tring inclosure map and awards, 1799.
69   Richards, *Tring*, p. 26; HALS, DP111/8/19 Tring vestry minutes, 1782–1815; Mingay, *Arthur Young*, pp. 98, 113, 115.

of a market town suggests that Tring only marginally achieved that status, and the picture emerges of a small town with an economy based on grazing cattle, straw plait and a local market but little real industry, which was well connected to the turnpike road and had a number of property owners, albeit three large estates dominated and employed a significant proportion of the inhabitants.

BERKHAMSTED

Berkhamsted was situated along the main road formed by the Sparrows Herne turnpike. It has been considered a fine example of a 'street town', with its marketplace to the west of the church.[70] Despite its two water mills and grammar school it was small, dominating a large parish with a small population; the *UBD* lists ninety-eight different local tradesmen in Berkhamsted, implying that most were working alone or with unrecorded 'family' labour; there were about fifty 'shops' as we might recognise them.[71] The map confirms this impression: the common was huge and the only other settlements were on its edge, but there were several significant estates, notably the duke of Bridgewater's Ashridge estate. The social centre seems to have been the King's Arms Inn, which also hosted the meetings of the Sparrows Herne turnpike trustees, and in 1799 Lipscombe observed that 'the town has in it many genteel houses, and the neighbourhood being pleasant, it is much resorted to by persons of fortune and fashion, so that a lively air of gaiety prevails here'.[72] But there was a discrepancy between these elegant mansions and the poverty of many of the townspeople, living mainly in the High Street and on its north side in Castle Street, Mill Street and Water Lane.[73] It was of Berkhamsted, but surely relating to the whole area, that a Somerset visitor observed in the 1770s that 'the people are so countrified as in any town I know. They will stare at you as if they had never seen no one before.'[74]

The valley of the Bulbourne, below the town on the north side of these streets, was marshy, even swamp-like, and unhealthy; but it did have agricultural value and, like most such areas, it was meadow and pasture

---

70 Jennifer Sherwood, 'Influences on the growth and development of medieval and early modern Berkhamsted', in Slater and Goose (eds), *County of small towns*, pp. 224–48.

71 Abstracted in Percy Birtchnell, *A short history of Berkhamsted* (Berkhamsted, 1972), pp. 78, 79.

72 'Georgian town' <https://rollitt.co.uk/georgian-town/>, accessed 1 May 2018.

73 Birtchnell, *Berkhamsted*, pp. 14–15.

74 Clark, 'Small towns', p. 737.

land rather than arable.[75] Many of the farmers, especially on higher ground, would nonetheless have grown wheat, as Young observed to be widespread in 1804 and Per Kalm had done over fifty years before him.[76] The two flour mills, Upper and Lower, seem likely to have been busy enough.

The main industry, here and over the hill at Chesham, had been wood-turning and related crafts, making bowls, dishes, spoons and similar ware, as well as pattens, clogs and shoe heels. But by the 1790s this had already declined severely, although woodworking was to continue as a local trade. Lace making was an important proto-industry for women, supported especially by the lace merchants Chambers Langston Hall & Co, based mainly at Leighton Buzzard but with interests in Berkhamsted.[77] Lace making was being superseded by straw plaiting in the 1790s, but the vestry minutes nonetheless reveal real poverty in the town, and Lipscombe also reported the market hall as being 'shabby and decayed', perhaps following the 'commodity to retail' path taken by many such market towns, as the commodity trade was replaced by retail sales of household goods and foodstuffs.[78] Even the *UBD* said that 'the market is much decayed, although the town is pretty large'.[79] The 1801 Census found that 395 families occupied 333 dwellings, indicating some urban overcrowding appearing even at this stage. It recorded 799 males and 891 females, a sex ratio of 86:100, suggesting that, as in Tring, there was work for women with some men having departed: while just 9 per cent of the population were 'employed in agriculture', only 10 per cent were 'in trade', again suggesting a significant number 'in service'.

There was, of course, brewing in the town: John Lane, the innkeeper of the Kings Arms, had his own brewery by 1800, and another Lane had one behind the Swan nearby. But they were small and local, and did not form a significant industry. Like most of the towns along the Sparrows Herne turnpike, Berkhamsted had a reasonable number of stage coach passenger services, but there was very limited capacity for freight: scheduled waggon services can be identified only on Tuesday and Friday.[80] The local industries do not seem likely to have required much more, although bespoke services

---

75 Birtchnell, *Berkhamsted*, p. 82.
76 Young, *General view*, pp. 80–91; P. Kalm, *Kalm's account of his visit to England on his way to America in 1748*, trans. and ed. Joseph Lucas (London, 1892) (Library of Congress <https://archive.org/details/kalmsaccountofhi00kalm>, accessed 1 February 2019, p. 150).
77 Birtchnell, *Berkhamsted*, pp. 70, 71.
78 Chartres, *Market integration*, p. 20.
79 Birtchnell, *Berkhamsted*, pp. 14, 75; Chartres, *Market integration*, p. 24; *UBD*, Vol II, p. 278.
80 *UBD*, Vol II, p. 278.

rather than common carriers would have been engaged by the wealthy inhabitants, and the tradesmen would have been supported by cart.

Berkhamsted, then, was not well off at the end of the eighteenth century: despite being ranked eighth by Goose and a place in which wealthy people had settled and to which they had continued to move, it was a rather small and shabby town, formerly prosperous enough to have 'pretensions' but now struggling.

HEMEL HEMPSTEAD

Hemel Hempstead was governed in a way rather different from the other towns of west Hertfordshire. Since the 1539 Charter of Henry VIII it had had a weekly market with a bailiff and jury supervising and managing it; this was in addition to the parish vestry, which carried out the other duties in respect of the poor, highways and church.[81] The bailiff took the rent revenue from, and set the rules for, the market, which in the late eighteenth century was a general one, with corn the main commodity but cattle and other animals as well as general merchandise also traded. The *UBD* reports that, surrounded by good corn-growing land, Hemel Hempstead was 'one of the greatest markets for wheat in this county, if not in England, £20,000 being often returned in it only for meal'.[82] This was a huge amount, and in 1822 the area round Hemel Hempstead was to be described by Cobbett as 'the very best corn land that we have in England'.[83] All of this supports the impression that the market revenue to the town, through the bailiff, contributed to general prosperity. In theory this was a pitched market, as described in Chapter 1, and there was a large market house, but by the 1790s this was in poor repair: the corn had to be pitched inconveniently in front of it, and the large volumes quoted as being traded despite this suggest that this had in fact become a sample market by this time. A butchers' shambles had a number of stalls near the market house, but by the 1790s these were also in poor condition, with moves afoot to replace them. Another commodity product sold at Hemel Hempstead's market was locally made straw plait, and indeed straw plaiting was clearly an important proto-industry in the town. The wool market in Hemel Hempstead was probably by now insignificant, as woollen cloth had declined in importance since the 1750s in the face of cotton, and the production of sheep for their wool does not seem to have featured much

---

81 Arthur L. Wood, 'The bailiwick and the market', in Yaxley (ed.), *History of Hemel Hempstead*, pp. 163, 172–3.
82 *UBD*, Vol III, pp. 254–6
83 William Cobbett, *Rural rides*, vol. 2 (London, 1822), quoted by Dorothy Cromarty, 'Topography and settlement', in Yaxley (ed.), *History of Hemel Hempstead*, p. 14.

in this area by this time.[84] An annual fair for animals and one for the hiring of labour provided important social opportunities.

The turnpike bypassed Hemel Hempstead to the south. The town accommodated many of the parish's inhabitants in a strip along the road running off the turnpike northwards along the river Gade towards Leighton Buzzard, but there were also settlements at Corner Hall, Two Waters, Boxmoor and further out at Crouchfield and Leverstock Green.[85] The very long list of traders and professionals in the *UBD* tends to support the high census figure of those 'in trade' (28 per cent), but it includes no carters or carriers. The further comment in the *UBD* that 'the road is by the eleven pairs of mills continually torn, so that it is one of the worst turnpike ways to London' is surprising, since the Sparrows Herne turnpike minutes report various other problems but not this one.

The limited extent of brewing in such a town is perhaps surprising: there were over twenty inns and beerhouses in the High Street alone, but there was no significant 'common brewer' at the end of the eighteenth century. There were inns and beerhouses, but it appears that they generally brewed their own, although what was to become an important brewery had been started at the Boot Inn at Two Waters by the Godwin brothers, who were already buying and leasing inns between 1740 and 1760.[86] The earl of Marchmont was among the sixteen people listed in the *UBD* as 'gentry', and the presence of a mantua maker[87] suggests that the gentry were responsible for at least some high-end business in the town. Nonetheless, most of the population were by no means prosperous: 14 per cent were 'employed in agriculture'; for agricultural labourers, even specialists such as ploughmen, rates of pay were as low here as in the rest of the county, and they lived under the same conditions of poverty. Hemel Hempstead also had, however, a nucleus of industry in the paper mills at Two Waters, taken over by the important London stationers Henry and Sealy Fourdrinier in 1792 or 1793, and Frogmore, taken over by them in 1803, as well as corn mills at Bourne End, Picott End and Noake Mill.[88] A degree of urban overcrowding was evident across the parish, with 481 dwellings housing 527 families in 1801,

---

84 Lionel Munby (ed.), *A history of Kings Langley* (Kings Langley, 1963), p. 112; Wood, 'Bailiwick and market', p. 170.

85 M. Gwennah Robinson and Valentine J. Wrigley, 'Hemel Hempstead in the nineteenth century', in Yaxley (ed.), *History of Hemel Hempstead*, p. 99.

86 Whitaker, *Brewers in Hertfordshire*, pp. 113–15.

87 A mantua was a high-class ladies' garment. Although the term 'mantua maker' may have been used to describe dressmaking more generally, the implication of quality is clear.

88 Robinson and Wrigley, 'Hemel Hempstead in the nineteenth century', pp. 100, 103; Hugh Howes, *Wind, water and steam* (Hatfield, 2016), p. 85.

with sixteen unoccupied, while the balance between the sexes (1,348 men to 1,374 women, a ratio of 98:100) was more typical of a rural parish, so there are slightly conflicting indicators. Despite its low ranking of fourteen by Goose, the impression is of a town with a prosperous market in grain and a large and thriving professional and trading community.

WATFORD

Watford parish included by some way the largest town in the area as well as the residences of the earls of Essex and of Clarendon and several other typically small estates. Running for a mile uphill north along the Sparrows Herne turnpike, Watford had developed on a different pattern from other Hertfordshire towns: 991 'families' lived in 661 houses, showing significant overcrowding and suggesting a high proportion of single people, small families and, especially, multiple occupation of dwellings, especially in the crowded alleys and yards.[89] The surprising sex ratio of 97:100 (1,736 males to 1,794 females) does not suggest employment biased to women, although the *UBD* reported that 'the principal manufacture is of silk thread', with three mills, two powered by horse and one, Paumier's large Rookery Mill, by water, which might have been expected to give that bias.[90] The market was for 'corn, cows, sheep and hogs', showing the influence of agriculture in and near the town.

Agriculture employed only 9 per cent of the population, however. There were manufacturers and vendors of an increasing range of goods as well as of farming implements – 20 per cent were 'in trade', although the *UBD* listing of traders was relatively short. The main outlet for Watford's trade was London, and coach services to London and to Tring, Berkhamsted, Chesham, Leighton Buzzard and Birmingham were advertised; in addition, two waggon services were scheduled weekly to London, but nowhere else. The *Directory* lists no specialist carters or carriers based in the town, but the whole traffic of the turnpike traversed the High Street; however, the turnpike records suggest that the volume of freight was relatively low. Analysis of the takings at the turnpike toll gates shows clearly that much of the traffic went through Watford, but with Berkhamsted the northern limit of trade to and from London. The river Colne, the most potent river in west Hertfordshire, with several branches and always liable to flooding, was crossed by the turnpike at the bottom of Chalk Hill. Although not navigable, it drove the silk and paper mills as well as the corn mill in the High Street.[91]

---

89 Mary Forsyth, 'The establishment and development of Watford', in Slater and Goose (eds), *County of small towns*, pp. 276–7, 279, 289, 295–6; Johnson, *Industrial archaeology*, pp. 138, 140.
90 *UBD*, Vol IV, pp. 698–704.
91 Henry Williams, *History of Watford* (London, 1884; reprinted Watford, 1976), p. 96.

By far the most significant brewing town on this side of the county, Watford had a large number of inns to serve both the local and the coaching trade on the turnpike. What became Dyson's, the largest brewery, had been established in the lower High Street before 1722 and had grown steadily.[92] But although it was to become one of the largest brewers in the area its scale was nonetheless limited – even in 1867 production was still only about 9,000 barrels a year, well below the probable mechanisation threshold of seventy years before, and it seems very unlikely that any of the other breweries in the area approached that output at this early stage.[93] The Watford Brewery had been established, also in the lower High Street, before 1758, and was sold with fifteen of its pubs to George Whittingstall in 1790: it, too, was growing steadily towards the end of the century, but even then it was not a large operation.[94]

In the 1790s, then, Watford, ranked fifth by Goose, was a large and fairly prosperous place with silk thread and paper manufacture, varied commerce and good connections to London and elsewhere. It showed many of the features of an industrial town, although that industry was limited, but few of the features of a regional centre, such as banks or assembly rooms.

RICKMANSWORTH

Rickmansworth parish covered a large area, and maps of the time show a sprawling collection of settlements in addition to the town. In 1801 its population exceeded those of both Hemel Hempstead and Berkhamsted, although Goose ranks it only nineteenth. Its high proportion of agricultural inhabitants (17 per cent) suggests that, although its market was in some decline and there were several mills, farming was the main economic activity.[95] The large size of Strutt's Batchworth Mill, however, should be noted (Figure 2.3): built next to an ancient corn mill probably in the late 1750s, it appears to have been one of the largest industrial complexes in the area, on a par with the Rookery silk mill in Watford.

Providing the main industrial employment, with both paid labour and paupers often drawn from London parishes, the brothers John and Joseph Strutt, nephews of the Derbyshire silk magnate Jedidiah Strutt, were clearly working on a considerable scale, combining cotton thread spinning (not necessarily for cloth – candle wicks were needed in large quantities) with

---

92 Whitaker, *Brewers in Hertfordshire*, p. 217.
93 Mathias, *The brewing industry*, p. 81.
94 Whitaker, *Brewers in Hertfordshire*, p. 224.
95 George Alexander Cooke, *Topographical and statistical description of the county of Hertford* (London, c.1805–1810), pp. 137–9, quoted in Jennings, 'The textile mills at Rickmansworth', pp. 4–7.

Figure 2.3. Batchworth Mill in about 1807 (TNA, MPH 1/451).

corn milling. Samuel Salter's brewery was relatively large, although still local in scope, having a significant tied estate within fifteen miles of the town, and had recently moved along the High Street from its original (*c.*1741) location.[96] And among the 15 per cent 'in trade' there were a number of 'professional men', with a firm of solicitors active and representing local businessmen, as we will see later.

Although the rivers Colne, Gade and Chess powered the paper, cotton thread and flour mills, none was navigable and all transport was by road. Although some way from the Sparrows Herne turnpike, Rickmansworth was on the Reading and Hatfield turnpike (see Figure 2.2), which crossed the river Gade from Watford at Cashio Bridge and then went past Croxley Green before following Rickmansworth High Street and going on towards Amersham. Rickmansworth had, therefore, road connections to several sizeable towns, including Watford, five miles away, although the London road through Pinner and Harrow had yet to be turnpiked; and there were several inns providing calling points for coach and waggon traffic through the town.[97] Although relatively large and having some industry and

---

96 Whitaker, *Brewers in Hertfordshire*, p. 173.
97 A.W. Hayman, 'The Bell Inn', *The Rickmansworth Historian*, 2 (1961), p. 19; Godfrey Cornwall, 'The Swan Inn', *The Rickmansworth Historian*, 7 (1964), p. 127.

several medium-sized estates, suggesting some degree of 'gentrification', Rickmansworth was not listed in the *UBD*, although it was in Holden's *Directory* of 1811.[98] The 1801 census recorded 1,477 males and 1,498 females, a sex ratio of 99:100, while 553 families living in 490 houses shows some evidence of the sort of overcrowding seen in Watford and other industrial settings and perhaps suggesting the industrial scope of the cotton mill. The impression is of a dispersed parish heavily dependent on agriculture, despite a leavening of other occupations; but a meeting of the Hertfordshire paper makers in Rickmansworth in 1796 shows that paper making was an important feature of the town, with Mill End paper mill to the west and four others (Sarratt, Loudwater, Solesbridge and Scotsbridge) on the river Chess just to the north.[99]

The rural parishes
None of the smaller parishes of the study had a real town, but most had features that would later be affected by the canal. Northchurch, originally the main parish of Berkhamsted St Mary, had been divided when Berkhamsted St Peter parish was carved out of the middle of St Mary's *c.*1100 to serve the borough that had grown up around the castle.[100] By the late 1790s it contained a single village very close to Berkhamsted, with outposts near Dudswell, Woodcock Hill and Little Heath, while Berkhamsted Lower Mill was divided by the boundary. Both the turnpike and the small river Bulbourne cut through both halves of the parish, and to a considerable degree Northchurch was an extension of Berkhamsted, but in so far as it was a single community it was an agricultural one, with 127 families in 127 houses, 370 males as against 365 females, and 22.5 per cent of the population in agriculture and only 4 per cent in trade.

Kings Langley was another sizeable but almost wholly agricultural parish dominated by the village itself, with the river Gade forming the boundary with Abbots Langley. There were a number of farms, with Langley Lodge, in the hands of Newman Hatley, perhaps the most prominent in this story.[101] Chipperfield Common, on the west side, had the only other significant settlement, while Apsley paper mill in the north and Toovey's flour mill to

---

98 Holden's *Annual London and County Directory for the year 1811, Vol. III* (London, 1811), consulted at HALS.
99 Finerty, 'Paper mills in Hertfordshire', May 1957, p. 420.
100 N. Doggett and J. Hunn, 'The origins and development of medieval Berkhamsted', *Hertfordshire's Past and Present*, 18 (1985), p. 22.
101 J.P. Haythornthwaite, *The parish of Kings Langley* (London, 1924); Munby, *Kings Langley*; Scott Hastie, *Kings Langley* (Kings Langley, 1991).

the south were both powered by the Gade. The turnpike passing through the village allowed it to be well served by coach and waggon services. It also had a brewery in the High Street, owned by 1790 by Francis Cromack and including a small malting, but again representing only a very local business. This all suggests a self-contained and reasonably prosperous agricultural parish, in which 189 families occupied 181 dwellings and whose sex ratio of 93:100 suggests the reasonably settled, non-industrial population that we might expect.

Abbots Langley lay to the east of and above the Gade, with its main hamlet, Bedmond, a little to the north. Hunton Bridge and its corn mill lay on the river, which the turnpike from Watford crossed and from which the road led off to the village above. On the hill to the west of the river was the main mansion, Langleybury, but there were other 'residences'. This, too, was a good-sized parish, albeit without any industrial activity outside the Nash paper mill, and 224 families lived in 222 houses. Thirty per cent of the population was recorded as being in agriculture and only 8 per cent in 'trade', and the sex ratio was almost exactly 100:100. The vestry particularly noted during the 1790s the growing imbalance between the unable and the unemployed in the overseers' disbursements, a problem by no means unique to this parish: but by 1801 it seems that 10 per cent of the 1,205 parishioners were on poor relief, with thirty-seven of them in the small Poor House, eighty-six others on out-relief and five-sixths of the overseers' money going to two-thirds of the poor, many able-bodied with families but not enough work.[102] It was a stark statistic, but not untypical.

The remaining smaller parishes form a group of small agricultural settlements. Aldbury was very much dominated by its farms.[103] High on the Chiltern crest, enclosed only to a limited degree and by agreement, its farming was in open fields dominated by the Stocks estate and by nearby Ashridge, and aside from the usual village trades and crafts the inhabitants were employed on the land. The turnpike passed along the southern boundary of the parish, but road connections from Aldbury were with Tring and Hemel Hempstead, and with Buckinghamshire to the north. The 1801 census recorded 105 families in 100 houses. Puttenham is added here only because the Aylesbury arm of the canal was to come through it in about 1815. It was a tiny agricultural settlement north of Tring, with a population in 1801 of about 130: twenty-four families in twenty-four houses. The only settlement outside the village was at Astrope, and all occupations were related to agriculture. Wigginton had a single village on the ridge

---

102 C.W. Clark, *Abbots Langley Then* (Cockfosters, 1997), p. 65.
103 Davis, *Aldbury*.

overlooking the Bulbourne valley. Its eastern extremity touched the small settlement at Cowroast, on the ancient drove road to London, and the turnpike skirted the eastern boundary, with its New Ground toll booth just in the parish; but the agricultural nature of the parish remained intact, and sixty-five families occupied sixty-two houses. None of these parishes had a 'gentleman's residence', although all were extensively owned by such people.

St Albans is relevant to this study as a comparator, having been offered but never getting a canal of its own, and so is considered in some detail. In the 1790s one of only two parliamentary boroughs in Hertfordshire (the other was Hertford), it returned two MPs. It had had a long and relatively illustrious history as an ecclesiastical centre dominated by its abbey until the Dissolution, when its extensive land holdings were broken up and passed to a variety of new owners, some of whom were to feature in the story of the Grand Junction Canal. In the 1790s the town, still small, was split between three parishes – St Michael's, St Peter's and the Abbey or Town parish.[104] It was ranked second by Goose, behind only Hertford.

Politics was an important element of St Albans life, dominated by the Spencer family and the Grimstons, with one parliamentary seat each in their gift. George John, 2nd Earl Spencer, provides a good example of the role of 'the gentry' in such towns at this time. Aligning himself with Pitt on the outbreak of war, in 1794 he became first lord of the admiralty and effectively the chief executive of the Royal Navy, at this time the largest industrial organisation on earth. His sister was Georgiana, duchess of Devonshire, and his wife a central figure in London society, and they were particular supporters of both Lord and Lady Nelson.[105] Spencer was heavily engaged in the detailed management of the navy and of its operations, including the appointments of senior officers. He was also an early investor in the Grand Junction Canal and an important committee member. He was truly eminent, and of himself something of an attraction to St Albans. His mother, the dowager countess Spencer, had returned to live in the town in 1785 and was very influential politically and socially, establishing something of a centre at Holywell House.[106] So people wanting patronage knew that being in St Albans would be helpful, and perhaps because of that they came there in the 1790s, so forming a nucleus of wealth that generated both trade and work in service. But there were no great estates – the town was 'open', with multiple

---

104 For the avoidance of confusion, the 'Liberty of St Albans' refers to Cashio Hundred with twenty-two parishes centred on Watford, and not to St Albans. No part of the Borough was in the Liberty, and no part of the Liberty lay in the Borough.
105 Sugden, *Nelson*, pp. 20, 21, 38, 373, 374; Freeman, *St Albans*, pp. 197–200.
106 Kate Morris and Julia Merrick, *St Albans: gentry town* (St Albans, 2014), p. 17.

owners of property, several political factions and no one person able to dominate the town, which was run by the corporation and the vestries.[107]

St Albans was an important staging centre originally about a day's travel outside London on what was then the important turnpiked road joining London to Holyhead and so to Ireland, and to Chester and so to Manchester. The Chester road was crossed on Holywell Hill by the Reading and Hatfield turnpike referred to earlier. In the 1790s there was no alternative, non-agricultural industry: hay was a significant crop, straw plait vitally important to many and the silk mill yet to appear. St Albans was a commercial centre, not an industrial one, and its development was largely based on its transport links.[108] Some of the effects of this are revealed by the 1801 census, which recorded the populations of the three parishes comprising the town at 3,038, with just 3 per cent of the inhabitants involved in agriculture, 19 per cent in trade, and a spectacular imbalance between the sexes (74:100), typical of a population dominated by females in service and in straw plaiting.

With no alternative to road transport, pedestrians, herds of livestock, waggons, carts and coaches all passed through the town towards and from London on the Chester road, on which were located several important inns.[109] An 1815 report of pack horses as part of the traffic seems unlikely to refer accurately to this period: they had been superseded by wheeled vehicles on roads like this during the mid-eighteenth century, and that freight traffic will have been dominated by the growing number of long-distance waggons of Pickfords and others connecting London to Manchester.[110] The press of vehicles and the difficult configuration of the roads prompted the cutting of a new London road, completed during 1796, which at a stroke took several of the major coaching inns off the new main road. The volume of traffic, however, continued to present a problem. Although the market's corn element, perhaps perversely, declined somewhat during this time, the market itself, supported by the good transport links and by the growth in straw plait dealing, held up well, and this local traffic, mixed with the long-haul, would have added to the congestion of roads and town.[111]

There was no country bank in St Albans until 1800, but there were two common breweries in the 1790s, both with their own maltings. The location

---

107 Freeman, *St Albans*, pp. 195, 202–4.
108 Elsie Toms, *The story of St Albans* (St Albans, 1962); Freeman, *St Albans*, pp. 186–9.
109 See Fig. 2.2, and http://www.turnpikes.org.uk/map%20Hertfordshire%20turnpikes.jpg, accessed 11 October 2018.
110 Solomon Shaw, *History of Verulam* (London, 1815), quoted in Freeman, *St Albans*, p. 190; Turnbull, *Traffic and transport*, pp. 23, 24.
111 Freeman, *St Albans*, p. 186.

of Kingsbury brewery, linked to the Hatfield brewery, is unknown, but it is clear that several houses were tied to it in and around the town. The St Albans brewery reputedly dated from 1776, although the number of its houses was small. It appears, therefore, that most brewing in St Albans was done by the inns themselves: it did not give rise to any business of importance outside the town.[112]

St Albans was, therefore, a very busy and important but small commercial town on a major road from London. The town and its parishes were dominated not so much by manufacturing as by businesses serving the users of the main roads – and by straw plaiting and trading. On the face of it, St Albans merited a canal in its own right, and the fate of the St Albans Canal project will be seen in the following chapters; for now, St Albans provides a comparison with its neighbours who were to be served directly by the waterway.

Conclusion

The general state of affairs in Hertfordshire was that suggested by the county historian Lionel Munby: the villages, and to a large extent the towns, were small, self-sufficient and still affected primarily by events in their own neighbourhood.[113] Wider society was about to intrude on this local stage: but what did the inhabitants of west Hertfordshire expect would happen as the canal approached and became established? Some would have eagerly anticipated opportunities for change; some would have resisted it; and some would have been wholly indifferent. It is important to compare expectation and reality: that comparison begins in the next chapter.

---

112 Whitaker, *Brewers in Hertfordshire*, pp. 186, 187.
113 Munby, *Kings Langley*, p. 115.

Chapter 3
The promise of the canal

The rise of manufacturing industry in Birmingham and the West Midlands depended heavily on good transport links to the consumers of the goods produced, and many of these consumers were in, or were accessed from, London. A route to London via the river Thames at Oxford had been started in the 1770s, although the Oxford Canal had been completed only in 1790. The route was long and circuitous, however, and in any case the Thames, encumbered by many navigation weirs, was highly problematic as a reliable artery for freight traffic. There was nonetheless a great and immediate increase in trade, and it was quickly clear that a more direct canal would be advantageous. The first moves to provide one came in 1791.[1]

Early in 1792 the inhabitants of small towns and rural parishes in western Hertfordshire would have started to hear of the approach of the Grand Junction Canal, and to see the chains and theodolites of the surveyors. The first newspaper article about it appeared in the *Northampton Mercury* in April 1792,[2] but few local people would have understood what it might mean or what was promised. Some will have done, however. By this time the value of canals to both national and local industrial interests, and to those investing in them, had been established for nearly thirty years. The headline attraction was that the price of coal was reduced in towns on or near a canal.[3] But the range of goods carried and the benefits conferred were far greater: finished goods of all sorts, machinery, raw materials, foodstuffs and fuel all found new markets from the 1760s.[4] During the 1770s and 1780s the enormous expansion of manufacturing industry in the Midlands

---

1   Faulkner, *Grand Junction Canal*, p. 1.
2   Quoted in Faulkner, *Grand Junction Canal*, p. 18.
3   Hadfield, *British canals*, p. 95; D.D. Gladwin, *The waterways of Britain* (London, 1976), pp. 13–17.
4   G.W. Crompton, 'Canals and the Industrial Revolution', *Journal of Transport History*, 14/2 (1993), pp. 93–110.

and north demanded a commensurate expansion in transport at a time when waterways were the only realistic option: the trade carried on the canals radiating from Birmingham gave industrialists and investors ample evidence of the value of canal transport. Arthur Young was impressed by the changes to Birmingham:

> The port, as it may be called, or double canal head in the town crowded with barges is a noble spectacle, with that prodigious animation, which the immense trade of this place could alone give. I looked around me with amazement at the change effected in twenty years; so great that this place may now probably be reckoned, with justice, the first manufacturing town in the world.[5]

John Hassell, writing in 1819, recognised the earlier impact of the new canals on Birmingham in particular, observing that:

> Formerly the whole of the manufactories of Birmingham were conveyed from that town by land carriage. The expense attending the conveyance of heavy goods induced the trade of Birmingham to procure the Coventry navigation [by] which ... they conveyed their goods to Braunston by water, and from thence in waggons to London.[6]

When, therefore, the prospect of a canal from the Oxford Canal at Braunston, near Rugby, directly to London was canvassed there was great and widespread interest.[7] In general promoters and proprietors of the early canals had been local people personally interested in their own business and that of their town, county or area, but by 1792, as the Grand Junction was being planned, benefits to investors were much more widely anticipated. Hence the enthusiasm to invest that gave rise to 'Canal Mania', especially coming as it did at the end of the economic depression following the American War of Independence.[8] By 1792 the perceived benefits of these projects were attracting serious money to a number of wildly optimistic schemes, but none of them yet offered the industrial Midlands a direct link to London. The Grand Junction therefore promised

---

5   Arthur Young, *Annals of agriculture* (London, 1791), quoted in Gerard Turnbull, 'Canals, coal and regional growth during the Industrial Revolution', *Economic History Review*, 2nd ser. 40/4 (1987), p. 544.

6   Hadfield, *British canals*, pp. 33, 34; John Hassell, *A tour of the Grand Junction Canal* (London, 1819; reprinted London, 1968), p. 61; David Blagrove, *At the heart of the waterways* (Bugbrooke, 2003), p. 10.

7   Faulkner, *Grand Junction Canal*, p. 18; Turnbull, *Traffic and transport*, pp. 77, 78.

8   Ward, *Finance*, pp. 86–8.

something genuinely new, and this was summed up concisely by William Jessop, the engineering consultant employed by the Grand Junction Committee in late 1792 to review the survey completed by the engineer James Barnes earlier in the year. Jessop confirmed his understanding of the Committee's intention:

> Making a Direct Communication between the Great Northern Manufactories and the Port of London.
> Reducing the cost of Coal to the Inland Counties where it is now extremely expensive.
> The carrying of provisions of all kinds to the Metropolis, where the consumption is almost unbounded,
> [which] ... must banish all doubt from the minds of those who have an opportunity of observing the effect produced by Canals already existing, in situations where the objects are much more limited.[9]

William Jessop at this time was by far the pre-eminent canal engineer in the country,[10] and this would have been a very strong encouragement to invest; it was taken as a green light to the project.[11] But Jessop gives no hint of any other *industrial* benefit to places between London and Birmingham, although in the same report he does refer to branches ('collateral cuts') already envisaged to places off the main line. There is no suggestion here that the main line itself might deviate to take in Buckingham, Dunstable, Daventry, Watford, St Albans or Hemel Hempstead: London was the destination, and nothing would interfere with that. Successful canals were built to exploit economic opportunity and to link main centres of population at each end, and this was to be no exception.[12]

Developing industry

Industry required both fuel and raw materials as well as a labour force, and in Chapter 1 we saw how these factors worked together elsewhere in England. Raw materials had always been lacking in Hertfordshire: it had no mineral resources, so whatever was needed had to be brought in, at great expense. Nearby London was a huge manufacturing centre, so manufacturing did

---

9 BL, General Reference Collection, shelfmark 713.i.27(2.) William Jessop, *Report to the Committee of the Subscribers to the Grand Junction Canal*, Northampton, 1792.
10 Hadfield and Skempton, *William Jessop*, pp. 9, 261.
11 Hadfield and Skelton, *William Jessop*, p. 112.
12 Bagwell and Lyth, *Transport in Britain*, p. 14; Turnbull, 'Canals, coal and regional growth', p. 539.

not flourish in Hertfordshire and in any case the pool of available labour was too small to encourage it. Fuel was a particular problem, as we saw in Chapter 2.[13] In Hertfordshire, as in much of England, the scrub, gorse (furze), broom, heather and bracken used for fuel was becoming depleted. Across the country, coal was becoming essential to life and work: the need to transport it in large quantities drove the development firstly of river navigations and subsequently of canals in the industrial areas of the north and Midlands – the duke of Bridgewater himself held that 'a good canal should have coals at the heels of it'.[14] For many decades London was protected from these pressures because it was served by sea from the north-eastern coalfields, and was to remain so even after the arrival of the railways – and it was to protect this monopoly that the Grand Junction would at first be prohibited from bringing coal closer to London than Watford.[15] Sea-coal shipped to London was carried out to west Hertfordshire by cart along the turnpikes at considerable extra cost and in relatively small quantities. An idea of the cost of road transport before the 1790s comes from experience on the Trent and Mersey Canal between Manchester and Birmingham in the late 1770s – using canal rather than road transport reduced carriage costs from £4 to £1 10s per ton.[16] As late as January 1802 the advertised cost of road carriage of Newcastle coal, which was priced in London at 52s per chaldron (about 1.25 tons), was 2s per chaldron for the first mile and 1s per mile thereafter, adding about 50 per cent to the cost at (say) Berkhamsted – it would have been more ten years before.[17] The aim of the Grand Junction promoters, as expressed by Jessop above, to reduce the cost of coal in places between Birmingham and London was by no means a throwaway line. Coal would not have been widely available, especially not to agricultural labourer families or the poor, and fuel poverty would have been a real concern. Whether the coal came from London or from the Midlands, it was both its availability in volume and its reduced cost that were the promise, and attraction, of the Grand Junction Canal (Figure 3.1).

Road transport in west Hertfordshire

We noted in Chapter 2 the roles in the 1790s of the Sparrows Herne turnpike and the main road passing through St Albans. The Grand Junction's line was planned to follow the former and would inevitably affect its traffic, perhaps

---

13 Bagwell, *Transport revolution*, p. 88.
14 Bagwell, *Transport revolution*, p. 23.
15 Faulkner, *Grand Junction Canal*, p. 110.
16 Turnbull, *Traffic and transport*, pp. 78, 79.
17 Advertisement by Henry Golding, London coal merchant, *The Times*, 15 January 1802.

Figure 3.1. Canal boats on the Grand Junction Canal in west London (LMA, City of London Collage: 23231). These are all narrow boats, and their general layout remains familiar, although the artist has shown various users of the towpath while omitting the canal horses for which it was intended.

at first beneficially, as a customer with material to move, but subsequently as a competitor with a closely parallel route. A similar relationship was observed elsewhere:

> When the canals were built, the takings of turnpike trustees of roads that ran parallel with canals fell sharply: for instance, those of the Loughborough–Leicester road fell from £1,800 in 1792 to £1,162 in 1802 after the Leicester Navigation opened in 1794 ... . Roads that suffered from canal competition had two consolations, that the removal of heavy traffic saved road users a great deal in upkeep costs, while the waterway was useful to carry roadstone to the nearest part of the road.[18]

The minutes of the Sparrows Herne trustees, however, make no reference at all to the canal at this time. This may have been because they were alarmed but did not record it; they may have seen the communal benefit; or they may not have perceived any threat. Analysis of the financial model presented in Appendix D suggests that this turnpike was not, in fact, a major artery of industrial traffic to or from London. Even in 1793 the total toll revenue was

---

18   Hadfield, *British canals*, p. 102.

only £1,428. The remarkably consistent pattern of toll revenue at the different gates (Watford the busiest, Ridge Lane 70 per cent of that figure, New Ground 38 per cent, Veetches in Buckinghamshire 18 per cent – see Appendix D) over these years suggests that the traffic was generally local and concentrated around Watford – a further hint comes from the description of the road in an 1818 survey as the 'Berkhamsted to London' turnpike.[19] Furthermore, perhaps as much as half was passenger traffic, for which the canal was generally not a competitor.[20] The road itself seems to have been reasonably diligently managed: Young, widely travelled and unsparing in his criticism of poorly maintained roads, observed of Hertfordshire merely that the roads were good, 'with six great turnpikes'.[21] The Sparrows Herne turnpike was responsible for about twenty-six miles, most of it in Hertfordshire, and the treasurer's account books show that between 1786 and 1793 the annual spend on the road per mile rose from £22 to £49, averaging £31, which suggests that investment in this turnpike was in line with national practice.[22] Travelling, however, was still not necessarily easy on this road, which, like many others, including the St Albans turnpike, was surfaced with gravel: anyone who has walked on a pebble beach or pushed a wheelbarrow on a gravel driveway will be aware of the difficulty. Writing some seventy years after the initiation of the Grand Junction Canal, Samuel Smiles devoted an entire chapter to a graphic if perhaps jaundiced picture, drawing on the accounts of Arthur Young, of the very poor state of the roads and their effect on the transport of both passengers and goods at, and before, this time: the turnpike itself may have been satisfactory, although limited, but connecting roads were probably not.[23]

Rather than an alternative to an existing freight artery through this area, then, the Grand Junction Canal seems to have promised a completely new one. For the first time the west Hertfordshire towns would be on a major, high-capacity through route. The Sparrows Herne trustees – some of whom, notably the clerk, William Hayton, were early Grand Junction Canal shareholders – must have been aware of the threat, and the promise, of the canal.

---

19 Parliamentary archives, HL/PO/PB/3/plan22 deposited plan, St Albans Canal. See also Figure 5.11.

20 D. Bogart, 'Turnpike trusts and the transportation revolution in 18th century England', *Explorations in Economic History*, 42/4 (2005), pp. 479–508. However, the lack of detailed traffic records from any turnpike trust make it almost impossible to make this statement with any confidence: at best, it reminds us that goods and passenger traffic should be recognised, at least in this context, as different.

21 Mingay, *Arthur Young*, p. 154; Young, *General view*, p. 221.

22 Bagwell, *Transport revolution*, p. 39.

23 Samuel Smiles, *Lives of the engineers*, vol. 1 (London, 1862; reprinted Newton Abbot, 1968), pp. 196–207.

The promise to investors

By the time the Grand Junction Canal became available as an investment, canal projects were already very familiar to those with money to spare. English canals were generally funded by residents in the areas served.[24] But in the case of the Grand Junction, as we have seen, it was the manufacturing and coal-producing areas of the Midlands and the importing and exporting interests of London that would be 'served' by the waterway, rather than those areas through which it would pass. It is, therefore, perhaps unsurprising that relatively few Hertfordshire residents were keen to make major contributions: there were a number of residents of Midlands towns and of towns in other home counties, such as, for example, Aylesbury, but there were few, at least in the first tranche of subscriptions, in Hertfordshire.[25] By this stage of the canal age a significant proportion of the investor cadre were speculators: this project would have been particularly attractive to them because of the wealth being generated at each end.[26]

Some Hertfordshire residents did take up investment options. A comparison between Land Tax and Grand Junction records reveals a few names from the area. Some were landowners, whose position with regard to the canal passing through their land is discussed below.[27] A few, such as the London banker Drummond Smith, who had moved to Tring Park in 1786, were invited directly to invest in order to encourage them to join the committee or a sub-committee, and others were no doubt attracted by the investment returns. Motives to invest included benefiting business, improving the value of land, making a reliable family investment, supporting a special interest in the canal as a professional engagement (notably the canal engineers) or making quick money.[28] By the start of the 1793 'Canal Mania' investors' returns in the early canals were considerable and well known. Dividends were high, with average returns at this time in the range 30–40 per cent.[29] Furthermore, the price of shares had rocketed: shares in the Birmingham Canal, which cost £140 in 1767, had reached £370 by 1782 and £1,170 in 1792, just at the time when investors began to consider the Grand

---

24 Ward, *Finance*, pp. 79, 97.
25 Ward, *Finance*, p. 45.
26 T.C. Barker and Christopher Savage, *Economic history of transport in Britain* (London, 2012), p. 41.
27 Many of the names of landowners are recorded in TNA, RAIL 830/37 GJC lower district committee minutes 1793–1797 in and after June 1793; Ward, *Finance*, p. 43.
28 Hadfield, *Canal age*, pp. 37, 38.
29 Ward, *Finance*, p. 135.

Junction.[30] One of the surprisingly few references to canal investments in the *Gentleman's Magazine* is a letter expressing concern about the effect of the wild speculation of the time. Suggesting that interest on canal speculation should be limited by parliament to 10 or 12 per cent, the author went on:

> I know that it has been said that the proprietors of the shares in some canals (particularly the Grand Junction) will, in a few years after they are completed, obtain at least 25 or 30 per cent interest on their money ... canals are now become quite a lottery; and there is a much gambling going forward ... as in the Alley.[31]

In fact the Grand Junction was to pay nothing until 1801 and only about 8 per cent on average between 1801 and 1841, but investors would have been conscious of the 30 per cent rate, comparing it in particular with the 'blue chip' investments of the day: government 3 per cent Consols, and Bank of England and East India Company shares at about the same rate.[32] Nonetheless, it does not appear that the promise of the Grand Junction Canal was a widely attractive investment in western Hertfordshire.

The promise to landowners

Landowners could capitalise on an approaching canal project either by selling land to the company or by taking advantage of the fact that their land was suddenly on the line of a major through route and transport artery. In 1793 Hertfordshire landowners had the opportunity to do both. It was recognised that landowners could not be allowed simply to refuse to sell land to a canal once approved by parliament. Compulsory purchase was enshrined in the various canal acts, as it was for both river and road improvements, with commissioners appointed to ensure that land was correctly valued and appropriate compensation paid. The services of such commissioners were required very little in Hertfordshire, where most of the landowners were content with the price offered, although some agreements were greeted with relief by the committee.[33] Across the country a landowner often had more at stake than just improving his estate and exploiting the mineral wealth, if any, beneath it. Sometimes there was a need to maximise capital by selling land for canal building: land is an illiquid asset, and this

---

30 Burton, *Canal builders*, p. 62.
31 *The Gentleman's Magazine*, vol. 62 (1792), quoted in Burton, *Canal builders*, p. 65.
32 Faulkner, *Grand Junction Canal*, pp. 109, 110, 166, 224; Hadfield, *British canals*, pp. 158, 159.
33 For example, Harcourt of Pendley, who had flatly refused the first offer – TNA, RAIL 830/39 GJC general assembly and general committee minutes, 28 March 1794.

offered one way of monetising it, although holding out to optimise one's returns had to be balanced against the risk of unintentionally holding up the project by doing so.[34] Chapter 4 will consider how the Grand Junction's land purchases were realised, but here it is worth noting that, whereas purchasing land typically required a canal company to lay out about 10 per cent of the total cost, for the Grand Junction it was more like 20 per cent, partly as a result of very high compensation payments in Watford and partly because of relatively high prices in Middlesex.[35] The right of selling landowners to buy shares (one for each acre sold, up to a maximum of ten) at face value of £100 was clearly attractive: the company set aside 1,000 shares in trust to cover this commitment, and many, but not all, were taken up. Overall, some 50 per cent of the Grand Junction landowners did so, whereas, for example, only about 10 per cent of the landowners did so for the contemporaneous Kennet and Avon Canal, connecting Bristol to Reading and the Thames.[36]

There is, however, little evidence here of the other suggested reason for landowner enthusiasm: a benefit to their business interests – the 'economic motive'.[37] With most of the land used for agriculture rather than industry, and with little prospect of new canal-related businesses developing quickly, Hertfordshire landowners could not expect to suddenly set up manufacturing premises. Indeed, among the paper makers only Griffith Jones of Nash Mill seems to have invested in the new canal, while none among the silk throwsters did so. On balance, then, there was little perceived benefit to either agricultural or industrial interests: the promise to Hertfordshire landowners was limited to the prospect of selling their land for cash.

The promise to the towns
Chapter 1 explained how towns generally developed during this time. By 1770 Arthur Young was among several already writing in highly approving terms of the developments and workings of the Birmingham Canal and of the duke of Bridgewater's operations at Worsley.[38] In 1792 John Phillips was already able to write that 'the canals have entirely changed the appearance of the counties through which they flow'.[39] It was widely anticipated that

---

34 Ward, *Finances*, pp. 143, 153, 156.
35 Arthur Young, *Enquiry into the progressive value of money in England* (London, 1812), quoted in Ward, *Finances*, pp. 148, 149.
36 Ward, *Finances*, pp. 44, 157.
37 Ward, *Finances*, p. 126.
38 Mingay, *Arthur Young*, pp. 145–54.
39 John Phillips, *A general history of inland navigation, foreign and domestic* (London, 1792), p. viii.

considerable economic benefits would accrue wherever a canal passed. Townspeople, traders and professionals along a proposed canal, well aware of the opportunities offered by canals elsewhere over the previous thirty years, would have been keen to exploit those opportunities as well.

But we saw in Chapter 2 that Hertfordshire towns at this time were small, principally dedicated to agriculture, and local rather than regional in influence.[40] Most of those on the western side of the county had a small element of local manufacturing as well as the trades and services usual to a market town, and some benefits, in the form of new jobs, businesses or goods and foodstuffs in shops, would have been expected from the canal.[41] Many factors, however, affected those benefits, and not all were encouraging to Hertfordshire interests. As already noted, the main drivers of the Grand Junction were at either end, while the greatest influence on rapid development elsewhere was the presence of minerals, which were wholly absent from Hertfordshire: there was nothing to generate major urban development. In the early 1790s Hertfordshire had little manufacturing, not least because fuel was expensive and hard to obtain, whereas agriculture was well-organised and relatively prosperous, with its main market in London reasonably accessible by road. In other places canals brought new prosperity to a new range of local entrepreneurs: but some prosperity was already being brought to west Hertfordshire by those who had made, or were still making, their money in or through London, and they had little need to set up new enterprises in the county.

Nonetheless, with the canal approaching, the traders of Watford, St Albans and Hemel Hempstead, none of which was planned to be on the main line, were all keen to have their 'collateral cut'. These were promised for Watford and St Albans in the original or amending parliamentary acts, and the towns protested strongly when it began to become clear that the cuts would not be made.[42] Even if major local manufacturing was unlikely to start up, manufactured goods arriving from elsewhere would be anticipated, as had happened elsewhere, and dealers and shopkeepers as well as potential customers would have been well aware of it. Connection to a canal was widely expected to increase both prosperity and population: indeed, some inland towns (for example, Birmingham and Coventry) that had been given

---

40   Slater and Goose, *County of small towns*, Ch. 1.
41   Trinder, 'Market town industry', pp. 75–89.
42   Alan Faulkner, *Grand Junction Canal in Hertfordshire* (Hatfield, 1993), p. 9; H.C.F. Lansberry, 'The St Albans canal', *Hertfordshire's Past*, 7 (1967), pp. 3–8; Faulkner, *Grand Junction Canal*, pp. 68–9.

canal access had become ports as well as manufacturing centres.[43] Towns needed a constant supply of both food and fuel, and the cost of transporting these was a key economic consideration in Hertfordshire as elsewhere. West Hertfordshire was already reasonably well provided with road transport, but it was local rather than national in scope: a new waterway might have allowed at least some of these towns to take advantage of being on a major high-capacity transport route and to develop as ports. But some successful towns that did grow in this way, such as the Westmorland town of Kendal, made active preparations for their new opportunity, with roads improved and wharves and warehouses prepared in advance, suggesting that, although major manufacturing was not necessarily a prerequisite for canal-generated prosperity, preparatory action of some sort was helpful.[44] There is no sign of this having been done in west Hertfordshire.

The promise to agriculture
There was some promise of benefit to farmers, although Jessop did not refer to it in his synopsis. As already noted, one consequence of steadily improving transport in the eighteenth century was a national market for agricultural produce, as grain and more durable foodstuffs, such as cheese, could be moved far outside their area of origin. Hertfordshire farmers, who would have been well aware of these developments, might have expected to benefit considerably from the Grand Junction Canal and the huge distant markets it opened up. The same applied to those retailing produce, whether from shops or market stalls: no longer was the stock of the shopkeeper limited to what was grown locally. The use of canals to transport produce to markets was already well known; indeed, some parliamentary acts, including the Grand Junction's, made special provision for the short-distance transport of agricultural materials.[45] Further, as Young noted, the long-established backload of manure of many sorts from London and elsewhere would have been expected to be greatly increased: a waggon carrying perhaps four tons might be replaced by a barge carrying sixty tons for the same, or less, effort.[46]

But Hertfordshire farmers were already relatively close by road to their main market, London: would they be able to increase their production to enable them to send it north to new markets rather than (or as well as) to their main established one? In any case, as we have seen, a particular problem emerges when serving farms by canal: the area to be served might be several

---

43 J. Douglas Porteous, *Canal ports* (London, 1977), pp. 24, 25.
44 Porteous, *Canal ports*, p. 33.
45 Faulkner, *Grand Junction Canal*, p. 23.
46 Young, *General view*, p. 17.

hundred acres, and many tracks and roadways would be needed, whereas industrial sites were much more compact and easily served by a single dock or wharf. So for farmers whose fields lay more than a few hundred yards off the line of the canal much of the benefit of canal transport would be lost once goods or materials had to be put into carts to get to the canal: they might just as well continue to their destination by road.[47] The promise to west Hertfordshire agriculture may well, therefore, have been rather more limited than that to other sectors of the local economy.

Conclusion

In the early 1790s western Hertfordshire was overwhelmingly agricultural, with villages scattered around small towns. The main turnpike road brought little benefit to most of them, despite providing reasonable links to both London and the Midlands. The small rivers powered corn mills and small pockets of industry, mainly silk spinning and paper making, and London dominated the market for the main agricultural product, wheat.

As the Grand Junction Canal began to materialise in early 1792 it offered a range of opportunities to various people, including local landowners and business people, all well aware of the success of the earlier canals and of the remarkable developments that they had enabled in the new industrial towns. The main aim was to connect Midlands industry and London, but the new canal offered towns along the line a chance to develop in a new way, and also a redress to the growing threat of fuel poverty. The overall promise of the Grand Junction Canal was a strong and attractive one: the extent to which that promise was realised in western Hertfordshire will be examined in the following chapters.

---

47 Wrigley, *The path to sustained growth*, p. 139.

Chapter 4
The coming of the canal

The earlier chapters considered the context within which the canal was planned and the general state of Hertfordshire's agrarian, largely arable economy, as well as the expectations of both potential investors (some of them in Hertfordshire, but most not) and local people along the proposed route of the canal. This chapter discusses what happened once the plan was formalised by the royal assent to the parliamentary act: the purchase of the land, the effects on the other users of water in the area and on their industries, and the way in which the workforce was recruited and employed.

Before any work could start it was necessary, firstly, to gain parliamentary approval in the form of an enabling act that permitted the company to issue shares to raise money and to obtain the land through which the canal would be cut.[1] As we shall see, the provisions of the act were to constrain the company's actions considerably, and will feature at several points in this account. The first thing to be done was to obtain the land.

Buying the land

When a major operation such as the building of a canal was intended, the company itself – given that government involvement was minimal – had to obtain the land required, and all canal acts made provision for this. Financial estimates had to be made before negotiations with landowners could start: a canal with a surface width of forty-eight feet needed about ten feet more for the towpath, and where an embankment or cutting was required the whole of the footprint, often very much greater, had to be bought – the Grand Junction's basic width allowance was sixty feet.[2] So the land required was

---

1   The parliamentary process did not relate specifically to Hertfordshire, and has been described very well by Alan Faulkner in particular: it is not repeated here. See Alan Faulkner, *The Grand Junction Canal*, 2nd edn (Rickmansworth, 1993), pp. 2–6; Burton, *Canal builders*, pp. 49–60.
2   John Phillips, *A general history of inland navigation, foreign and domestic*, 5th edn (London, 1805; reprinted Newton Abbot, 1970), pp. 305, 306.

at least seven acres for each mile of length, and could easily be ten acres, sometimes more, especially if a wharf was planned – for this, the Grand Junction was allowed up to forty-five yards. This is confirmed by the details of the purchase at Boxmoor, Hemel Hempstead, where the length of one mile three furlongs ten poles needed nine acres and two roods and cost £300 – £32 per acre for rather boggy pasture.[3] Furthermore, the act required the company to purchase, if asked by the owner, any remaining parcel of land of area less than two acres when the rest of a plot had been bought.[4] Such extra purchases were not usually determined until the detailed plan had been laid out. The area of land that the canal needed in Hertfordshire was therefore theoretically over 200 acres: in fact, very much more was to be bought eventually, and in addition it was necessary to provide reservoirs to supply the summit at Tring and at Aldenham to replace water taken from the river Colne south of Watford. Although the company had powers of purchase conveyed by the parliamentary act, agreement on price was still required. The land would first be measured by surveyors and valued by the company's valuers, and then an offer would be made. If the landowner refused it, the dispute was referred to a body of commissioners named in the act, themselves often landowners, and their decision could be appealed to a jury, whose verdict was final.[5] The general value of land was about 'thirty years purchase' – that is, thirty times the annual rent, which at this time in Hertfordshire was less than £1 per acre – but more was usually paid to cover the likely inconvenience, such as separating a farmhouse from its land or cutting off a field from a road. Some purchases were for very much more than that, and we saw in Chapter 3 that the Grand Junction spent about 20 per cent of the total cost of the canal on the purchase of land alone – about twice as much as usual.[6]

The very first meeting of the general committee of the company accordingly made arrangements for a detailed survey and valuation of the required land, and agreed the overall terms of the purchases.[7] The engineer, James Barnes, was encouraged to complete laying out the line of the canal – making a precise survey along the whole broadly agreed line of the canal and marking it with pegs – quickly, so that land ownership could be accurately assessed and negotiations begun. Purchases proceeded apace, with valuations varying

---

3   A mile = 1760 yards = 8 furlongs. A furlong = 10 chains each of 22 yards, 4 rods = 1 chain. An acre is a chain by a furlong = 4840 square yards. 40 perches = 1 rood, 4 roods = 1 acre.
4   33 Geo.3 c.80 Grand Junction Canal, Clause XXVIII.
5   Hadfield, *British canals*, pp. 47, 48.
6   Ward, *Finance*, p. 144; 33 Geo.3 c.80.
7   TNA, RAIL 830/37 GJC lower district committee minutes 1793–1797, 1 June 1793.

widely but generally in the range £50–£80 per acre. Bridges were required to carry roads, and were often demanded by landowners too, but these were often 'bought out' by the payment of compensation, to the landowner rather than to the farmer whose operations were inconvenienced by the separation of fields from farm or road and who may or may not have been given any part of the compensation. A sample of the land purchases in Hertfordshire (Table 4.1) is derived from the minutes of successive committee meetings and from the records of the clerks to the company, the Aylesbury solicitors Gray and Chaplin.[8]

It seems that purchases were still being made, at least in Hertfordshire, surprisingly late – in many cases, after work had already started. Although the landowners must have agreed to give access ahead of the purchase being formalised, there was clearly pressure to keep the work moving once it had begun. For example, in May 1796 the clerks of the company asked Caius College for permission to enter their land at Croxley to proceed with the work, even though the land purchase there was not concluded until later that year.[9] The notes of Gray and Chaplin show some of the substance behind the simple facts. For example, in 1798 Paul Vaillant of Northchurch 'insisted on an agreement in writing for expressing the time of payment of the purchase money, the creation of bridges and other matters before he would permit the company's workmen to enter his land'. The purchase from Joseph Allen of Hemel Hempstead involved an exchange of land on each side of the canal between him and John Field to avoid the need for an accommodation bridge. And the purchase from Francis Cromack of Abbots Langley was complicated by the death of the previous owner, who had already agreed a lower price than Cromack was seeking, and by a dispute over the valuation of some trees that had been removed during the cutting.[10] All along the canal the owners, and no doubt the occupiers, of the land were involved in disputes great and small, and this will have had an unsettling effect on the area. The work proceeded nonetheless.

There was, however, a difficulty relating to land ownership that was not immediately apparent. Some of the land to be procured was copyhold, as described in Chapter 1. This should not have created any problems, since the purchase procedure laid down in the act ought to have superseded the

---

8   TNA, RAIL 830/37 GJC lower district committee minutes 1793–1797, various dates; CBS, Gray and Chaplin Archive GJC/9, 1798/9. Edward Oakley Gray was actually of Buckingham, while Acton Chaplin was from Aylesbury, where their business was based. They acted as clerks until 1805.
9   TNA, RAIL 830/38 GJC upper district committee minutes, 3 May 1796.
10 CBS, Gray and Chaplin Archive GJC/9 1798/9.

Table 4.1. A sample of land purchases and valuations by the Grand Junction Canal Company in Hertfordshire.

Parish and landowner	Area bought[1] (acres. roods. perches)	Price paid	Value per acre (approx.)
Rickmansworth			
H.F. Whitfeld	1.1.3	£74.0.3	£56
Samuel Leightonhouse	3.0.34	£171.4.8	£53
Joseph Skidmore	3.3.17	£308.10.0	£77
Joseph James	0.1.35	£37.10.0	£81
Joseph Hone	0.0.25	£4.13.9	£36
Aldenham Commoners (for reservoir)	10.0.0	£300.0.0	£30
Lot Mead			
Unnamed	1.0.18	£66.15.0	£60
James Bovingdon	8.0.0	£640	£80
Solomon Weedon	4.0.20	£318.2.6	£77
Jedidiah Strutt	2.3.0	£206.5.0	£75
Geo. Philip Ehret	2.0.0	£160.0.0	£80
Robert Clutterbuck	1.3.20	£140.12.6	£75
Joseph Skidmore	1.0.0	£75	£75
Caius College (Common Moor)	4.3.11	£108.8.5	£23
Caius College (Croxley Hall, Cashio Bridge Farms)	6.1.17	£226.17.6	£36
Hemel Hempstead			
Boxmoor Trustees	9.2.0	£300.0.0	£32
Corner Hall	2.0.0	£160.0.0	£80
Corner Hall – Tan Yard Meadow (Mrs Rebecca Shipton – for the wharf?)	2.0.0	£120	£60
Watford			
Earl of Clarendon (The Grove)	1.2.7	£100.6.10½d	£63
Northchurch	4.2.33	£282.7.6	£60
Kings Langley			
Mrs Elizabeth Blayney	0.2.23	£33.5.11	£52
Earl of Essex (occupier, Newman Hatley)	7.0.6	£433.15.7	£63
Abbots Langley			
Matthew Sutton	0.2.0	£42.10.0	£85
Francis Cromack	0.0.25	£16.8.1½	£100
Belsize Farm	2.0.14	£62	£30
John Strange	1.0.6 (meadow) 1.1.15 (arable)	£123.6.3[2]	£53

1   40 perches = 1 rood; 4 roods = 1 acre; 1 acre = 4840 sq yards = 1 furlong (220 yds) × 1 chain (22 yds).

2   The valuer's valuation was £90, but, pragmatically, the company paid what was demanded.

provisions of copyhold tenure, but some of the copyholders were uneasy about this and sought special assurances. Forty years later at Rickmansworth it was to lead to a very unusual dispute that would take over fifteen years to resolve, when the then lord of the manor decided that he still owned the land.[11]

Damage to nearby property was also a feature of canal building, and it was anticipated in the act. Compensation was usually paid without demur, having been assessed by the surveyor.[12] In Rickmansworth, for example, three farmers were paid a total of £120; in Kings Langley an orchard was damaged and £12 was paid, after an initial offer of £7 had been rejected; damage at Northchurch was due to a spoil bank and broken fencing, for which £2 14s 6d was paid, while similar damage at Tring and Aldbury attracted compensation payments of £12 6s 0d and £37 5s 6d respectively; and £50 was paid for damage to a plantation of trees during a widening operation at Tring.[13] Many of the claims were made two or three years in retrospect, but were generally met: the company was keen not to alienate its neighbours any more than it already had.

Progress through Hertfordshire

Building the canal started at both ends immediately after the act received royal assent on 30 April 1793, and the length through Hertfordshire is shown in Figure 4.1.[14] It opened northwards progressively from the Thames at Brentford, reaching Uxbridge in November 1794, Rickmansworth in the summer of 1796, Kings Langley by September 1797, Two Waters (Hemel Hempstead) early in 1798 and Berkhamsted in the autumn of that year. Crossing the Chilterns at Tring was always recognised as being a major task, and William Jessop had confirmed as much in his report of October 1792.[15] A canal of any length has to cross undulating terrain using embankments and cuttings to maintain the level, with locks to change levels, and often has to climb up the side of a hill, cross its summit and descend the other side. And so the Grand Junction climbs southwards up the escarpment of the Chilterns towards Tring, where it enters Hertfordshire, has a three-mile summit, as shown in Figure 4.3 (below), and then descends the dipslope in a thirty-seven-mile-long drop of 142 metres through fifty-five locks to the

---

11 Faulkner, *Grand Junction Canal*, pp. 123, 124.
12 33 Geo.3 c.80 Grand Junction Canal, Clause LII.
13 For example TNA, RAIL 830/38 GJC upper district committee minutes 1796–98, 8 May, 17 October 1796, 14 March, 21 April 1797; DHT, DAHCT 51.015, receipt for payment (Richard Bard Harcourt), 20 May 1801.
14 Faulkner, *Grand Junction Canal*, pp. 27–41; Charles Hadfield, *The canals of the East Midlands* (Newton Abbot, 1981), pp. 110–13.
15 BL, General Reference Collection 713.i.27.(2.), Jessop, *Report to the GJC Committee*.

Figure 4.1. The route of the Grand Junction Canal through west Hertfordshire (abstracted from *Plan of the Grand Junction, Grand Union and Union Canals* by C.S. Smith [London, 1810]) (By permission of Canalmaps Archive, www.canalmaps.net, A0863).

Thames. Water had to be supplied into this summit pound (a pound being the stretch of a canal between two locks), as boats heading downhill in either direction use it to fill and empty the locks as they descend and others ascend.

There were two problems at Tring. One was the physical task of cutting though the chalk to reduce the level to that at Bulbourne on the north side and Cowroast on the south; the other, much harder to resolve, was the supply of water, to which we will return below. The first task of making the cutting was commenced in the summer of 1793. Probably employing about 1,000 men at the peak of activity, it continued through both of the very cold, wet winters of 1795 and 1796 and was completed in early 1797, along with the Wendover arm running north of Tring.[16] Meanwhile, progress from

---

16   Richards, *Tring*, p. 48, Faulkner, *Grand Junction Canal*, p. 39.

the south passed Berkhamsted and connected with the finished summit in early 1799, completing the whole Hertfordshire section, connecting it to the Thames and allowing trading traffic from Wendover and Tring to join that already using the southern section to and from London via the river. The line northwards between Tring and Birmingham was completed in early 1801, except for the expensive and inconvenient need to trans-ship cargoes for a further four years across Plainwood Hill at Blisworth, near Northampton, while that tunnel was being painfully completed.[17] By the start of 1801, therefore, the new waterway connected London to the Midlands, and a few months later the important branch running from the canal's main line at Southall to Paddington took traffic much closer to the heart of the capital. The Grand Junction was ready for business.

On the way, however, there had been one important change of plan, and it directly affected west Hertfordshire. The original plan was to tunnel 900 yards under Langleybury, north of Watford, in order to avoid the parks of the earls of Essex and Clarendon. William Jessop disliked tunnels, not because he was not capable of directing such work but because a tunnel always threatened the schedule and budget of his client, and he was ever mindful of the need to reduce such threats (the later shambles at Blisworth was particularly painful to him).[18] Early in January 1794 the company, with its chairman William Praed taking the lead, opened negotiations with Essex and Clarendon, among others, and was eventually successful in getting their agreement that the canal line could follow the river Gade through their parks (Figure 4.2).[19]

Indeed, the greatest of all 'damages compensations' were those paid to the earls for the right to divert through their parks at Watford (Cassiobury and The Grove respectively) to avoid tunnelling at Langleybury – £15,000 to Essex and £5,000 (which included the land) to Clarendon. As noted in Table 4.1, Clarendon was also paid over £100 for other land, but there seems to be no record of Essex being paid per acre – on 1 September 1795 the cash book records a part-payment to 'the Earl of Essex … for liberty to cut through Cashiobury Park £2,000'.[20] As a member of the company's general committee, perhaps he felt he had received enough.

This diversion had two significant consequences. Firstly, the complication of a tunnel (and of an aqueduct at Kings Langley, which it would have necessitated in turn) was removed. Secondly, the new line of the canal came

---

17 Faulkner, *Grand Junction Canal*, pp. 22–4.
18 Hadfield and Skempton, *William Jessop*, pp. 114, 117.
19 TNA, RAIL 830/39 GJC general committee minutes 1793–1798.
20 TNA, RAIL 830/63 GJC treasurer's cash book 1794–1801.

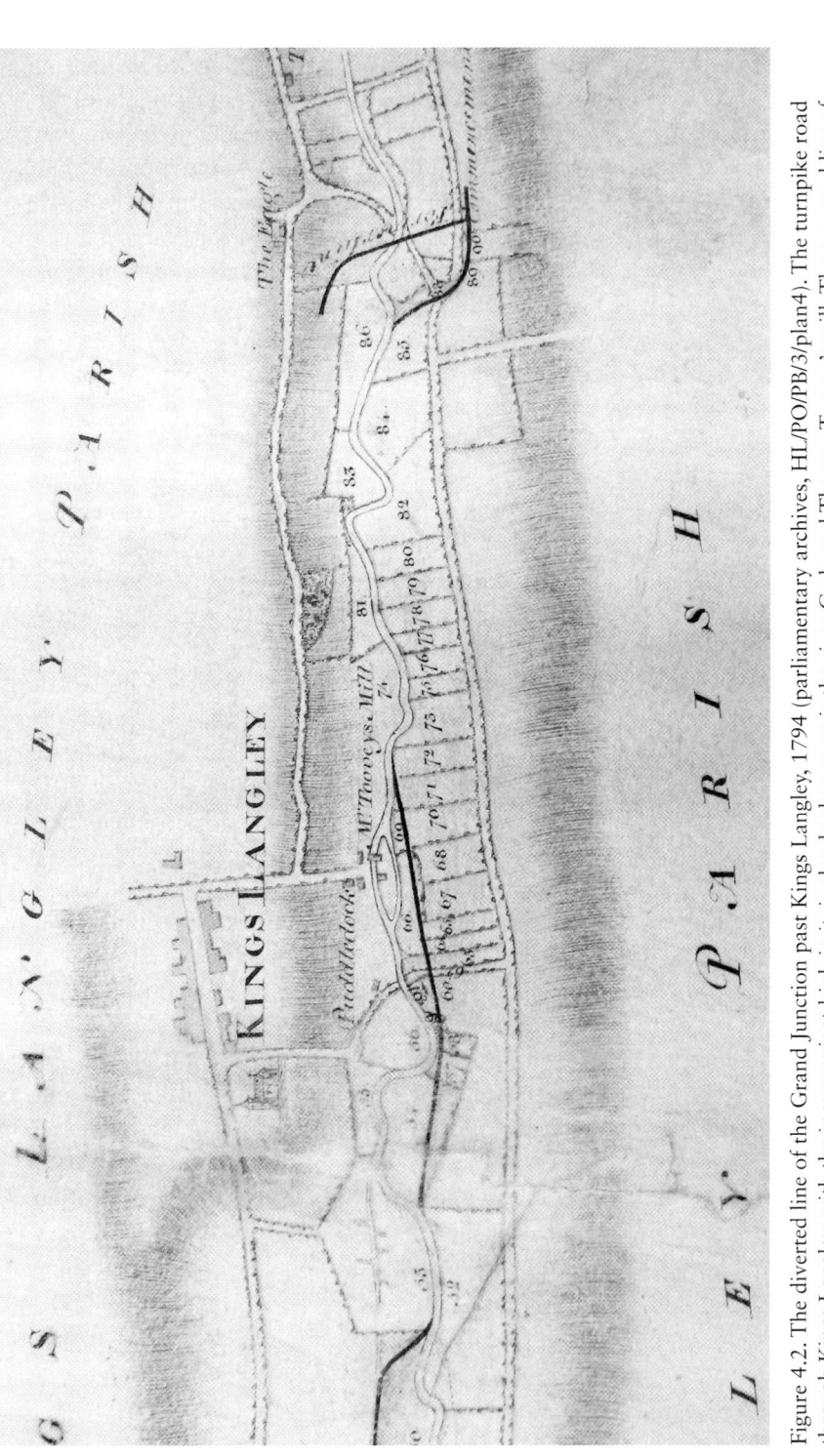

Figure 4.2. The diverted line of the Grand Junction past Kings Langley, 1794 (parliamentary archives, HL/PO/PB/3/plan4). The turnpike road through Kings Langley, with the inconvenient kink in it, is clearly shown, as is the river Gade and Thomas Toovey's mill. The surveyed line of the canal making use of the river is shown as a black line, and the 'former line' is also shown. The diversion, principally to avoid the need for Langleybury Tunnel, also obviated an aqueduct over the river and a bridge under the turnpike, as is shown on the right of the plan.

sufficiently close to Watford to make it at least arguable that the branch to the bottom of the High Street there, authorised in the original act, was no longer needed. Wharfs on the new line, to be provided at Cashio Bridge and The Grove, would suffice to serve the town at a distance of a couple of miles, and were in any case required by the enacted prohibition on carrying coal any further south than Lady Capels' (*sic* – there were two Ladies) Wharf near The Grove. Despite the appeals of the town, led by Lord Clarendon in particular, the Grand Junction Company, increasingly strapped for cash and with the Paddington arm having much higher priority, became unwilling to provide the Watford branch, stating as early as 1796 that it would do so only if the town paid for it.[21] This invitation was declined, and we will see later how Watford was affected by the decision.

Perhaps more importantly, the St Albans canal, sponsored by the Earl Verulam and for which a separate act had been obtained in 1795, was a fully surveyed extension of the Watford branch along the rivers Colne and Ver.[22] When the Watford branch was deleted, so, effectively, was the St Albans Canal, although that was not formalised until 1808: the effect on St Albans will be considered briefly in Chapter 6.

Aside from the Tring cutting there are no eye-catching engineering features on the canal south of the Chilterns, but a number of problems had to be overcome nonetheless and some of the engineering difficulties affected the surrounding countryside. There was plenty of cutting, and more importantly embanking, to be done, notwithstanding that the existing courses of the rivers Gade and Bulbourne were adopted in several places. Many of the lock approaches had to be heavily embanked, such as those at Winkwell, north of Hemel Hempstead, at Cashio Bridge and Croxley Green near Watford, and at Rickmansworth, where the rivers Colne, Chess and Gade come together in a very complex set of interacting channels which had to be negotiated. At Berkhamsted, the valley of the river Bulbourne, marshy and unhealthy, had to be drained by the new waterway; and at Boxmoor, too, a low-lying meadow had to be crossed. Many of the work sites were wet, a situation exacerbated by the heavy rainfall of 1795 and 1796, so the lock workings had to be pumped out.[23] In all of these places the canal cutting intruded visibly on the local countryside, and although disruption to the local economy was probably not great the canal cutting was by no means unobtrusive.

---

21 Faulkner, *Grand Junction Canal*, pp. 68, 69.
22 35 Geo.3 c.85 St Albans Canal; TNA, RAIL 830/39 GJC general committee minutes 1793–1798; Lansberry, 'The St Albans canal'.
23 Faulkner, *Grand Junction Canal*, 2nd edn, p. 13.

The impact of the wet and very cold weather of 1794/5 and 1796/7 demands consideration. As we have seen, by the end of 1794 the French wars were already having an economic effect, and the poor harvest that year was to be one of a series, with the very wet autumn resulting in widespread floods and the last weeks of the year turning cold all across the country. The winter was exceptionally severe, with very cold conditions setting in on Christmas Eve 1794. The frost lasted, with some breaks, until late March. A rapid but temporary thaw, accompanied by heavy rain, began on 7 February, and resulted in flooding across large areas of England, with extensive damage: bridges, canals and turnpikes were rendered unusable. The severe cold returned after 12 February and continued well into March. On 23 February the Severn and the Thames were frozen, and there was frequent snow in easterly winds.[24] Prices increased sharply, not only of wheat but also of the quartern loaf (4lb 5oz – 2kg), which was the staple diet of the families of the farm labourers who formed the greatest part of the population. Between 1765 and 1794 the price of that loaf, of which a family would eat several a week, had varied only between 6d and 8d (about a twelfth of a typical labourer's weekly income); but during 1795 the price doubled to around about 1s 2d, while agricultural wages hardly changed.

Real and potentially fatal hardship threatened widely, and the west of Hertfordshire was not immune.[25] At Rickmansworth in February 1795 the vestry was concerned at the 'very broken and decayed state of Batchworth Bridge (occasioned by the late floods)' and took various actions, including building a temporary bridge.[26] The spring weather did not improve, and the situation became serious. On 11 July 1795 a meeting was chaired by Thomas Rous of Moor Park of 'the Gentlemen and Principal Inhabitants to consider the best way of relieving the poor from the alarming and increasing high price of bread, and to secure to the inhabitants of Rickmansworth sufficient wheat or other grain for the use of the said Inhabitants until the next Harvest'.[27] As a result a number of actions were taken to relieve the poor and control both the supply and price of bread. At Tring and Watford different but equally exceptional measures were taken to provide food directly to the poor.[28] The following year, 1796, was better, with a dry summer and a fair harvest, but

---

24 Martin Rowley, 'British weather from 1700 to 1849', <http://www.pascalbonenfant.com/18c/geography/weather.html>, accessed 21 March 2019; James Woodforde, *The diary of a country parson 1758–1802*, ed. J. Beresford (Oxford, 1978), pp. 477–86.
25 Horn, *Rural world*, pp. 38–44.
26 HALS, DP/85/8/9 Rickmansworth vestry minutes 1783–1796.
27 HALS, DP/85/8/9 Rickmansworth vestry minutes 1783–1796, 11 July 1795.
28 HALS, DP/111/8/19 Tring vestry minutes 1782–1815; DP/117/8/2 Watford vestry minutes 1785–1812, 31 March 1795 and 4 February 1796.

measures for relief of the poor continued during that year, and the following winter was again notably cold and wet. What is remarkable is that in the midst of all this the builders of the canal, who were hard at work in the area between 1794 and 1797, seem to have been unaffected – at least, the committee of the Grand Junction Company recorded no reports of delays, nor any problem feeding the workforce. Why this was so is unclear – perhaps it shows that they made wholly separate arrangements to acquire bread or flour, which would scarcely have made for good community relations, but again there seems to have been no comment on this on either side at the time. Certainly, when the London and Birmingham Railway faced the same problem forty years later the engineers reported real difficulty and delay, but the Grand Junction Canal seems to have been immune.[29]

Water supplies for the canal
We have already touched on the problems of supplying the canal in Hertfordshire with water, but they deserve closer attention. Any canal has, in effect, its source at its summit, and boats using the canal take their water with them as they descend – in theory. Each pound is therefore supplied from the lock descending into it, and boats going up use the lock vacated by the boats coming down, and fill the lock with the next boat's water. So, in theory, each boat uses only one lock full of water in its whole descent, carrying about fifty tons of cargo. This is supplied relatively easily by reservoirs built a little above the level of the summit, with their water running gently into the summit pound and moving from there downhill to feed the whole canal.

There are, however, several problems with the theory, and they were and remain particularly relevant to Hertfordshire. First, leakage and evaporation have to be compensated for. Second, by no means all boats climb to or descend from the summit: many will start and finish much lower down, and their water must be provided at that intermediate level. Thirdly, although lock capacities are reasonably constant (in broad terms, those of the Grand Junction were 56,000 gallons or 250,000 litres – 250 tonnes), the boats using them vary in size and capacity: a single narrow boat uses as much water as a pair of boats or a barge but carries much less cargo, and so is much less efficient in its use of water. The overall requirement for water was therefore much greater than the theory suggests. Furthermore, the Chilterns are notably dry and porous land: these problems were recognised both

---

29 Peter Lecount, 'A history of the railway connecting London and Birmingham' (London, 1839) and Robert Stephenson's reports to the Board of the London and Birmingham Railway, quoted in Ian Petticrew and Wendy Austin, *The railway comes to Tring* (Tring, 2013), pp. 19, 20.

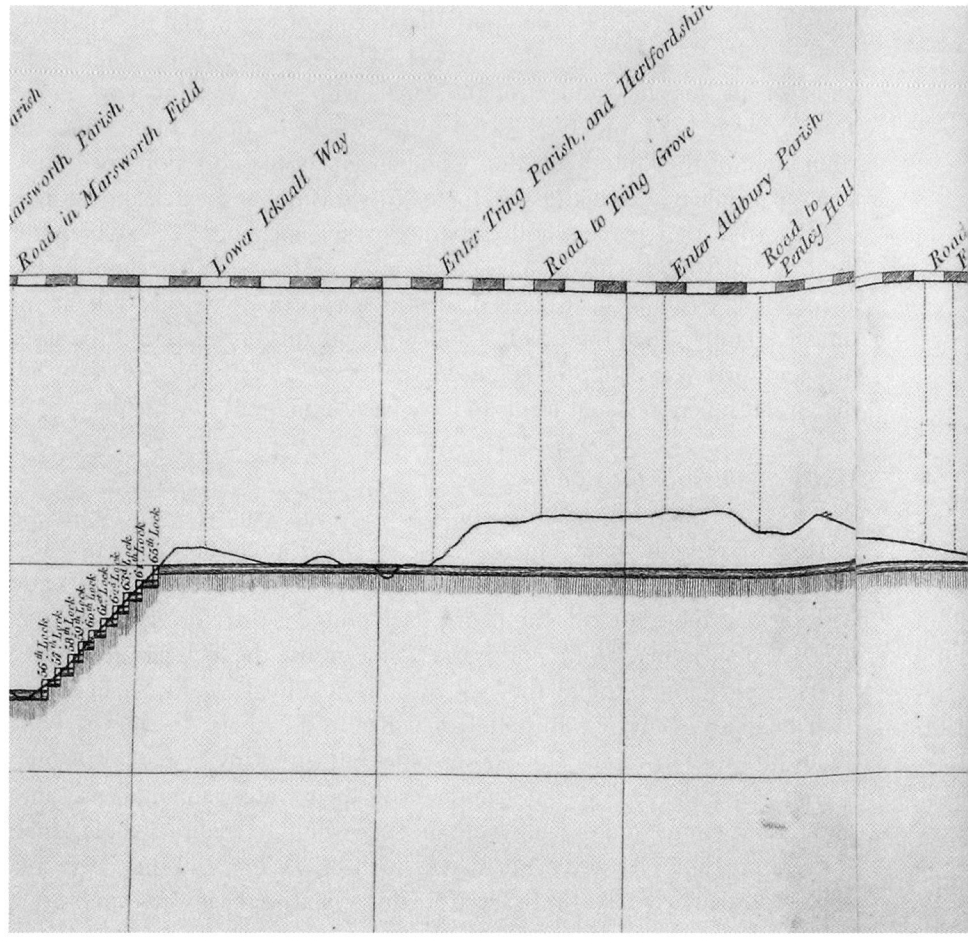

Figure 4.3. A section through the Chiltern hills along the Tring summit, as planned in 1792 (by permission of NWA, BW99/12/1/7). North is to the left, south to the right. The flight of locks at Marsworth (to the left) would have been spectacular but impracticable – a different line was taken. The rest is 'as built'. The heavy lockage on both sides of the summit and the formidable depth of the cutting required can be clearly seen.

by James Barnes in his first survey and by William Jessop in his review of Barnes's survey.[30] Figure 4.3, a section through the Chilterns along the line of the canal (as planned, not in the end as built), shows both the heavy lockage in both directions, which had to be served by the supply of water into the summit, and the depth of the cutting required on the summit.

---

30   BL, General Reference Collection 713.i.27(2), Jessop, *Report to the GJC Committee*.

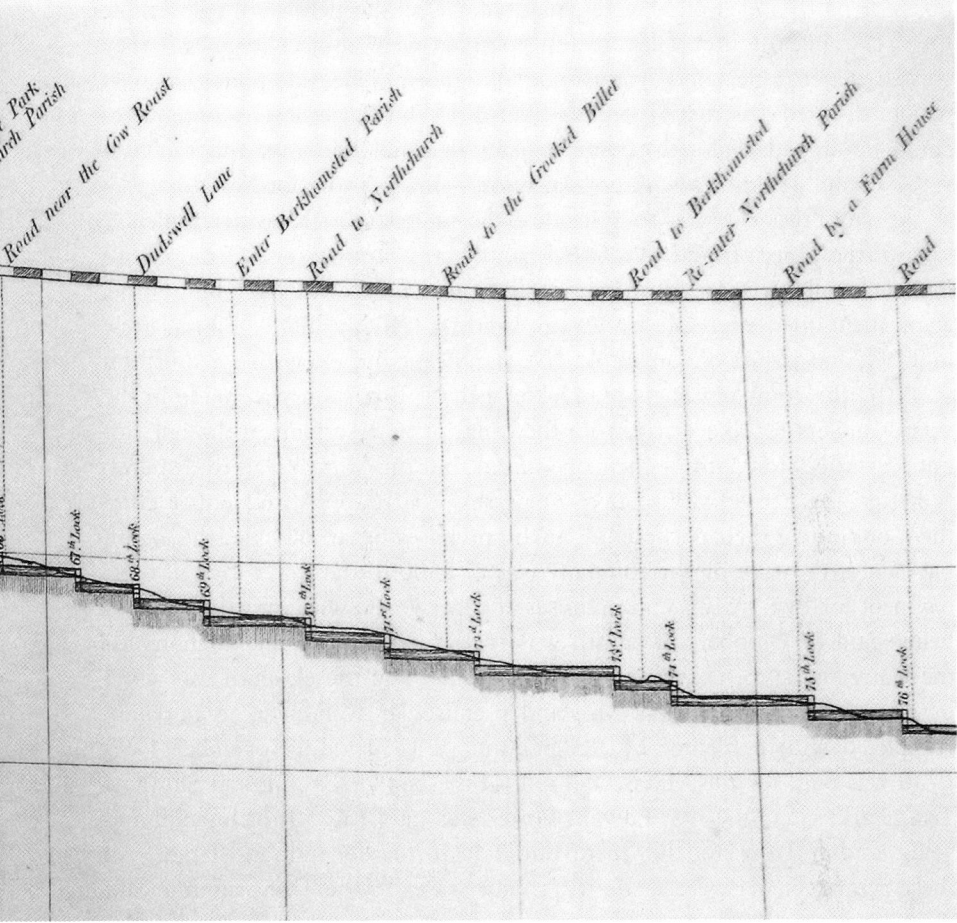

There were a number of possible solutions, all of which were used by the Grand Junction Canal Company.[31] Firstly, the reservoirs could be large: those at Tring were expanded several times after 1798, and would eventually cover about 250 acres. But they were below the summit level, and steam engines had to be installed to pump water up to the summit: this had been anticipated by Jessop in his 1792 report, and the first, in 1798, seems likely to have been one of the earliest such installations in Hertfordshire. Secondly, provision could be made for the economical use of water. It was not long before side-ponds were being tested and then installed at particular points, including Berkhamsted and Marsworth, although one drawback was that they slowed the traffic because they took extra time to operate, and single

---

31   TNA, RAIL 830/38 GJC upper district committee minutes 1796–98, 6 September 1796.

boats or partly laden craft were penalised.[32] Lock-keepers were responsible for overseeing the use of locks, and boatmen were subject to fines if they wasted water, especially by misusing or ignoring the side-ponds, against which detailed instructions were issued.[33] Third, natural watercourses could be tapped. This was commonplace in canal building, and each act – the Grand Junction's was no exception – made provision for doing so, at the same time seeking to safeguard the interests of the water millers.[34] One of the plots of land purchased from Mrs Mary Seare of Tring Grove included Bulbourne Head, the spring from which rose the river Bulbourne, again mentioned expressly by Jessop. It cost £1,400, a huge amount, early in 1794, and is just one example of a significant but expensive acquisition made by the company in its search for water.[35] Provision was made in the act for millers to take water from the canal or its reservoirs, although 'not unnecessarily', to continue their operations, but this was to lead to disputes. A better alternative was to take ownership of the mills and either close them or control their occupiers.[36] Such purchases began quickly: the eighth payment ever made by the company was of £500 to the Rev. Lloyd in part-payment for Pym's Mills and premises at Marsworth, with a further £1,000 being paid in October; the ninth was to the marquis of Buckingham for the water rights to his mill at Weston Turville; and the eleventh was £464 in part-payment for Lucas's Mill and premises at Wendover, a purchase completed with a further £1,285 in January 1794.[37] In November 1793 £750 was paid for the Marsworth mill of the banker Drummond Smith of Tring Park; later, in 1795, Edward Foster was paid £1,250 for his mill and some land at Tring and Elizabeth Butler £850 for her mill and land.[38] All these arrangements were made to provide water to the Tring summit, and

---

32 Faulkner, *Grand Junction Canal*, p. 104.

33 For example, the Regulations of 2 June 1807, Clause XXXI (NWA, BW99/5/3). It is not clear who was to read these, for the boatman almost certainly could not – his employer was responsible, but the boatman took the fine.

34 33 Geo.3 c.80 Grand Junction Canal, Clause X. Provision was also made for any water 'wasted' from the summit, which was to be sent southwards for the Bulbourne and Gade.

35 TNA, RAIL 830/63 GJC treasurer's cash book 1794–1801, 22 January 1794; NWA, BW99/1/2/1 sale agreement, 31 January 1794; BL, General Reference Collection 713.i.27(2), Jessop, *Report to the GJC Committee*.

36 35 Geo.3 c.8 Grand Junction Canal – Cashiobury variation, Clause XX, corrected an error in the original Act.

37 TNA, RAIL 830/63 GJC treasurer's cash book 1794–1801, 26 July, 9 August and 11 August 1793.

38 TNA, RAIL 830/63 GJC treasurer's cash book 1794–1801, 21 November 1793, 23 March 1795; CBS, Gray and Chaplin Archive GJC/9, p. 110.

were augmented by wells sunk in the same area – the latter were to become very contentious, as they abstracted from the aquifers and came later to be recognised as threatening surface water supplies, but this was not identified at this early stage. The Wendover Arm was originally a feeder to the main line of the canal simply to carry water from several streams and wells as well as the reservoirs, and it was only after work had started that the potential for reaching Wendover was realised; an act was obtained in March 1794 and the feeder expanded to be navigable.[39]

Other millers had to be compensated for the taking of water supplies: one reservoir was built especially to compensate the millers of Aylesbury for the loss of water from the river Thame (the clerks recorded a decision to buy these mills because of the heavy compensation demanded by their owners, but this may not have been the final outcome), and further south the Aldenham reservoir was required by the original act to replenish the river Colne because it drove the duke of Northumberland's mills on the river below Uxbridge.[40] Meanwhile, the 1794 act authorising the deviation of the canal through Cashiobury Park and The Grove at Watford made specific provision for the mills of Thomas Toovey at Kings Langley and William Smith at Hunton Bridge, near Abbots Langley, which were not to be 'damaged', but the resultant disputes with the Tooveys were to be problematic for another fifty years, as we will see.[41]

We will consider in the next chapter the important dispute between about 1809 and 1818 over water supplies to the paper mills south of Hemel Hempstead. Flowing water was a vital economic resource, and interference with it threatened not only the viability of the affected mill but also the ability of farmers to have their corn ground, and so flour supplied, locally. This is just one example of an adverse economic effect of the Grand Junction Canal in Hertfordshire.

Manpower and people
Although it is not possible to give an exact number of men employed on the canal, it is reasonable to suggest some general figures. There were several hundred men, mostly labourers but some tradesmen, at many of the work sites and, as noted above, perhaps 1,000 at major project sites such as the cuttings, tunnels and aqueducts (Figure 4.4). It seems that up to 3,000 were

---

39 34 Geo.3 c.24 Grand Junction Canal – authorisation of collateral cuts, 1794; Faulkner, *Grand Junction Canal*, p. 73.
40 Faulkner, *Grand Junction Canal*, pp. 124, 125, 132, 133.
41 35 Geo.3 c.8 Grand Junction Canal – Cashiobury variation, Clause XIII.

Figure 4.4. Canal building gang (Peter Dunn, by permission of Historic England). The various activities required to cut a canal are depicted in a shallow cutting in which tools typical of the time are being used. The completed canal is held back behind the structure over which the bridge is being built, and is no doubt being used by the work gang.

employed along the whole line of the canal at any one time.[42] But where did they come from? By the time work on the Grand Junction Canal began the early model of canal building, followed in the 1760s, had been found unsatisfactory. It had involved labourers drawn from estates local to the canal learning 'on the job' and using tools and techniques familiar to them, with estate carpenters building lock gates and fences, masons employed on locks and miners tunnelling.[43] But few areas had enough men sufficiently skilled or willing to do the work, and most had to come from elsewhere. A different model was in place widely by about 1780, in which large gangs of itinerant but dedicated men, usually employed by specialist contractors, undertook to cut, build or tunnel defined lengths of the canal and its structures for an agreed and contracted price before moving on to the next job, possibly many

42 Faulkner, *Grand Junction Canal*, 2nd edn, p. 9.
43 Christine Richardson, *The waterways revolution* (Hanley Swan, 1992), p. 102.

miles away.⁴⁴ There were, however, pitfalls in the use of contractors because their work was not fully under the control of the resident engineer, and, for example, the contemporaneous Lancaster Canal and Leeds and Liverpool Canal suffered from them.⁴⁵ Except for its major specialist projects, notably the tunnels and major aqueducts, the Grand Junction was built by directly employed rather than contractor-supplied labour, and in July 1793 its first paymaster was appointed, with cash for the men then passed to him by the resident engineer James Barnes, to whom tens of thousands of pounds were transferred by the treasurers.⁴⁶ The men doing the work were the same: but their supervision and direction were more direct.

Some observers, including farmers and their landlords, were concerned that the workmen were farm labourers whose absence at critical times, such as harvest, caused disruption. In 1793 a bill to prevent the employment of agricultural labourers on canal workings during the harvest was defeated, at least in part on the grounds that many of the canal labourers had no farming background – *The Times* reported the debate at some length.⁴⁷ In fact the canal-cutting workforce was very mixed and varied from place to place: some were English and may well have come initially from farms, often but not only in the north, but a significant proportion were from the Fens or from deeply impoverished Ireland and Scotland.⁴⁸ Some might have been locals, which raises the question of whether Hertfordshire agriculture was affected by the call from the canal.

There are three reasons for arguing that the impact was limited. First, the skills required were not transferable from agricultural labouring. A typical unit of work for one man was to dig twelve cubic yards (about twenty tons) in a day.⁴⁹ The technique required to dig that volume day after day was a specialist skill for a labourer even had he been physically fit enough, and there is good reason to think that the typical Hertfordshire agricultural labourer was too undernourished to be so.⁵⁰ Furthermore, labourers needed

---

44 Burton, *Canal builders*, pp. 158–71, 188–209; Gladwin, *Waterways of Britain*, pp. 49–75; Hugh Ferguson and Mike Chrimes, *The contractors* (London, 2014), pp. 22–5, 110, 111.
45 Burton, *Canal builders*, pp. 134–6; Mike Clarke, *The Leeds and Liverpool canal* (Barnoldswick, 2016), p. 234. The latter considers many of the matters addressed in this chapter, and the reader may find the comparison of particular interest.
46 TNA, RAIL 830/37 GJC lower district committee minutes 1793–1797, 17 July 1793; RAIL 830/63 GJC treasurer's cash book 1794–1801.
47 Ferguson and Chrimes, *The contractors*, p. 114; *The Times*, 11 April 1793, quoted by Burton, *Canal builders*, p. 161.
48 Hadfield, *British canals*, pp. 39, 40.
49 Gladwin, *Waterways of Britain*, p. 53; Burton, *Canal builders*, pp. 156–8.
50 Burton, *Canal builders*, p. 134; Agar, *Behind the plough*, pp. 153, 154, 158.

to understand how the work site was organised: the operation of a barrow run, removing spoil up a steep plank in a horse-drawn wheelbarrow from the bottom of a cutting; how explosives were used; even where to stand to avoid being 'run down' by others working more confidently. Thus it becomes clear why, by the 1790s, canal labourers were generally being found in the organised and specialist gangs described above.

Second, the impact on the harvest, which would have been especially sensitive in arable Hertfordshire, appears not to have been much remarked upon locally. The cutting of the canal occupied the harvest seasons of 1794–98, with the parishes of Tring, Aldbury, Wigginton and Northchurch especially vulnerable all that time; but there is no suggestion in the available records of those parishes of any undue effect, although, as we have seen, several of those harvests were very poor, which may have concealed an underlying shortage of labour to gather them.[51] Jessop may have noted in a 1794 report that the completion of the Wendover Arm would be delayed until 'after harvest': but that does not seem to have been a significant matter at the time.[52] Hadfield does relate the harvest to labour shortage at this time, but acknowledges that most of the labourers were 'professionals'.[53]

Third, had agricultural labour migrated wholesale to the canal the call on parish support for the poor would have been reduced: those left behind would have been needed to do at least some of the work vacated by those who had gone to work on the canal, and so become less reliant on relief. But vestry minutes and overseers' accounts of the parishes under review make no reference to this sort of effect, nor do they suggest that pauper men might be sent to work on the canal. There are a few mentions of casual relief to families of 'navigators', but generally they were separate and did not fall on the parish.[54]

A related effect might have been an increase in agricultural wages in response to the higher ones being paid by the Grand Junction Canal. As we saw in Chapter 1, there was a general shortage of labour: the country was at war with France throughout the period of the cutting of the canal, with large numbers of men absent from all callings and communities. Indeed, from his considerable experience the chief engineer Jessop anticipated this as early as 1792: 'In two or three works in which I am concerned they are nearly

---

51 HALS, DP/2/8/1 Aldbury vestry minutes 1702–1822; HALS, DP/111/8/19 Tring vestry minutes 1782–1815; HALS, DP/74/8/1 Northchurch vestry book 1650–1806.
52 Ian Petticrew and Wendy Austin, *The waterway comes to Tring* (Tring, 2014), p. 19.
53 Hadfield, *Canal age*, p. 57.
54 For example in HALS, DP/19/12/3 Berkhamsted overseers' accounts 1800 and DP/47/12/3 Hemel Hempstead overseers' accounts 1797.

at a stand for want of all descriptions of workmen – and I cannot conceive how the Numerous Schemes now in agitation can be executed in less than double the time that was formerly necessary.'[55] And in his initial report to the Grand Junction committee he had said 'I have thought it necessary to make very large allowances for the encreased and encreasing price of Labour, in consequence of the numerous works of this kind now in agitation.'[56]

He did not make enough allowance, and wage inflation was one of the causes of cost overrun on the canal, with a labourer's wage increasing from 2s to 3s a day, about 18s weekly.[57] But this inflation did not spread to agricultural wages, and the canal labourer's wage was already far in excess of the local agricultural labour rates reported by Arthur Young five years later in 1803/4: 14s per week in winter in the Watford area, 10s per week round Berkhamsted (up from 7s in the 1790s), and an average across the county of 10s to 12s per week.[58] We have seen that agricultural wages, in Hertfordshire as elsewhere, had not changed much in the interval, and had failed to keep up with the rising cost of food throughout the war: there is no suggestion that they had risen temporarily while the canal labourers were working, and it does not seem that farmers had had to make a serious effort to compete for labour.

There is little evidence, therefore, of a strong call by the canal on Hertfordshire agricultural labour, despite a shortage of manpower on the Grand Junction, as on other canals. An alternative view of labour availability is that the gangs of itinerant labourers who augmented the agrarian work force at harvest time had themselves been diverted to the canals. Their lifestyle would have made this a relatively natural move, as it would have given them much more regular work through the year, and they might have been better able to adapt to the work as a group than would individuals coming straight off the fields. This would have had a serious impact on agricultural production: a farmer used to having his 'heavy gang' appear just in time for harvest would have been hard pressed to replace those men, even by offering more money to his own small workforce. There is little evidence that this happened on any scale, but it would explain why there was a shortage of labour for harvest and at the same time no apparent reduction in the size of the local working population. There was certainly a problem: but it was not addressed by buying in local labourers.

---

55 Hadfield and Skempton, *William Jessop*, p. 38, quoting Jessop's letter to Lord Sheffield of 3 September 1792, in East Sussex Record Office.
56 BL, General Reference Collection 713.i.27(2), Jessop, *Report to the GJC Committee*.
57 Faulkner, *Grand Junction Canal*, p. 72.
58 Young, *General view*, pp. 217–20.

It is worth considering also where and how the imported labour force was accommodated, although there is little surviving evidence. The general custom was for encampments to be set up, and one may have been on Roughdown Common, south of Two Waters, near Hemel Hempstead. But by definition such camps were transient, and would have moved quite quickly through the fields (or, more probably, waste land) with their occupants as the work sites progressed northwards. Some men would, no doubt, have taken lodgings, especially if they had families: longer-term arrangements are likely to have been made around Tring and Pendley, where the work extended over several years.[59] The local economy does not seem to have benefited greatly: although the labourers were relatively well paid many probably sent their money home, and while it is clear that beer houses were among the services set up for the workforce, there are few references to them in local records. As we have seen, even in the devastating winters of 1795 and 1796 no comments were apparently made about the canal workers as the principal inhabitants of Tring and Rickmansworth dealt with the plight of their own parishioners. There are surprisingly few references either to the arrangements for accommodating the canal workers or to any problems arising from their presence in the area, but this may well be simply a function of the lack of surviving records: there were no truly local newspapers in Hertfordshire at the time.

There may, however, have been a different impact of canal-building on agricultural output: its use of high-value horses, for which it competed with agricultural work. For example, with bricks for locks and bridges in short supply as the canal approached Berkhamsted and Tring, the real constraint was insufficient horses to pull the barges carrying them from Southall, which was attributed to the spring sowing of 1798.[60] There was a tussle between the demands of the canal and of the farmers, but the farmers, who owned many of the horses, seem to have won: their core business took priority over short-term gain from helping the canal company. The adverse effect was on the canal rather than on the local economy.

Effect on local transport – the Sparrows Herne turnpike

The Sparrows Herne turnpike trust had been set up in 1762, and the proximity of the road to the canal all through Hertfordshire is shown in Figure 4.1.[61] As suggested in Chapter 3, it might have been expected that the turnpike would suffer damage to its long-distance traffic, but would pick

---

59   Burton, *Canal builders*, pp. 169, 170.
60   Faulkner, *Grand Junction Canal*, p. 38; Gladwin, *Waterways of Britain*, p. 53.
61   2 Geo.3 c.63 Sparrows Herne turnpike.

up other traffic more locally. A simple model of the finances of the trust for the years 1786–1806 derived from the account books and trustee minute books is presented as Appendix D.[62] The toll revenue was always relatively modest: the bulk of tolls were paid at the gates on either side of Watford (Watford and Ridge Lane gates), and increased only slowly in the years prior to the start of canal-cutting in Hertfordshire, but with outgoings growing much more strongly. This resulted in an operating loss in almost every year after 1793, although, perhaps surprisingly, the tolls did not peak until 1796, when the canal began to carry from London into Hertfordshire. Thereafter they declined until 1800, as the canal was opened throughout the county, recovering slowly after that. From late 1805 the tolls were farmed – let out to a contractor, who took the tolls and paid an agreed fee to the trust – and in 1821 the engineer/surveyor McAdam was appointed to act, in effect, as a maintenance contractor.[63] As a result the accounts do not contain enough detail to justify analysis after 1806; however, a number of conclusions can be drawn.

First, and acknowledging the benefits to commerce usually provided by the turnpikes leading into London, it seems unlikely that the Sparrows Herne road was ever an artery of industrial traffic between the Midlands and London.[64] The big long-distance carriers did not use it, and it does not feature in Albert's analysis of the major routes following the turnpikes northwest from London, which went via either Uxbridge or St Albans.[65] The toll distribution is too concentrated on Watford for much to have been moving along its full length: flow to and from London as far as Berkhamsted can be seen, but not as far north as the New Ground gate, which lay between Berkhamsted and Tring. The canal did not, therefore, act in competition with the turnpike as a long-distance route. Second, the cutting of the canal may account for some of the increase in toll revenue between 1794 and 1799, and increased wear on the road may account for some of the increase in costs: but, if so, the effect on tolls was small and that on costs disproportionately high. Third, the reduction in toll revenue after 1797 was due almost entirely to the fall in takings at the Watford gates, which suggests that it was these that were bypassed by the canal carrying goods from London to Watford,

---

62 HALS, TP4/28–32 (Sparrows Herne Turnpike – Journal accounts of income and expenditure, 1786–1865).

63 HALS, TP4/2/4 Sparrows Herne turnpike , minutes of meetings of the trustees, 12 March 1821.

64 Wrigley, *The path to sustained growth*, pp. 142, 143.

65 Albert, *The turnpike trusts of England*, pp. 35, 38, 225–8. The latter pages list the roads from London to Birmingham and Manchester: all went through either St Albans or Uxbridge, none through Watford.

Hemel Hempstead and Berkhamsted. The takings at the toll gates further north, always small, saw almost no change. In any case, in broad terms about 50 per cent of the traffic on a typical turnpike was passenger traffic, and the relationship between west Hertfordshire and London suggests that the Sparrows Herne road was unlikely to be much different in this respect.[66] The decline in the tolls must therefore have been due to a reduction in freight traffic on the road. It appears, then, that while the canal and the turnpike were not in competition for passengers or long-distance freight, the traffic on the southern end of the turnpike was affected by the canal carrying traffic between London and Hertfordshire. Whether this was significant to the long-term financial health of the turnpike in view of the inexorable rise in costs is doubtful, and in Chapters 5 and 6 we will see what happened to freight transport later.

Passenger transport

It has been generally considered that the canals were for freight and were not expected to provide much, if any, passenger transport.[67] Nonetheless, the Grand Junction Canal Company was open to the idea of passenger services. For example, on 24 January 1798 the upper district committee 'ordered that two of the barges, part of the ten ordered to be provided at the last meeting of the General Committee, be covered or decked barges for the conveyance of passengers and separate parcels upon the canal',[68] and on 4 July 1801 the committee was ready to grant pleasure boats licences to attend the opening of the Paddington branch. Furthermore, in 1802, renewing their position from the opening of the branch in 1801, they were 'ready to contract with persons willing to farm the passenger and pleasure boats on the canal between Uxbridge and Bulls Bridge and the first lock towards Brentford'.[69] A dedicated passenger boat service operated spasmodically between Uxbridge and Paddington from the opening of the branch, and Thomas Homer, employed in a superintendent role in September 1793 and later to be dismissed for financial irregularities, was contracted to operate the service: but, although initially successful, it seems to have petered out in about

---

66 Bogart, 'Turnpike trusts', pp. 479–508.
67 Phillips, *Inland navigation*, 5th edn, pp. x–xxii; Joseph Priestley, *Navigable rivers and canals* (London, 1831; reprinted Newton Abbot, 1969), p. xi; Hadfield, *Canal age*, pp. 22–31.
68 TNA, RAIL 830/38 GJC upper district committee minutes 1796–1798.
69 *The Times*, 4 July 1801, p. 1; 20 May 1802, p. 1. This was Norwood Top Lock – perhaps the company was unwilling to allow lockage water to be wasted on passenger traffic, requiring it to be confined to lock-free sections, of which the Paddington Arm is one.

1810.⁷⁰ Passengers usually travelled in their own vehicle, by stagecoach or waggon, or walked. But that is not to say that there were no opportunities for people to travel quite long distances by canal. The army certainly did so by 1806, moving (for example) whole units from London to Liverpool for Ireland and demanding both toll-free and priority transit.⁷¹ Certainly, in the early nineteenth century there was some recorded passenger traffic, which was slower than the stagecoach but probably cheaper: it was used by parish removing officers, for example.⁷² Although the instances recorded, often because the fate of the traveller came to the attention of the courts and press, may be few, there is enough other evidence to show that it was reasonably commonplace for the working poor to migrate long distances by canal, fitted in around the general cargo being carried in a boat. There is no surviving evidence that Hertfordshire people moved like this – if they were going to London it was probably not worthwhile, with the waggon services even cheaper and not much slower – but we should bear in mind that there was an option for them to use the canal in this way.

Conclusion
The planning and arrival of the Grand Junction Canal in west Hertfordshire affected the area in several ways, not all beneficial. A considerable amount of land, most of it agricultural, was bought to accommodate the canal, and these purchases were more to the benefit of the landowner than of the farmer. A major change to the landscape was made near Tring as the canal was cut through the Chilterns, and this took several years to finish. Other, lesser but still significant, changes were wrought as the line descended through Hertfordshire from Tring, with cuttings and embankments appearing as scars on the rural landscape and the courses, and indeed sources, of rivers altered. Daily life for the arable farmer would have been affected considerably as a result of the purchase by the Grand Junction Canal Company of a number of water corn mills, and perhaps to a limited extent by the competition for his workforce; but most of the work on the canal will have been done by the significant number of itinerant labouring men brought into the area, some of them with families and with the largest group near Tring.

By early 1800 the canal was ready to take goods traffic from Tring and Wendover to London and the river Thames, and the connection northwards

---

70 Faulkner, *Grand Junction Canal*, p. 81; TNA, RAIL 830/64 GJC treasurer's cash book 1806–1811, April 1807.
71 *The Times*, 19 December 1806.
72 Harry Hanson, 'Canal travel', *Journal of the Railway and Canal Historical Society*, 25/2 (1979), pp. 70–3.

to Birmingham was complete in the spring of 1801. There was an early effect on transportation through the county: the freight traffic on the Sparrows Herne turnpike, which ran alongside the canal from Watford to Tring, was skewed significantly to its southern section, and the turnpike suffered a noticeable loss of revenue at that end as soon as the canal reached Watford. This suggests that at least some of the freight moving between London, Hemel Hempstead and Watford was diverted onto the canal, but the volumes seem likely to have been relatively small.

The next chapter will look more closely at how the agriculture and industry of western Hertfordshire were affected over the next few decades by the canal in operation, and the extent to which local businesses were able to use it.

Chapter 5
The Grand Junction Canal in operation

What were the economic and social effects of the canal in the early days of its operation? It is, of course, difficult to be clear about what can be directly attributed to the canal and what to other factors, but it is possible to observe extra economic activity along the line of the new canal as it passed through the parishes, villages and towns to connect London with the Midlands and north. First we should consider the transport systems in west Hertfordshire.

Freight transport

As already discussed, the Sparrows Herne turnpike was not a major route for industrial traffic from the north and Midlands: that passed mainly through St Albans on the Chester road to London. But, like towns everywhere, west Hertfordshire towns were nonetheless served by road carriers, and Pigot's and Robson's *Directories* allow us a glimpse of what was happening throughout the period until just before the London and Birmingham railway began to have an effect on road transport.[1]

First, St Albans. The listings of local carrying firms in the *Directories* became more comprehensive over the years. Pigot's (1823) advertised only two waggon services on Monday and three on Thursdays, but the entry notes that 'waggons to & from London pass through St Albans daily' and we would expect these to embrace those from Liverpool, Manchester and other industrial towns, offering an integrated service that included both canal and road services, with interchanges as needed.[2] By 1832 the synopsis in Pigot's was more explicit: three local carriers were listed as operating waggons on Mondays and four on Thursdays, and Robson's lists similar services,

---

1   *Pigot's Royal National and Commercial Directory and Topography for the Counties of Essex, Herts and Middlesex* (London, 1823); Robson's *London Directory and Classification of Trades*, Part IV (Waggons), (London, 1832), pp. 32–84.
2   Pigot's *Directory* (1823), pp. 363, 363; Turnbull, *Traffic and transport* (London, 1979), p. 106.

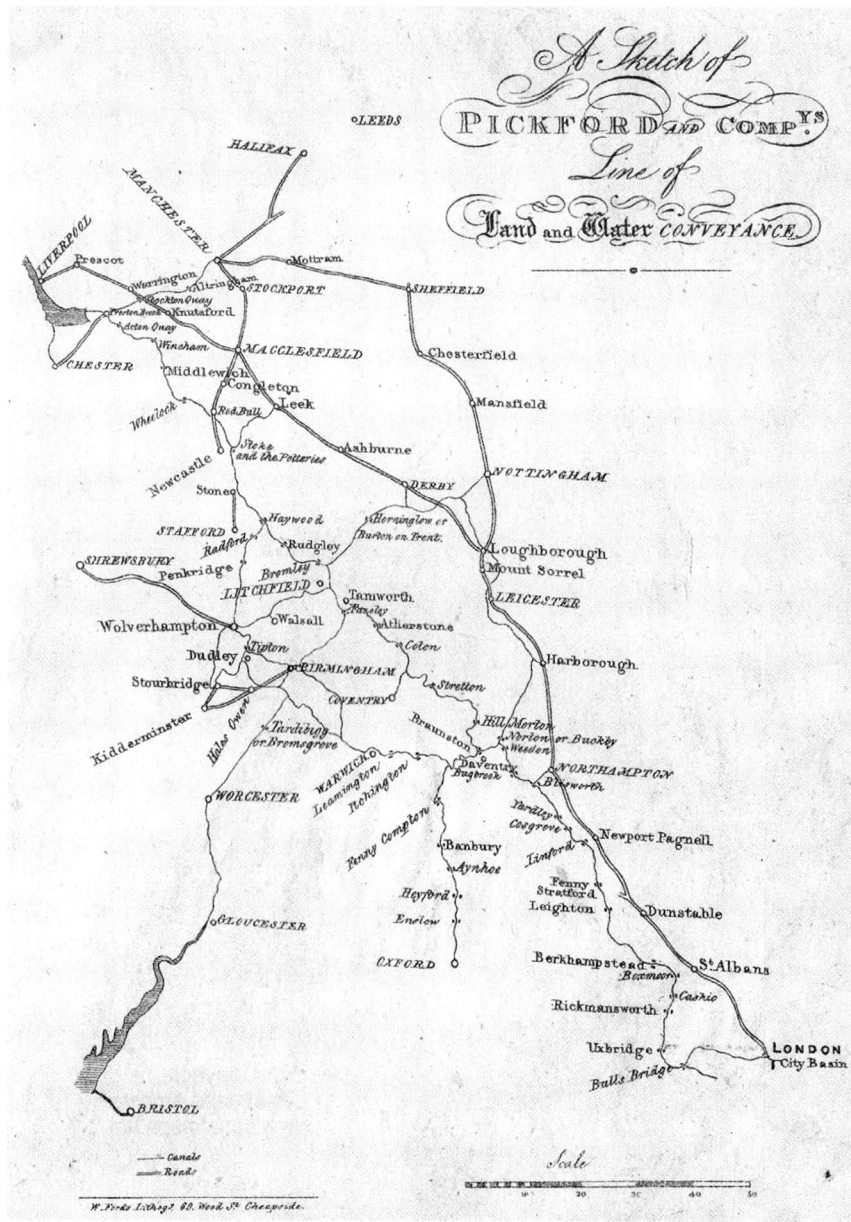

Figure 5.1. Pickfords route map, showing both road and canal services, c.1832 (by permission of Canalmaps Archive, www.canalmaps.net). The Sparrows Herne turnpike and the towns served by it do not feature at all. The role of local carriers (by both road and canal) in connecting places not directly served by this major carrier can be seen.

although with some different names. The long-distance services were from Birmingham, Daventry, Leeds, Nottingham and Sheffield 'continuously during the week', although Manchester was quoted only in connection with Pickfords' vans.[3]

Compare this with the other towns, all significant but not on a trunk road. The 1832 listings are not long and show mainly services to London: Tring was offered one waggon on Wednesday, Thursday and Sunday, two on Tuesday and Friday and the mail cart daily, with another apparently bespoke cart service. Berkhamsted had only one service on Tuesdays and Fridays.[4] Hemel Hempstead's listing was much more comprehensive, however, and included the national carrier Worster and Stubbs – but only once a week, with two more local carriers passing through twice weekly. There is, however, a note that 'besides the above, carriers to and from London, the North etc pass through Two Waters daily', so there were some long-range connections, although we do not know which; but they do not seem to compare with those through St Albans.[5] Most of those listed were the short-range carriers, filling the gaps between the long-range providers, and we note that the 'Public Carrier' services offered to west Hertfordshire do not include any of the major long-range firms.[6] Although this picture is not complete (the services listed went through all the towns on the route, but we really do not know how they captured trade), it seems reasonable to infer, given the development and history of the towns, that it had always been so: the Sparrows Herne road provided local services, and its towns, devoid of significant industry, were served mainly by local carriers with limited capacity.

The listings for Hemel Hempstead, however, give a very comprehensive statement of the *canal* carriers from wharfs described as Crouchfield (probably Fishery, as we now know it – see Figure 6.4) and Independent as well as Boxmoor and Frogmore End, and these are worth capturing in some detail. Unsurprisingly, Pickford & Co was one, carrying to 'London, Birmingham and Dudley etc' daily (Figure 5.1). But also listed were Kenworthy & Co, Whitehouse and Sons, Robins Mills & Co, Crowley Hickling & Co, Worster & Stubbs, Deacon & Harrison, Shipton & Pratt, Thomas and William Tildesley and Sturland, Thomas Bache & Co, the Horseley Iron Works Co, Robinson & Co and George Ryder Bird & Son. Thomas William Ebbern is

---

3   Pigot's *Royal National and Commercial Directory and Topography for the Counties of Essex, Herts and Middlesex* (London, 1832), pp. 754–8.
4   Pigot's *Directory* (1832), pp. 761–3, 727.
5   Pigot's *Directory* (1832), pp. 737, 738.
6   Robson's *Directory*, Part IV (Public Carriers), pp. 85–91.

listed, and we will meet him again in Chapter 6; Ann Landon and Sons of Aylesbury, also listed, was a more local firm, but still operating over long distances. The destinations offered included Birmingham and Manchester as well as Coventry, Leicester, Market Harborough, Northampton, the Potteries 'and all intermediate places'.[7]

This is almost (not quite) a complete 'Who's Who' of pre-railway canal as well as road industrial carrying, and all of these canal services also passed through Rickmansworth and Berkhamsted and close to Watford and Tring. That is not to say that all stopped in each place; the true frequencies of services are unknown, with some scheduled 'fly' (non-stop) to fixed destinations and schedules, others 'stage' boats, stopping as required. Nevertheless, there was clearly very significant business being done in 'building materials [stone, timber, slate and bricks], salt, iron, manufactured goods' and agricultural products as well as coal. Furthermore, few of the named carriers offered road services in any of these towns, tending to confirm that the Sparrows Herne turnpike did not carry significant industrial traffic.

As anticipated in Chapter 3, the canal placed all these towns on a major industrial freight route for the first time, offering new opportunities to both industry and commerce. However, it was by no means certain that the canal would be selected as the desired mode of transport from the west Hertfordshire area. If goods or produce had to be taken far by cart or waggon to the canal from its start point, especially a farm, the cargo might as well have stayed in the cart until reaching its destination. An example is in an undated note reflecting on the merits of using the canal to transport billets (logs cut and split for firewood) to London from Rickmansworth.[8] Its text is shown verbatim:

Expense of delivery of Billit Wood
500 In Number is a Wadgon Load wich will way 2 tons 5 hundred

Caridge from the wood to Rickmersworth warf	0 - 18 - 0
Warfidg and Loading Into Barge	3 - 0
Tunidge & Barge Caridge from Rickm. to London 6s a tun	13 - 6
On Loding of the Barge In London	2 - 0
Warfidg In London	2 - 0
Caridge In London to Fire Place	<u>6 - 0</u>
	2 - 4 - 6

---

7   Pigot's *Directory* (1832), p. 738.
8   Manuscript note (unreferenced) found by the author unattached in the back of TNA, RAIL 830/42 GJC general committee minutes 1807–1811. Presumably it dates from about that time, but there is no indication of its provenance.

Land Caridge for A wadgon Load of Billit No 500 from the
   woods To London In [?] the Naiberhood of Rickmersworth   2 - 2 - 0
The Hole Vawley of 500 of the above Billit Wood wen
   delivered [*illegible*] is   <u>£4.5.0</u>

Billets were a common product of the woods in this area but seem to have been quite expensive to transport; the statement above suggests that 500 'Billits' weighed about 5000lb, or about 10lb each. The cost of 500 billets was £2 – 1d each – while the carriage charge to London, whether by road or water, was over £2, making the full cost to be recovered £4 5s, double the original sum.[9] The mode of transport chosen by this individual is not recorded, but it is clear that the decision was close-run and that the relative costs were calculated and considered in some detail even by small traders and carriers. It tends to confirm that, if a cart or waggon had to be used to take a load to a wharf for trans-shipment, the owner might well have it continue to its destination. For loads moving to London from as close as Rickmansworth, the canal did not necessarily provide the best mode of transport.

The canal in the towns and parishes

The best indicator of canal-based economic activity is the presence of a wharf, the interface between the canal and a town or village: where there was a wharf, there was business of some sort being done. A wharf was not just a 'feature' waiting to be used: it was a business asset owned by someone, sometimes the canal company but often an individual who had built it on his own land or on land leased for the purpose, and who either managed it himself or employed a wharfinger to manage it for him. Nor was the wharfinger a mere minion: in May 1812 the committee of the Grand Junction Company appointed John Beales, 'loyal toll clerk at Boxmoor', to be their wharfinger there at a salary of £120 plus an advance of £25 to buy a horse and commission of 6d per ton for the coal he sold at the wharf above 2,000 tons a year.[10] Indeed, the wharf was often the base for a coal or timber business, and in any case a fee ('wharfage') was charged for the use of a wharf, which would typically have a crane and access to a warehouse of some sort. Although some were probably little more than landing stages with few facilities, those on which we will concentrate here were much more significant, and Figure 5.2, showing wharfs near Paddington, gives an idea of the configuration.

---

9   This could, of course, be interpreted as meaning a sale price when delivered of £4 5s, in which case the disparity between the cost price and the transport cost is even greater.

10   TNA, RAIL 830/42 GJC general committee minutes 1807–1811, 12 May 1812.

Figure 5.2. Wharfs near Paddington (LMA, City of London Collage: 322394). Although not typical of wharfs in smaller towns, all the features of Boxmoor Wharf as advertised in 1815 are seen here in about 1828. Most of the waterside wharf area is covered with a canopy, and there are large warehouse buildings. A light crane is just to right of centre, and a large crane 'suitable for timber' appears above the bow of the Pickford's boat at centre. Note also the universal use of shafts to move boats around such a basin. A covered loading dock is on the right of the picture (see Figure 5.3).

Labourers were employed to move goods around and to load or unload boats (Figure 5.3), and road access was essential. Several of the boat owners or operators, or their relatives, also had interests in wharfs: Appendix B lists boat owners and operators based in or close to Hertfordshire during this period, and John Holladay of Watford, Wilkins and Ashness of Boxmoor, Emmott Skidmore of Rickmansworth, Thomas Howard of Troy, near Rickmansworth, John Hatton of Berkhamsted and Kings Langley farmer Newman Hatley were all at various times involved in wharf and related operations in these early years.

A few wharfs were established soon after the canal opened, and more were to follow. The earliest public wharf operations are recorded in the parish overseers' accounts, although farmers could already have been loading and unloading informally alongside their own fields. At Tring, William Grover was tenant of Tring Wharf at Gamnel on the Wendover Arm, a mile north of the town, for some years following James Tate's 1800 occupancy, until in early 1810 he was allowed to buy it for £400.[11] In Berkhamsted's accounts

---

11   TNA, RAIL 830/42 GJC general committee minutes 1807–1811, 9 January 1810.

Figure 5.3. A covered loading dock (LMA, City of London Collage: 321981). The boat under cover in this dock might have been depicted today. Labourers are using light cranes to load items weighing up to perhaps three cwt, or perhaps the cut timber seen on the left. A foreman or tally clerk is keeping track of the process, and a gauging clerk is ready with his staff to measure the weight loaded by comparing the freeboard of the boat against the gauging table for it (see Figure 5.9). A dock of this sort might well have been used for trans-shipment between canal and road vehicles – the well-known 'Samuel Oldknow's warehouse' on the Ashton Canal near Manchester is a survivor of this type.

the canal company itself appears from 1800, when a surveyor was paid to measure it for valuation, and the company was certainly paying rates from 1803, but there is no mention of wharfs until 1806, when Daniel Norris was rated for one. In the next year 'Mr Gilbert' was also rated for a wharf,[12] which in 1809 was taken over by William Tompkins, and the pattern was set for the next twenty years: by 1831 William Tompkins and John Tompkins ('coal dealer, wharfinger') were rated together for 'house and wharf', almost certainly Castle Wharf.

Other Berkhamsted wharfs were mentioned occasionally, including, from 1810, that of the earl of Bridgewater for his Ashridge residence. Hemel Hempstead accounts first mentioned the Grand Junction Company in the summer of 1798, with land valued at £7 and Boxmoor Wharf (Wilkins and Ashness) at £47: William Howard (who was also a boat operator) had the

---

12 HALS, DP/19/11/2 Berkhamsted overseers' accounts 1806–1823.

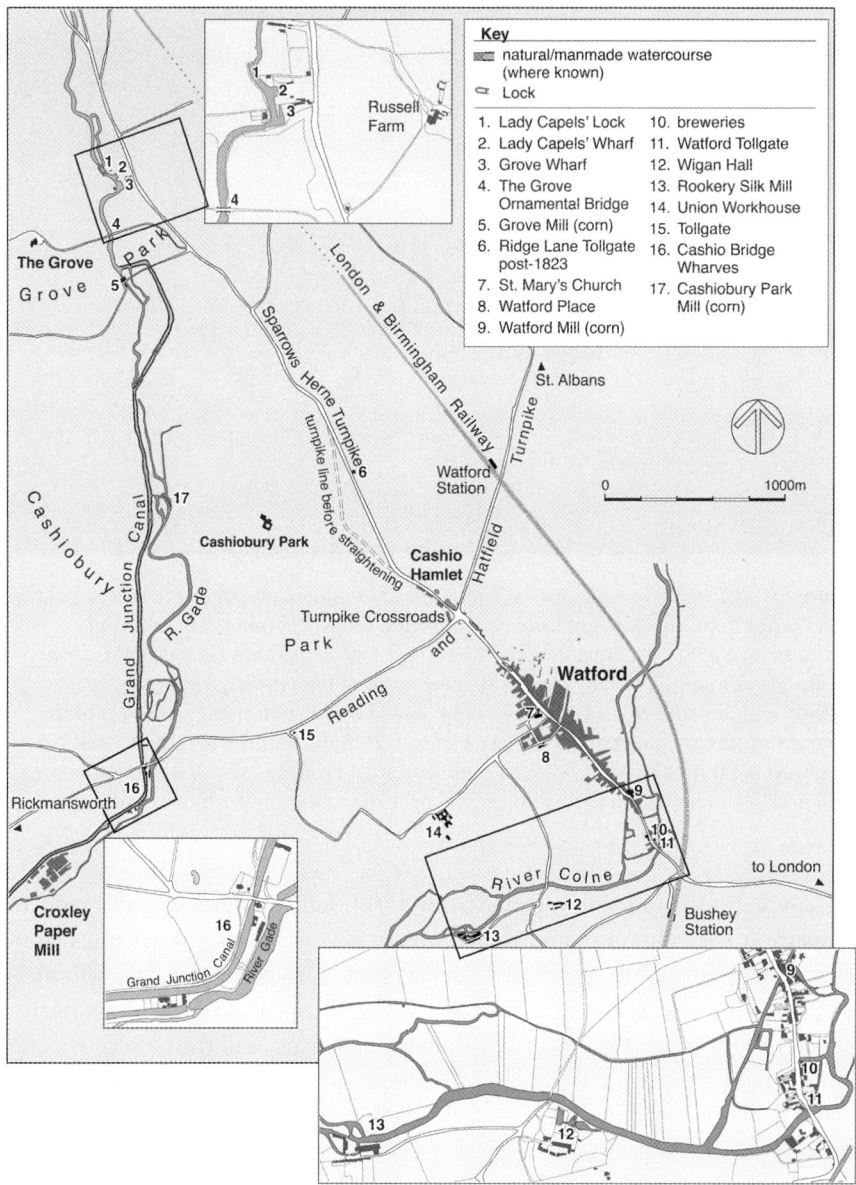

Figure 5.4. Watford and its wharfs *c*.1838. This map shows the distances from Watford of the wharfs serving it from Cashio Bridge along the Reading and Hatfield turnpike and from Grove and Lady Capels' wharfs along the Sparrows Herne turnpike. Even from the turnpike crossroads there was still a considerable distance to the industrial area on the Colne at the bottom of the town, with the Rookery silk mill isolated and the Hampermill paper mill to the west of it not even appearing on the map. The advantages of the railway are obvious, especially once the main line station had been moved in 1858.

next 'wharf' entry (£49) in 1800.[13] So the value of these wharfs was already considerable, although it appears that no rates were charged until the canal was actually working and the wharf ready.[14] The Hemel Hempstead rate books showed successive acquisitions by Howard and others until, by 1812/13, Johnson (£10), Pickford (£22), White (£40) and Howard (£125) were all paying rates on wharfs of varying sizes. Howard's, especially, was a large undertaking, part of the wharf complex seen in Figure 5.6 and described in the 1815 advertisement placed by the Boxmoor Trustees before renewing Howard's lease:

> a capital Wharf ... in the iron, coal, timber, stone, soot, ashes and other trades ... now in the occupation of Messrs Howard and Son ... furnished with a large Dock, branching out of the Grand Junction Canal, capable of holding 10 or 12 barges, and is adjoining to the road from Hemel Hempstead to London ... a spacious warehouse ... 32 feet 8 inches by 52 feet 9 inches ... a ground and upper floor ... with a crane ... for raising goods out of the barges; also a shed next to the water, 10 feet wide the whole length of the warehouse ... . A strong crane, fit for loading large timber, deals &tc.[15]

Figure 5.2 shows all these features. Among the likely users of the canal here were the Fourdriniers' paper mills, and the possible relationship between them and the canal, together with the importance of these wharfs, will be discussed below.

Watford's wharfs (Figure 5.4) included two in Rickmansworth parish, and the Grand Junction Canal Company itself appeared in the Rickmansworth overseers' accounts only under the Croxley hamlet, in one corner of that parish. There John Holladay was rated for a wharf, presumably one of those at Cashio Bridge.[16] In August 1805 the company minuted that 'the waste land by the Company Wharf at Cashiobury be purchased for the enlargement thereof, and that the said wharf ... be offered to Mr Holliday ... '. Later the earl of Essex made a proposal to let 'his wharf at Cashiobury' to the company, which was accepted for seven years at £50 a year.[17] These two wharfs served Watford along the Reading and Hatfield turnpike, while

---

13 HALS, DP/47/12/3 Hemel Hempstead overseers' accounts 1791–1804; TNA, RAIL 830/64 GJC treasurer's cash book 1806–1811, 15 December 1806.
14 Boxmoor Wharf had been built by the Boxmoor Trustees with the proceeds of the sale of their land to the canal, and had been ready in the previous year. It is not clear why rates were not charged then.
15 *The Times*, 17 June 1815.
16 HALS, DP/85/8/2 Rickmansworth vestry minutes 1796–1818.
17 TNA, RAIL 830/42 GJC general committee minutes 1807–1811, 13 August 1805 and 14 March 1809.

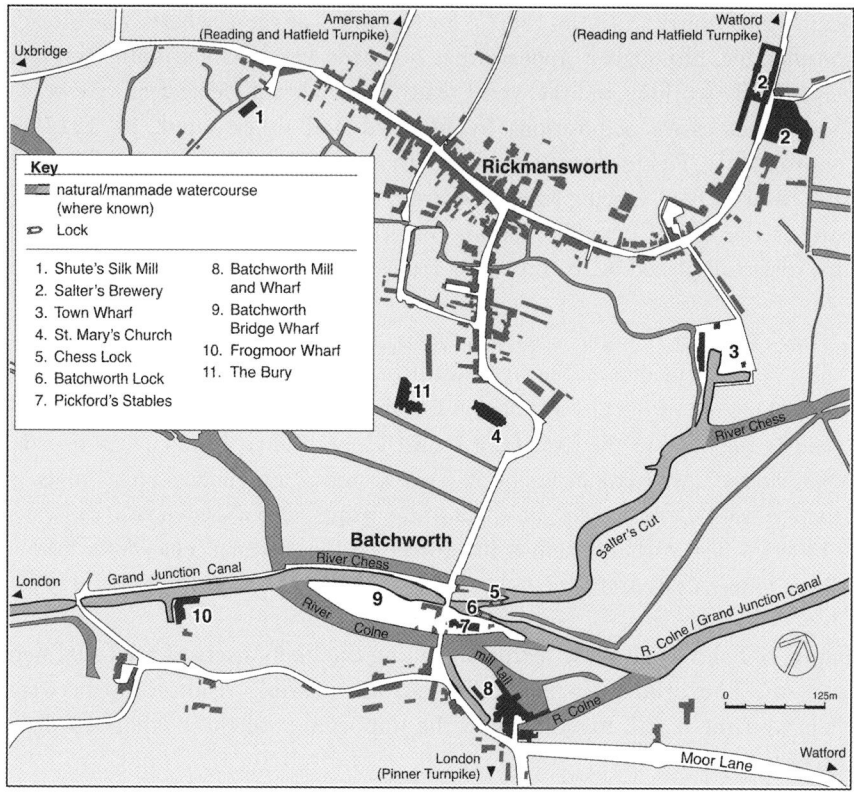

Figure 5.5. Rickmansworth, c.1830. Note the relationship between Salter's brewery (2) and the Town Wharf (3), and between the newly rebuilt steam powered silk mill (1) and the main wharfs at Frogmoor (10) and Batchworth Bridge (9). Batchworth Mill (8) had by now been significantly modified by Dickinson from the earlier cotton and corn mill of the Strutts (see Figure 5.7).

further north, along the Sparrows Herne turnpike, were two further wharfs, Lady Capels' and Grove adjacent to it. Lady Capels' wharf was identified, as soon as the diversion through Cashiobury Park was approved in 1795, as the point past which coal was forbidden to pass towards London; even when that prohibition was lifted in 1805 there was still a tax to be paid to the City of London,[18] so this wharf was quickly established as a coal depot, and was joined in close proximity by Grove Wharf. Even though Watford lay more than two miles from either set of wharfs, it merited a considerable degree of canal-based service.

---

18   35 Geo.3 c.8 Grand Junction Canal – Cashiobury Park variation, 1795; Faulkner, *Grand Junction Canal*, 2nd edn, p. 75.

Two wharfs at first, and later a third, were provided at Rickmansworth (Figure 5.5). The large Frogmoor Wharf, in the hands of Emmott Skidmore, was just off the London Road out of Rickmansworth at Batchworth, while by 1805 a lock connected the river Chess to the canal to serve Town Wharf, which lay between Salter's brewery and the town. A map of 1805 notes 'Skidmore's and Salter's coal wharfs', so both Frogmoor and Town wharfs were already working at this time, providing coal and other goods for local use.[19] The 1811 Holden's *Directory* lists William Pimstome as coal merchant at Town Wharf, as well as Emmott Skidmore at Frogmoor.[20] The parish record is patchy, however: the Rickmansworth vestry minutes concerning the church rate record Samuel Salter's rating as including 'Batchworth Water', although not expressly a wharf, and William Plaistowe appears with a 'wharf' for a few years from 1813.[21] Over the next thirty years Mill End paper mill, Rickmansworth silk mill, described below, and possibly other mills along the river Chess became steam powered, so increasing the demand for coal through these wharfs. It is not clear from the Grand Junction records when the small wharf immediately below Batchworth Bridge was first established, but in 1828 it featured in the sale of Rickmansworth Park after the death of the widow of the long-term owner, Henry Fotherley Whitfeld. The sale included both Rickmansworth Park mansion (lot 1) and The Bury (lot 2), as well as property on Scots Hill nearby (Lot 4). Lot 3 was:

> a very valuable freehold wharf, containing 1 acre 32 roods and 1 perch upon the banks of the Grand Junction Canal and situate between it and the River Colne at Batchworth … its situation is far preferable to any other … abutting as it does the Turnpike Road [the Pinner turnpike, 1809] and its triangular form renders it perfectly secure from depredation bounded as it is on two sides by the Colne River and the Grand Junction Canal and on the other by a substantial lofty brick wall with entrance gates opening onto the turnpike road. There have been recently erected … on this wharf at a considerable expence a Dwelling House and inclosed yard and warehouse with the necessary erections of William Eggleton, Carpenter … . Also 3 cottages and gardens … . The above premises are in the occupancy of Emmett Skidmore as yearly tenant at the very low rent of £25.[22]

First offered for sale on 31 July 1828, the lots did not at first reach their reserve, but a year later they did, and the wharf was sold to George Alfred Muskett for £910.

---

19   HALS, 44209B map: '16 Square Miles round Chorleywood', George Thompson, 1805.
20   Holden's *Directory*.
21   HALS, DP/85/8/2 Rickmansworth vestry minutes 1796–1818.
22   TNA, C101/3295 'Sale of Land at Rickmansworth' in Chancery, July 1828.

Several other, smaller, wharfs were established on the canal in addition to these main ones.[23] A wharf at New Ground, on the summit above Berkhamsted, is evidenced by the delivery of road stone there in April 1813.[24] This might, however, have been the same as nearby Cowroast wharf: it is not known exactly when that wharf was established, but Thomas Landon was operating boats there by 1810 (Appendix B); however, it seems unlikely to have been large. The entry in Pigot's *Directory* of 1832 for Tring refers to him as wharfinger at Cowroast and serving the town, and since it was on the turnpike it may well have been more convenient for deliveries to Tring than taking boats off the main line of the canal and down to Gamnel on the Wendover branch. A wharf was established at Kings Langley waterside by December 1815, when Mrs Sarah Nicholls was rated for it at £10.[25] That at Hunton Bridge, serving Abbots Langley, was established some time after 1805, when the company ordered the purchase of a meadow for a wharf, while in February 1810 the earl of Bridgewater notified the company of his intended private wharf at Berkhamsted.[26] But these less prominent facilities emphasise the main point: there was plenty of canal-based business to be done by people operating public wharfs, as well as by factory owners such as Dickinson and the Mines Royal copper mill operating their own. Vestry records valuing landholdings in the parishes mention wharfs, and indeed the canal, only very intermittently, and while we do not know exactly what was being traded though these public wharfs there was sufficient trade to make or keep their proprietors reasonably prosperous.[27] As the advertisement for Boxmoor wharf shows, they were certainly dealing in goods such as iron, coal, timber, stone, soot and ashes, and we will see below something of what else was passing on the canal. Ashness and Wilkins were paid from November 1798 to supply increasing amounts of coal from Boxmoor wharf to the Hemel Hempstead poor house, and presumably wealthier inhabitants would have been purchasing it as well.[28] Although there are insufficient

---

23 One wharf-like provision deserving comment is the boat horse station at Dudswell, Northchurch, just below the Cowroast summit lock. Built in 1805 for the Pickford's company, which leased it, it was reached during the second day's travel from Paddington or Brentford, but it was not a wharf. J.E. Hunt, 'A history of Dudswell Mill', *Hertfordshire's Past*, 27 (1989), pp. 27–32.

24 HALS, TP4/30 Sparrows Herne turnpike accounts, April 1813.

25 HALS, DP/64/12/6 Kings Langley overseers' accounts 1815–1821, December 1815.

26 Clark, *Abbots Langley then*, p. 83; TNA, RAIL 830/42 GJC general committee minutes 1807–1811, 13 August 1805, 22 October 1805, 13 February 1810.

27 HALS, DP/85/8/9 Rickmansworth vestry minutes 1763–1796; DP/85/8/2 Rickmansworth vestry minutes 1796–1811.

28 HALS, DP/47/12/3 Hemel Hempstead overseers' rates and accounts 1791–1811.

surviving records to allow detailed conclusions about the cargoes being delivered, they clearly included materials not available in the area earlier.

Aside from the wharfs, the canal itself appears to have been considered an attraction to the towns from an early stage, as evidenced by advertisements in *The Times*. For example, in April 1799 a cottage in Woodcock Hill, Berkhamsted, offered 'a pleasing view of the Grand Junction Canal and the surrounding country'; in December, timber on a freehold estate between Tring and Berkhamsted was 'about 1 and 2 miles from the Grand Junction Canal'. Five years later, a farm and cottage were for sale: 'Felden Cottage or Sporting Box and Farm, at Two Waters within a mile of the Turnpike and Grand Junction Canal, 236 acres … ', and (albeit in Buckinghamshire) an estate for sale near High Wycombe was advertised as being '8 miles from the Grand Junction Canal'.[29] A mill was advertised for sale in Hertfordshire as 'A desirable leasehold estate … an excellent Corn Mill, which contains four pairs of stones, situate on a powerful stream, within a short distance of the Grand Junction Canal, and in the centre of several capital market towns'. Details were to be had from 'Mr Munn': Lewis Munn was the owner and occupier of Mill End paper mill in Rickmansworth at this time, but this seems to have been another mill, further north.[30] A residence and land were for sale at Berkhamsted: '14 acres with a large house and barns, well supplied with water and with the Grand Junction Canal running through it'.[31] So the presence of the canal in the west Hertfordshire towns in these early years was seen to be, and was presented as, an advantage to residents, mill owners and local businesses. But did they take the advantage offered?

West Hertfordshire trade and industry

Hertfordshire's manufacturing industry was small and included few elements of domestic or proto-industry. Even though Hertfordshire straw plaiters were sufficiently numerous to make a significant contribution to their local rural economy, their products were simply one of the components used by hat manufactories in St Albans, Luton and Dunstable – straw-plaiting was not nationally significant.[32] The county's main industries – plaiting, malting, brewing, milling – were generally based on agricultural products. There was scarcely any manufacturing, apart from paper making and preparing silk and cotton thread. Chapter 2 demonstrated how and roughly when

---

29 *The Times*, 10 July 1804, p. 4 and 17 November 1804, p. 4 (The Times digital archive, accessed 21 May 2015).
30 *The Times*, 12 December 1804, p. 4.
31 *The Times*, 5 September 1805, p. 4.
32 Freeman, *St Albans*, p. 177.

these industries fitted into the towns and villages of Hertfordshire before the coming of the Grand Junction Canal; we will now consider how they changed under the influence of the opportunities offered by it.

PAPER MAKING

Paper making is perhaps the most celebrated industry of west Hertfordshire, and we have seen how, in the 1790s, increasing demand for paper due to growing economic and industrial activity was driving production to such a level that its scale supplanted imports and indeed generated exports.[33] But the development of a mechanised production process did not occur until the early nineteenth century, when, coincident with the coming of the canal, paper-making machinery developed at the French paper mill of Leger Didot was brought to Frogmore and then to Two Waters, near Hemel Hempstead, by the London stationers Henry and Sealy Fourdrinier, and subsequently developed at their expense by the engineer Bryan Donkin (see below).[34]

The canal did not immediately greatly benefit the paper mills because they were not yet configured to use it: rather, competition for water as a power source caused many disputes between the mill owners and the canal company. Well into the nineteenth century water power was often preferred to steam because it was cheaper and easier to control: Croxley mill, opened in 1830, was driven in part by a water wheel, Frogmore was water powered until at least 1839 and water turbines were used at Nash until 1879. A steady water supply was vital and was not always found near a canal.[35]

When the canal arrived, the actual making of paper in these mills, all water powered and small-scale, was by hand: true industrialisation was yet to occur, and the industry was not economically dominant even in Hemel Hempstead, Kings Langley, Abbots Langley and Rickmansworth. But it was the Hemel Hempstead mills, already well established by 1792, that seem to have used the canal quickly – and thus grown. The Fourdrinier brothers already had Two Waters Mill (they insured it in October 1792, and a canal survey map earlier that year shows it clearly as 'Mr Fourdrinier's Paper Mill'). They also had Frogmore Mill from 1798 and were about to start investing heavily in technology.[36] They may have had direct access from their mills to the canal but, even if they did not, convenient wharfage was available nearby (Figure 5.6).

The rateable value of the two mills, £114 and £120 in 1798, increasing to £120 and £200 in 1803, suggests sizeable businesses, as does the £47

---

33 Hills, *Papermaking*, pp. 45, 46, 53.
34 Finerty, 'Paper mills in Hertfordshire', p. 425.
35 Hills, *Papermaking*, p. 161; Joan Evans, *The endless web* (London, 1956), p. 96.
36 Finerty, 'Paper mills in Hertfordshire', pp. 424, 425.

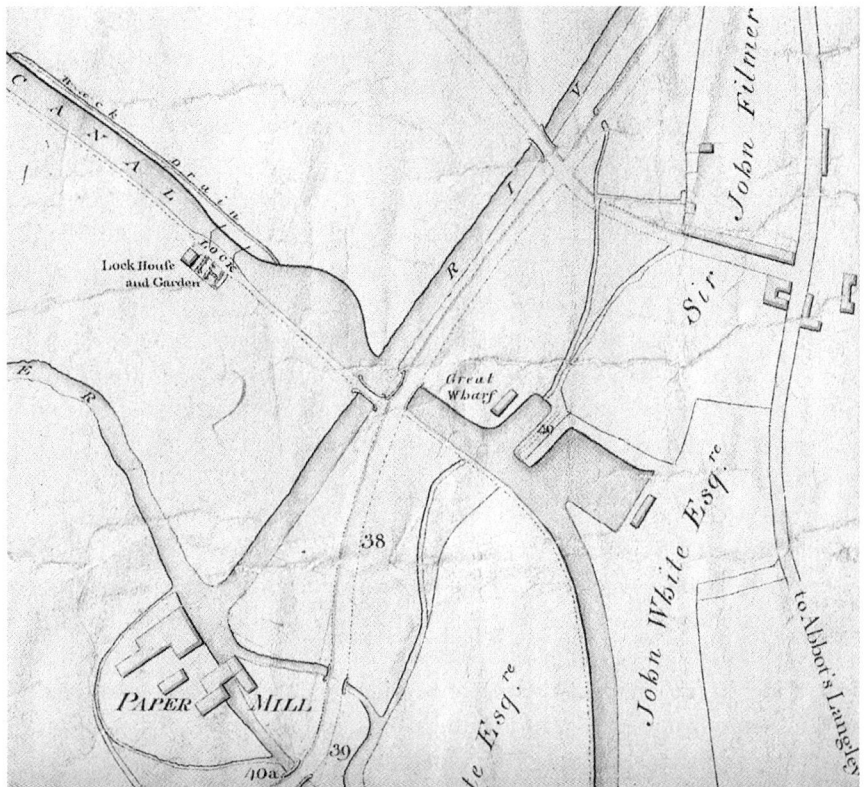

Figure 5.6. Hemel Hempstead: Two Waters and Boxmoor, c.1810 (by permission of Canalmaps Archive, www.canalmaps.net). Two Waters paper mill was at the confluence of the Gade (from the north) and the Bulbourne (from the west). There was certainly a wharf at the mill some time after this, although the towpath bridge over the Gade seems here to be fixed. Even before that, the distance to the Boxmoor wharfs was only a few hundred yards. The Sparrows Herne turnpike ran parallel to the canal just off the bottom left corner of the picture.

valuation of Boxmoor wharf, and all were to grow considerably.[37] Meanwhile, the boat-gauging[38] registers show a range of long-distance canal carriers as well as local firms working past Hemel Hempstead, and it would

---

37   HALS, DP/47/12/3 Hemel Hempstead overseers' rates and accounts 1791–1804.
38   'Gauging' was the process by which a boat's freeboard was measured at various weights of loading, with the results recorded in a book, the gauging register. This was done for each boat by each canal company on which the boat was expected to trade, and copies of the book were issued to each toll clerk along the canal. As the boat proceeded along the canal the weight of the cargo, and so the toll payable, could be determined by the clerk by measuring the freeboard ('dry side') presented to him. Figure 5.11 is an example of an entry for one boat.

be surprising had the Fourdriniers not engaged their services both south to London and north towards Birmingham to bring raw materials (rags) in and paper out. When in 1803 the Fourdriniers' water-powered paper-making machinery was being delivered from Bryan Donkin's works on the south bank of the Thames at Bermondsey it could have come by waggon up the turnpike, but it is far more likely that these entrepreneurs would have used the river Thames and the canal for this, as well as for the boilers, installed in 1810, and fuel to heat the water for paper drying.[39]

The inventory of Two Waters Mill, drawn up later in 1810 in support of the Fourdriniers' bankruptcy proceedings and the sale and lease-back of the mill, shows the sheer mass of material required just for the lead piping, most of which was probably for the water delivery: a quarter of a mile of pipework of diameters from three-quarters of an inch to seven inches, accompanied by dozens of brass cocks, pump barrels and other fittings.[40] Even more tellingly, there were '54 yards of six inch cast iron piping laid on the loft floor for drying the paper by steam';[41] a two-inch copper pipe thirty-three feet long 'to convey the steam from the boilers to the iron pipes'; another of nine feet 'to communicate with the pipes in the loft above the engine house'; thirty-eight yards of cast-iron steam pipe; fourteen feet of copper steam pipe; and a cast-iron boiler in the engineer's room for heating the loft by steam, with twenty-two feet of two-inch copper steam pipe. Add to this a very large amount of tools, including a lathe and other equipment, and we see the scale of such an establishment. Cast-iron pipes were, at this time, being cast horizontally, probably in lengths of about nine feet – and this was specialist work, done in the West Midlands by the large foundries. All this, bulky and very heavy, could have come from there by road in dozens of waggons, but it is much more likely to have come by water, and indeed the canal may well have been necessary to the whole project.[42]

---

39 Before mechanical paper making was established, hand-made paper was manufactured in small enough quantities to be dried naturally by simply hanging it in a loft. The far greater volumes made by machine required dedicated heating, and that was done by steam (briefing by Mike Stanyon, *The Paper Trail*, 4 December 2018); Hands and Davis, *Book of Boxmoor*, p. 48.

40 Michael Stanyon, 'Inventory of Two Waters Mill', *The Quarterly (Journal of the British Association of Paper Historians)*, 61 (2007), pp. 14–18. This is an analysis of the original document at HALS, D/Eb 1296 Z1.

41 Lead and iron pipe seems to have been measured in yards, copper in feet.

42 It seems unlikely that any of this related to steam power. Much later the new tenant, William Hunter, asked that because of a shortage of river water lasting three years the Company erect a steam engine of ten to twelve horsepower. They declined, but reduced his rent by 20 per cent. TNA, RAIL 830/7 GJC select committee minutes, 23 January 1839.

The Fourdriniers had therefore probably been using the canal for about ten years before Dickinson came to Apsley in 1809. Their presence may well have influenced Dickinson's decision about where to buy his first mill, and the availability of the canal nearby could have been another factor.[43] Their financial troubles of 1810 required them to sell and lease back their mills, however, and the role of the Grand Junction Company in this will be discussed below.

Other paper mills, such as that at Mill End, Rickmansworth, also used steam later, but we know little of their operations, and it was Dickinson's business that developed most quickly. His rapid expansion and mechanisation of a formidable industrial footprint, with mills at Apsley, Nash and Batchworth taken over and then Home Park and latterly Croxley built, could not have occurred without the canal, and Hemel Hempstead, like Abbots Langley, Kings Langley and Rickmansworth, owed much to the Grand Junction Canal. For example, Dickinson leased Batchworth pulp mill in July 1819 at a rent of £125 a quarter and increased its operating scale with new equipment to make pulp for use in his other mills: in October 1820 the Grand Junction Canal Company paid half of his costs (£569 5s 4d) in setting up a new bleaching house and the bleaching chests to go in it.[44] A canal arm was cut in the first few months of his occupancy and steam power introduced during the modernisation that followed.[45] All this investment was clearly part of an ambitious canal-based plan, and Dickinson had already taken a warehouse at Paddington at an annual rent of £124 14s 2d.

Other west Hertfordshire paper mills were not so well placed to use the canal, and in any case were not yet producing paper mechanically. So it would not be true to say that the first few years of the canal had a significant effect on the paper industry overall, although it was certainly helpful to Dickinson and probably to the Fourdriniers before him.

SILK AND COTTON

The silk industry in Hertfordshire at the start of the period is outlined in Chapter 2.[46] Silk thread throwing was unlikely to become dependent on the canal. As already observed, canal transport was particularly suitable for

---

43 Robinson and Wrigley, 'Hemel Hempstead in the nineteenth century', pp. 103–6.
44 TNA, RAIL 830/66 GJC treasurer's cash book, October 1820. There is no indication in the minutes of why the GJCCo felt obliged or even inclined to do this, and one can only suppose that Dickinson had such a grip on their business that they felt it necessary to oblige him in this way.
45 TNA, RAIL 830/35 GJC general committee minutes 1816–21, 10 June 1819; Evans, *Endless web*, p. 22 – she sets this a year earlier, however, than the GJC's official records, which in this account have been taken as correct.
46 Jennings, 'Ravelled skein'.

relatively low-value bulky goods moving in large quantities: raw silk meets none of these criteria, being of high value (over £100 per cwt), light and moved in relatively small quantities.[47] All the Hertfordshire silk mills were throwing mills that prepared the finished thread for weaving, the latter process not to be carried out in the county for several years hence. Mechanical throwing had been spreading in England since 1717, and the Watford mills had been running for a number of years – the Rookery mill, on the Colne below Watford, having been advertised for sale in the *Manchester Mercury* in 1768.[48] But the expansion of the number and size of throwing mills seen in Cheshire was not evident in Hertfordshire, where, notwithstanding Woolams's establishment at St Albans in 1802, the mills remained few in number and generally, until 1824, small.[49] A silk-throwing mill had three requirements apart from its labour force: driving power, transport of raw material from the point of import, and transport of the product to market. Neither the raw material nor the product was especially bulky: for years carried by road, it could easily have continued so.[50] But driving power was a different matter for the throwsters in Watford, St Albans, Rickmansworth and later Tring.[51] The Rookery mill, four storeys high, was powered by the river Colne at the southern end of Watford, about 500 yards downstream of the 1780 turnpike bridge.[52] Owned by the Paumier family until 1826, it was sufficiently large to be clearly shown on Bryant's 1822 map of Hertfordshire. By 1792 two more mills, both horse-powered and small, had been established in Watford, one probably also by Paumier and another on the High Street probably by Thomas Watson (see below).[53] Rickmansworth silk mill was established by 1806 by William Harty, a son-in-law of Peter Paumier of Watford's Rookery mill, and the lack of water near it indicates that it too was probably powered by mill horse.[54] Thomas Rock Shute took over Rookery Mill in 1826 and sought to expand production, but, finding that there was not enough labour in Watford, in about 1830 he opened two other mills – in Rickmansworth on the site of the 1806 establishment and in

---

47 Gerhold, *Road transport*, p. 121.
48 Jennings, 'Ravelled skein', p. 13.
49 Freeman, *St Albans*, p. 181.
50 Jennings, 'Ravelled skein', p. 4.
51 Jennings, 'The silk industry', pp. 96–7.
52 Johnson, *Industrial archaeology*, pp. 62–4.
53 Wendy Austin, *The Tring silk mill* (Tring, 2014), p. 4; Bryant's *Map of Hertfordshire 1822* (map 3) (Hertfordshire Records Society, 2003); Jennings, 'Ravelled skein', pp. 180, 181.
54 Jennings, 'Ravelled skein', pp. 178, 182; Howes, *Wind, water and steam*, p. 177.

Chesham, a few miles west of Berkhamsted.[55] In 1835 he complained that although he had 600 people at his mills he still needed pauper labour, which was not made available.[56] Both Shute's Chesham and Rickmansworth mills were powered by steam, which suggests that not only the fuel but also the steam plant and machinery came by canal, although there is no surviving record of the supply of this equipment.

No record has been found, either, of how the silk was carried, although a 1792 transaction between the Watford throwster Watson and the Ruislip workhouse suggests that moving raw silk and thrown thread across a distance of about eight miles by road presented little difficulty.[57] The throwsters did not need to use the canal, although they could have done so: at Rickmansworth both Frogmoor and Batchworth Bridge wharfs were within half a mile of the mill, although at Watford the journey from Cashio Bridge wharf to Rookery Mill was about three miles and that from Berkhamsted's Castle Wharf to Chesham was about five miles. These are not prohibitive distances for a valuable material – the raw silk had already come from the port of London by boat or more probably by waggon, and the thread would have gone south to London or north towards the Cheshire weavers in the same way.

The influence of the Grand Junction Canal, then, did not cause silk throwing to develop further as a major industry in Watford or Rickmansworth. In 1824 another throwing mill was established at Tring by the Manchester silk and cotton spinner William Kay, who had recently bought Tring Park.[58] Again, the transport modes used by him and from 1829 by his successor David Evans are unknown: but the canal was nearby and the steam engine bought from the well-established Manchester engine builder Peel Williams & Peel in the early 1830s is almost certain to have come by canal from their works on the Ashton Canal to Tring Wharf at Gamnel on the Wendover Arm, less than a mile from the mill.[59] It would be surprising if the coal had not come by the same route, but there is no hard evidence, although it has been suggested that thrown thread was sent to both London and Manchester, and some to Coventry, all on connected canals, and later to the weaving mill at Aylesbury.[60]

---

55   Jennings, 'The silk industry', p. 44.
56   TNA, MH12/4679 correspondence between T R Shute and Watford Board of Guardians, 1 and 3 November 1835.
57   HALS, DE/B1157 B11, Draft agreement between the Master of the Ruislip Workhouse and Thomas Watson of Watford to wind silk in the workhouse, 1792.
58   Austin, *Tring silk mill*, p. 8.
59   Austin, *Tring silk mill*, p. 16; Musson and Robinson, *Science and technology*, pp. 459, 470.
60   Johnson, *Industrial archaeology*, pp. 67, 68; Austin, Tring silk mill, p. 37.

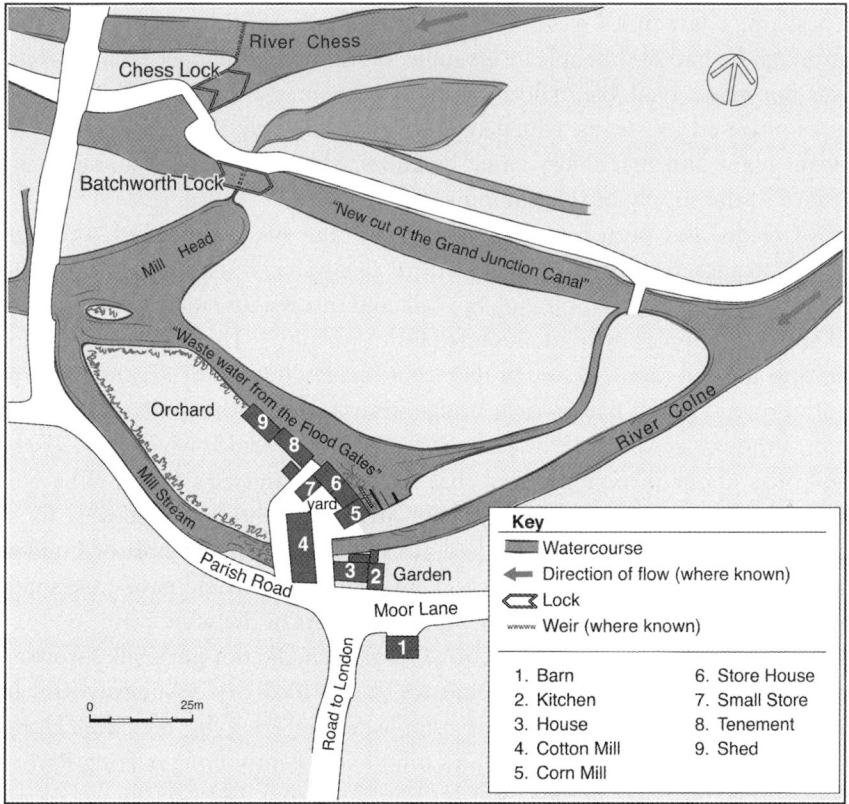

Figure 5.7. Batchworth Mills, *c.*1807 (after TNA, MPH 1/451, 'A Plan of the Estate of Mr Joseph Strutt'). This plan was drawn after the opening of the side cut via Chess Lock into the river Chess in 1805, and before the mill was sold to the Grand Junction Canal Company in 1811 to be used as a paper pulp mill, first by the Fourdriniers and then by Dickinson. The mill stream below the cotton mill (4) was canalised by Dickinson in 1819 to serve a wharf at the mill, from which paper pulp was moved to his other mills a few miles further north.

The cotton industry was also confined to thread spinning, in St Albans from before 1798 when the *UBD* listed the cotton manufacturer George Gill, and at Batchworth (Rickmansworth) from before 1786 in the mill described in Chapter 2.[61] There had been a corn mill on the Batchworth site since Domesday and a paper mill of some sort after 1755, but there is no evidence that its owners, the Strutts – whose uncle Jedidiah was a promoter of canals in Derbyshire – used the canal at all for their business, despite its proximity to Rickmansworth's large wharfs: Figure 5.7 shows the layout

---

61 UBD, Vol 5, p. 180 (St Albans) <https://babel.hathitrust.org/cgi/pt?id=njp.32101072916255;view=1up;seq=188>, accessed 1 May 2019.

in about 1807.⁶² Their interaction with the Grand Junction Canal related only to water supplies from the river Colne, and began very shortly after the canal came into use.⁶³ As will be outlined below, they sold out to the Grand Junction in 1811, and the mill was passed to the Fourdriniers and then to Dickinson. It cannot be said that the Grand Junction Canal brought prosperity to the small cotton industry in Hertfordshire.

Hertfordshire business using the canal

In the early days, with carrying on the canal already becoming well established and with well-recognised national carriers using it, volumes of trade were already high – over £1,100 in tolls was collected during 1797.⁶⁴ The Coventry carrier Thomas Bache, of whom we heard earlier as a road carrier, carried 5,000 tons of bar and pig iron annually to London via the Coventry and Oxford Canals and river Thames, or by the Coventry and Trent and Mersey Canals, river Trent and finally by ship from Hull. In 1806 he offered to switch that business to the Grand Junction Canal for a rate of ¾d per ton-mile, an offer that the company was very happy to accept.⁶⁵ Iron was important to every town at this stage: iron foundries had begun to appear in some, and it is likely that some of this iron went also to the still-small ironworking businesses in the Hertfordshire towns. An idea of the range of goods being carried on the canal in about 1816 comes from an exchange between the Grand Junction and a connecting canal that refers to sugar, molasses, porter, soap, tallow, oil and hides ('new and tanned') from London to Nottingham and cheese, ale and iron from Nottingham to London, and at about that time there are many references to glass, nails, salt, coke, stone and timber.⁶⁶ Spread throughout the committee's minutes are offers of deals being declined or accepted, made or withdrawn, which affected business along the length of the canal.⁶⁷

One local user was Thomas Toovey, corn miller of Kings Langley, to whose complex relationship with the canal we will return, but no other water corn mills seem to have been significant users of the canal for transport. There were a number of other water corn mills on the Bulbourne and Gade and therefore

---

62   TNA, MPH 1/451 'Plan of an Estate The Property of Mr Joseph Strutt Situate in the Parish of Rickmansworth in the County of Hertford', c.1807.
63   The story is given in more detail below.
64   TNA, RAIL 830/63 GJC treasurer's cash book 1794–1801, 4 Sep 1797, 22 Nov 1797.
65   TNA, RAIL 830/42 GJC general committee minutes, 11 February 1806.
66   TNA, RAIL 830/35 GJC general committee minutes, 2 May 1816; Hadfield, *Canals of the East Midlands*, p. 119.
67   TNA, RAIL 830/42 GJC general committee minutes, 8 April 1806.

on the canal, including Berkhamsted Upper and Lower mills, Bourne End, Hunton Bridge, Grove and Lord Essex's private mill in Cashiobury Park. It is surprising that they did not use the canal more, as increasing quantities of grain were being imported after the end of the Napoleonic war, but it is quite possible that these mills were being supplied by road mainly with local grain. In any case, none developed into businesses as significant as Toovey's.

COAL DEALING

One major cargo coming to this area by canal which could not have done so by road was coal. Volumes carried were considerable: in 1809 the company directed 3,000 tons of Staffordshire coal to be supplied to Paddington, to be followed by a further 7,000 tons either there or to 'the Company's wharf at Cashiobury as required', indicating that business at Watford was already growing.[68] There is also a rare direct reference to its price in the county: the lowest bid to supply the back-pumping steam engine near Nash Mills with coal was 30s per ton at the wharf, plus 6d per ton to unload and stack it.[69] This was, of course, wholesale: the purchase by the Hemel Hempstead overseers of thirteen tons at £2 15s a ton (delivered) late in 1808 by the Boxmoor wharfingers suggests that a private householder would have been paying about £3 a ton.[70] This can be compared with some more recent examples to estimate the annual use of coal for a small canal-side cottage: over a century later a lock-keeper resident on the Worcester and Birmingham canal above Worcester was receiving an allowance of five tons per year, while even more recent recollections of deliveries to lock cottages on the river Weaver in the late 1970s are of an allowance of about three tons.[71] On both waterways these cottages were essentially the same as when first built, and it seems reasonable to suggest that about three tons of coal a year, costing in about 1810 around £9, was needed to provide a basic level of heating and cooking for a small cottage. Coal was perhaps beginning to be affordable to the working tradesman, if not yet the labourer.[72]

---

68 TNA, RAIL 830/42 GJC general committee minutes, 7 November 1809.

69 TNA, RAIL 830/42 GJC general committee minutes, 11 July 1809. A few years later in 1828 Dickinson had 175 tons delivered to Nash Mill at 27s a ton, suggesting that the wholesale price of coal in Hertfordshire had, if anything, declined in the interim. In early 1813 coal was advertised at the GJC wharf at Northampton at 27s 6d a ton (*Northampton Mercury*, 23 January 1813). Later it was in the range 18–24s a ton (see Chapter 6).

70 HALS, DP/47/12/4 Hemel Hempstead overseers' rates 1804–1811.

71 Pat Warner, *Lock keeper's daughter* (Shepperton, 1986), pp. 41, 42; Interview with Richard Horne, Narrow Boat Trust, 5 February 2018.

72 One Yorkshire labourer in 1841 was spending £2 on coal from his annual £50 income. Horn, *Rural world*, p. 267.

The relatively large amounts being used in the poor houses of Hemel Hempstead and Kings Langley especially demonstrate how the use of coal had grown: no record has been found of a parish buying it before the arrival of the canal, but Hemel Hempstead overseers in particular were buying small but increasing amounts from 1798, and ten years later it was in regular use.[73] The 1821 census shows that there were, in the parishes along the canal from Tring to Rickmansworth, about 4,300 inhabited houses. Allocating three tons of coal to each (and many would have used very much more) suggests that some 13,000 tons a year – about 520 boat loads – would be needed to supply this area with domestic fuel alone.[74] The *Directories* listed coal merchants in each town, and even if only half the households were in fact using coal it is clear that no system of road transport could possibly have provided a supply requiring at least 2,500 three-ton waggons. In this regard alone the Grand Junction played a significant role in this area.

AGRICULTURE

Arthur Young provides much evidence of use of the canal by farmers who had land alongside it.[75] Even though Young's attention was largely on the more progressive farmer, he provides important clues as to what was happening more generally. The development of Paddington was clearly important, and allowed the establishment of agricultural wharfs for produce into London and manure wharfs for material leaving it, all much closer to the centre of the city than the facilities at Brentford and much less risky than the Thames itself. Young records the experiences of the west Hertfordshire farmers to whom he spoke, with Newman Hatley of Kings Langley giving the most detail. The problem for Young was that the arrangements at Paddington basin, opened only in 1801, were not good enough in 1804 to serve Hertfordshire agriculture properly. He commented that 'the benefit of bringing back bulky manures is extremely questionable at present … . Vast quantities of hay and straw go to London, from the very banks of the canal, by land-carriage, the carts bringing dung back, which does not answer when brought by the navigation.' This 'apparent absurdity … arise[s] from the want of magazines and wharves at Paddington, where a hay and straw-market should be immediately established, so that both articles might be sold directly from the barges, which should be immediately loaded with manures from the wharfs'. Until proper steps were taken to do this the potential

---

73 HALS, DP/47/12/3 Hemel Hempstead overseers' accounts, November 1798; DP/64/12/4 Kings Langley overseers' accounts, 29 March 1805.
74 HALS, 1821 census – abstract of answers and returns, pp. 128, 129.
75 Young, *General view*, pp. 16–18.

Figure 5.8. Paddington Basin on first opening in 1801 (LMA, City of London Collage: 324191). This was soon to become a significant inland port with wharfs for manure and produce, as well as for coal and general goods. Some of the Hertfordshire famers used it, and its facilities were adversely commented on in 1804 by Arthur Young (see text).

benefits of the canal would not be realised. 'A beast and sheep market there should also be established,' he wrote, to benefit all the grazing counties – that is, those on the drove roads to London. 'Manures come at too heavy an expense, from the double cartage at London, which might very easily be prevented.' Once this was done,

> we shall see land carriage parallel to the line of the canal laid aside; and a considerable saving will be made by the non-employment of many horses; the roads will be consequently preserved; and the use of manures will be greatly extended among the farmers *who live within reach of the canal*.[76]

As we have already seen, the problem lay in the nature of farming. Its activity covers a large area, to reach across which 'dendritic' transport is required: tendrils such as farm tracks, lanes and roads. But a canal is 'linear': it connects points, such as wharfs in towns or industrial premises. For a farmer to use a canal he had to be close to it: if he had to cart his produce, or his delivery of manure, any great distance to get to or from the canal bank – usually no wharf would be required – he might as well have

---

76 Young, *General view*, p. 17 (my italics added).

continued with his load by road, especially if his market or source were close by, which in Hertfordshire it almost invariably was. So even if Young was correct in his analysis of the situation at Paddington, which would have disappointed the company, as it had in fact opened a hay and straw market at Paddington in 1802 (Figure 5.8), few Hertfordshire farmers would have been significant users of the canal.[77] Some did use it: the early gauging records and descriptions of wharfs note hay as a cargo for Paddington and the Thames as well as manures as a return load, and Newman Hatley set up a canal carrying business, as we shall see below – but few other Hertfordshire farmers did so, although some of the carriers who set up may also have been farming.

In 1801 Hatley commissioned a sailing barge to carry 'corn and flour' from Kings Langley to the Thames, although his original idea seems to have been to improve his supply of London manure (Figure 5.9).[78] In 1804 he gave Arthur Young, who described him as 'a considerable farmer', an account of his experiences.[79] His barge cost £262 10s, one man (with three horses, probably the biggest running cost) and a boy cost £2 12s 6d a week, another man 17s: these wages for boatmen were somewhat above agricultural wages for skilled men and labourers of about 2s a day in winter.[80] The tolls totalled £5 for a load of composted 'night soil and sweepings' costing £12. The time for the fifty-mile round trip quoted by Young was protracted, at ten days – in fact it is about sixty-six miles, and should have taken at most three days, suggesting considerable delays in loading and unloading.

And indeed it was Hatley who had complained to Young that the arrangements at Paddington were not good enough to avoid expensive trans-shipment of produce as well as manures onto road vehicles, so at this time his use of the canal was probably still tentative and wholly focused on agriculture (he later engaged in carrying other goods, especially coal) – he already owed tolls to the canal company of £65 0s 6¾d, due in 1802, for which the company was about to take legal proceedings.[81] Other agricultural canal users noted by Young included Kingsman of Kings Langley and Dorrien of Berkhamsted; at the latter place the use as manure of ashes from London was 'universal' and their cost had reduced owing to canal transport from 2s 6d to 1s 6d 'per sack', although Rooper of Berkhamsted continued to send carts, empty if necessary, to London for them. The canal brought the first London 'night soil' to Berkhamsted and Kings Langley, with one

---

77 *Northampton Mercury*, 10 April 1802 (opening of hay and straw market at Paddington).
78 NWA, BW99/6/5/1 GJC gauging register vol. 1.
79 Young, *General view*, pp. 16, 17.
80 Young, *General view*, pp. 16, 217, 218.
81 TNA, RAIL 830/42 GJC general committee minutes, 10 December 1805.

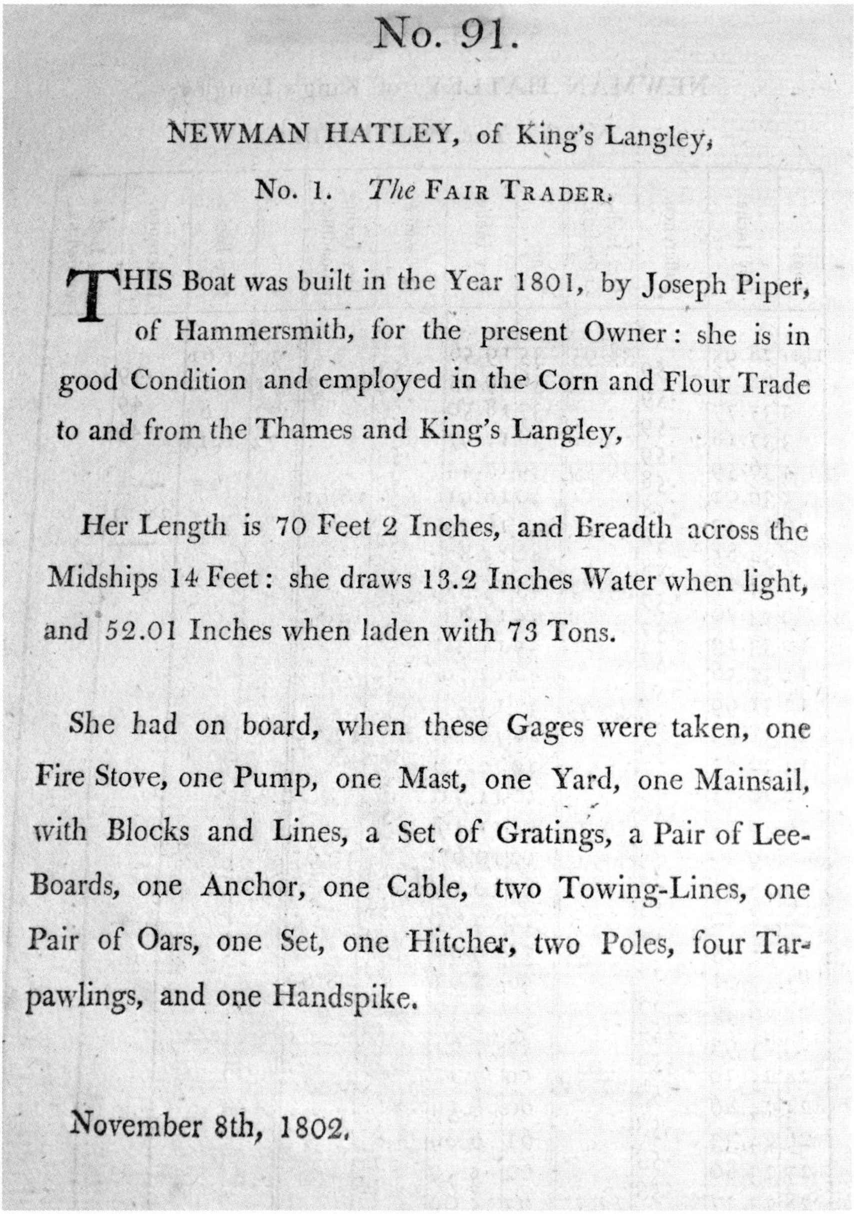

No. 91.

NEWMAN HATLEY, of King's Langley,

No. 1. *The* FAIR TRADER.

THIS Boat was built in the Year 1801, by Joseph Piper, of Hammersmith, for the present Owner: she is in good Condition and employed in the Corn and Flour Trade to and from the Thames and King's Langley,

Her Length is 70 Feet 2 Inches, and Breadth across the Midships 14 Feet: she draws 13.2 Inches Water when light, and 52.01 Inches when laden with 73 Tons.

She had on board, when these Gages were taken, one Fire Stove, one Pump, one Mast, one Yard, one Mainsail, with Blocks and Lines, a Set of Gratings, a Pair of Lee-Boards, one Anchor, one Cable, two Towing-Lines, one Pair of Oars, one Set, one Hitcher, two Poles, four Tarpawlings, and one Handspike.

November 8th, 1802.

Figure 5.9. Gauging entry, barge 'Fair Trader' (1802) (by permission of NWA, BW99/6/5/1, f.91). This typical page of the gauging book used by toll clerks the length of the canal shows the detail of the barge and its intended business when built for the Kings Langley farmer Newman Hatley.

customer paying £27 per barge-load to treat ten acres.[82] Despite his view that it was the inconvenient arrangements at Paddington that prevented the canal being used more to serve Hertfordshire agriculture, Hatley, for one, persisted: in 1826 he, with his landlord the earl of Essex, was allowed to unload boats over the towpath at the wharf that had been built for him by the company in 1822, mainly but not only for manure.[83]

It is noticeable, however, that all these farmers were close to the canal, and even then at least one used a cart as a ready alternative to a boat. For most of the 'manure' trade no wharf was needed – it was enough to pull the boat in to the bank next to the field, put planks across, and fork the material into carts or barrows. It was not infrastructure but distance that was the problem. Young recorded very few farmers elsewhere in the county using canal-carried manure or indeed taking produce to market by canal, and the canal had little effect on Hertfordshire's agriculture, its main industry.

BREWING

Every village had at least one beer house that brewed on the premises, but it was the larger 'common brewers' who brewed most of the beer sold.[84] Hertfordshire beer houses and breweries were as prosperous as any, but the scale of production is important. We saw in Chapter 2 that a small brewery could be powered by mill horse, and that the market of such a brewery typically remained small and local – carrying beer, a low-value product bulky to transport, more than about five miles by brewer's dray was difficult and uneconomic.[85] In west Hertfordshire brewing was indeed on a relatively small scale. Even in 1867 the production of the largest brewery in the area was still only 9,000 barrels a year, well below the mechanisation threshold of seventy years previously.[86] There were, nonetheless, successful common breweries in Tring, Berkhamsted, Watford and Rickmansworth, and another was established in Kings Langley in 1826, although Hemel Hempstead's inns and alehouses were largely brewing their own at this time.[87] But the supplies of malt to these common breweries came by cart or waggon, their product was delivered by horse-drawn dray, and their power for grinding malt and other parts of the process was provided largely by mill horse.[88] But, as we

82 Young, *General view*, p. 171.
83 HALS, D/ECp.T11 Indenture (Hatley and Essex vs GJCCo), April 1826.
84 Mathias, *The brewing industry*; Whitaker, *Brewers in Hertfordshire*.
85 Mathias, *The brewing industry*, pp. 14, 81.
86 Whitaker, *Brewers in Hertfordshire*, p. 217; Mathias, *Brewing industry in England*, p. 81.
87 Whitaker, *Brewers in Hertfordshire*, pp. 4–5, 74–8, 113–15, 162–6, 173–7, 202–16, 215–33.
88 Whitaker, *Brewers in Hertfordshire*, p. 15.

saw in Chapter 2, a great deal of hot water was used, and coal was needed in some quantity. In Tring, Berkhamsted, Kings Langley and Rickmansworth the breweries were less than a mile from the wharfs, and while Watford's two large breweries were over two miles from either Lady Capels' or Cashio Bridge wharfs the opportunity to use the canal clearly existed.[89] Coal carried on the canal could well have been delivered by cart, while new barrels, which many brewers bought from specialist cooperages, could have been carried by water from London.[90]

Samuel Salter of Rickmansworth certainly used the canal in a more significant way, but not only for his brewery in the High Street. In 1805 he paid for the canalisation of the river Chess from Batchworth to Town Wharf.[91] Suggestions that the canal was used to transport beer to London or to bring in barley and malt should be viewed with caution, however.[92] Just because a brewer *could* move beer by water does not mean that he *did*. Maintaining the condition of the beer was one reason for beer markets remaining local, cost another – transporting beer more than a few miles, even by waterway, added greatly to the distribution costs.[93] For example, one brewer based on the river Great Ouse made little use of it for beer sales despite dispatching between eight and fourteen barrels a week to London by road in the 1820s.[94] Even ten times this volume would only generate about one narrow boat load of around ninety barrels, weighing about eighteen tons and approaching half of Salter's likely total weekly production – so unlikely to justify the cost of the boat, let alone of a dedicated canal arm. Salter may well have been moving beer towards and into London by water, but this was not enough on its own to justify such special provision, especially since he would have been thereby relinquishing the use of his own drays for delivery. In any case, the distance from brewery to wharf, about 400 yards, would still have required a cart to move a barrel of beer, which weighed over 400lb. It seems unlikely that the cut would have been left so short if it had been planned to serve the brewery directly – its purpose is more likely to have been to provide a public wharf near the middle of the town. Salter's brewery would have used it for fuel and for the return or supply of expensive barrels, and for moving some beer, but

---

89   Whitaker, *Brewers in Hertfordshire*, pp. 74, 163–5, 202, 217.
90   Mathias, *The brewing industry*, pp. 55, 56.
91   Faulkner, *Grand Junction Canal*, p. 95.
92   Whitaker, *Brewers in Hertfordshire*, p. 173.
93   T.V. Gourvish and R.G. Wilson, *The British brewing industry 1830–1980* (Cambridge, 1994), p. 147. We note, however, the reference to 'ale' as a cargo from Nottingham to London quoted above, so there were exceptions.
94   Gourvish and Wilson, *British brewing industry*, p. 148.

Figure 5.10. The Rivers of England, 'More Park, near Watford, on the River Colne' (1824), by J.M.W. Turner (1775–1851) (© Tate, London 2018). Although Turner's title was accurate (More Park is seen in the centre of the picture, and overlooks the river Colne, not in view), his sketch gives an impression of Common Moor Lock in 1824, on the Grand Junction Canal just north of Rickmansworth. Work to build Dickinson's Croxley paper mill would start four years later, just to the left of the scene.

in this matter he was a local businessman taking an opportunity rather than a brewer serving the direct needs of his brewery. The canal did not have the transformative effect on the brewing industry that might have been expected and which was to be suggested later.[95]

BOAT BUILDING

There are only two recorded examples of boat building on the canal in Hertfordshire (Appendix B). The Grand Junction's gauging register for 1802 shows that in 1801 William Butler had had the barge *Berkhamstead Castle* built by Peacock and Willetts of that town to be used to carry hay and coal between Berkhamsted and London.[96] But none of these people appears again: the overseers' accounts list neither Peacock nor Willetts, while a William

---

95 Williams, *History of Watford*, p. 77, quotes the brewer Sedgwick as suggesting a canal to Watford in the 1870s.
96 NWA, BW99/6/5/1 GJC gauging register vol. 1.

Butler features as a ratepayer but without mention of his business.[97] The first reference to a definite boat builder is to John Hatton, also of Berkhamsted: he gauged as owner two narrow boats in April and May 1823, and then others at intervals up to 1841. He could have been building earlier: he was listed in Pigot's (1823) as 'boatbuilder', but not yet as anything else.[98] The gauging record is incomplete, and in any case does not show the builder of boats gauged after about 1809, but he appears in the Berkhamsted overseers' accounts in 1832 (the period 1823/4 to 1831 is also missing) as 'Mr J Hatton (boatwright, coal dealer) – Boat Building Yard £1 10s 0d'.[99] Pigot's (1832)[100] lists him as a boat builder and coal dealer, locating him at Castle Wharf, whereas the 1839 tithe award shows him a little further south (see Chapter 6), but Hatton was certainly working over at least twenty years, and both built and operated boats as well as his wharf. There is, however, no evidence of any other boat builder in Hertfordshire at this time.

BOAT OWNERSHIP AND OPERATION

Boat operations started promptly in Hertfordshire. As shown in Appendix B, Hertfordshire men (including those of Wendover, since the arm serving it passed through Hertfordshire) were noted in the first gauging registers, with barges and boats carrying hay, coal, timber and 'general goods' between Paddington, Brentford, Watford and Berkhamsted. We have seen how Newman Hatley operated, and already by 1802 barges had been sold by Ashness of Hemel Hempstead, Bentley of Cashiobury – one used for carrying coal and dung to Berkhamsted – and Perkins of Lady Capels' wharf. From at least 1802 wharf operators such as Howard of Boxmoor, Holladay of Cashio Bridge at Watford and (later) Landon of Cowroast all operated boats in a trade related to their wharf, largely in coal. Although no details survive, it is clear that these were the people who served the smaller wharfs most comprehensively, with the long-range carriers working to the larger towns, just as nowadays long-distance trains and local services serve different stations on the same line. Manufacturers often had their own boats: the Mines Royal Copper Company and the miller Thomas Howard operated from their own canal-side businesses on the southern edge of Rickmansworth parish, and the paper maker Dickinson was a significant operator with boats based at Nash Mills from 1818: up to the end of that year he paid 'tonnage' (tolls) of £26

---

97 HALS, DP/19/12/3 Berkhamsted overseers' accounts 1755–1804. A William Peacock appears as a blacksmith in Pigot's Directory (1832).
98 Pigot's *Directory* (1823), p. 351.
99 HALS, DP/19/11/3 Berkhamsted rate assessments, 1831.
100 Pigot's *Directory* (1832), p. 727.

4s 8½d, for the following year £50 19s 1¾d, then, increasing rapidly, £253 14s 10d in July 1820.[101] Thomas Ebbern (or Ebborn or Ebburn), the son of a Warwickshire farmer, boat owner, wharfinger and coal dealer, features in Chapter 6, but his presence at Watford and Hemel Hempstead suggests a definite link via the canal between Midlands coal producers and coal sales in Hertfordshire.[102] There were, then, a number of traders on the canal in Hertfordshire, and although we do not know the value of their trade, many continued for some years, although none became dominant in the field.

The Grand Junction Canal Company as a neighbour
The company made a direct but little-recognised contribution to the local economy through being, like all businesses, liable for rates in each parish through which it passed. The largest part of its contribution was to the poor rate, a sensitive matter: the tension between the need to relieve the poor and the size of the bill paid by each ratepayer was ever-present in every parish. The arrival in the parish of a potential large contributor will have been generally welcomed, but there seems to have been confusion over the basis on which the company was to be assessed – was it the value of the trade, potentially huge, or the value of tolls levied in the parish, or just the value of the land it occupied, which was much less? Generally, the company's rating valuations in Hertfordshire seem to have been based on the area of land owned, and it was so rated from about the time the canal opened, which is itself somewhat odd, as it had owned, and was cutting, land for some years before that. Most parishes measured the canal and its property, set and collected a rate and allowed life to go on, although it is perhaps surprising that farmers, always conscious of their liability for rates, and other traders and residents seem to have felt sufficiently prosperous to pay the relatively low poor rate without too much anxiety.[103] But when the Napoleonic Wars ended in 1815 the situation changed: as already noted, farmers were less prosperous and labourers less well employed, and the poor-relief burden on parishes all over the country started to increase. In the years 1815–17 some parishes, in this area principally Rickmansworth, Kings Langley and Hemel Hempstead, tried to follow an earlier lead by Paddington and Isleworth and reduce the burden on the parish ratepayers by setting an enormous valuation

---

101 TNA, RAIL 830/66 GJC treasurer's cash book 1820–1826.
102 TNA, HO/107/439/5 1841 Census – Watford; HO/107/1136/27 1841 Census – Sow (Warks).
103 The Poor Rates had, nonetheless, been rising inexorably, and Arthur Young's attention was drawn to it in 1804. At St Albans, 'despite straw plait', they were 6s in the pound, up from 4s in 1801; in Berkhamsted 9s, up from 5s; at Hemel Hempstead 4s, up from 2s or 2s 6d; in Kings Langley 7s, up from 3s; in Watford 3s 6d, up from 2s 6d; and at Rickmansworth, 4s 6d, up from 2s. Young, *General view*, pp. 32, 33.

on the property of the canal company, attempting thus to extract large amounts of cash from this rich incomer.[104] Rickmansworth's grounds for thus setting a value of £1,250 are the most clearly captured in their minutes: 'a ... proportional part of the profits ... arising from the Rates and Tolls received from or arising within ... the parish of Rickmansworth ... '.[105]

This would have been prohibitively costly for the company, who regularly appealed against these demands to the magistrates and usually won, albeit after a tussle. In May 1816 the clerk to the company reported to his committee that he had appealed against the assessments of Kings Langley and Hemel Hempstead, but that the sessions had confirmed that rates were chargeable on a valuation of £500 a mile. He was told to appeal against the poor rates in 'all parishes in which it shall appear that the Company was unreasonably rated ... '.[106] He duly did so, and Kings Langley provides an example of what transpired.

The canal there had been valued at £16 or £17 'for land' since 1803, paying 1s in the pound each quarter, so contributing about £3 10s a year to the parish poor. On 25 October 1815 the overseer Dorothy Parsley, the only woman noted as serving in this office, made a trip to Berkhamsted 'to enquire concerning the Canal Rate'. Her report is not recorded, but the rate subsequently demanded as part of a general rating review by external surveyors was based on a valuation of £457, with the demand being for £27 17s 6d – by far the highest in the parish (Dickinson's Apsley mill was valued at £325). In early 1816 the canal's engineer Benjamin Bevan came for 'discussion': the company then appealed as above, and the debate continued. In January 1817 the valuation dropped without explanation to £285. This time the parish appealed to the quarter sessions magistrates, supported by Harry Grover, the Hemel Hempstead solicitor who had suggested that Hemel Hempstead and Kings Langley join forces, but in February 1818 the rate paid fell to £6 'for land', little more than the company had been paying quite happily before the challenge.[107]

---

104 In 1809 Paddington parish had set a rateable value of £10,000 on the 'supposed value of the tolls' (LMA, MJ/SP/1810/07/009 Middlesex quarter sessions 1810). In 1804 Isleworth parish had set a rateable value of £500 on the rental of the land supposedly occupied (LMA, MJ/SP/1804/10/1015 Middlesex quarter sessions 1804).

105 HALS, DP/85/8/2 Rickmansworth vestry minutes, January 1817.

106 TNA, RAIL 830/35 GJC general committee minutes, 2 May and 8 May 1816; HALS, DP/19/11/2 Berkhamsted poor rate assessments 1806–1823; HALS, DP/85/8/2 Rickmansworth vestry minutes, January 1817.

107 HALS, DP/64/12/6 Kings Langley overseers' accounts 1815–1821; HALS, QSMB Vol. XIII, Hertford Easter quarter sessions 1818, pp. 202–9; HALS, DP/47/12/13 Hemel Hempstead overseers' accounts 1811–1816.

This was not a good result for the parishes, and little more is heard of this sort of attempt by parishes to extract cash from the Grand Junction Canal Company.

After the completion of the canal there was considerable scope for the Grand Junction's extensive operation to bring it into further conflict with local people. For example, at Cashio Bridge the canal cut through Cashio Bridge Farm, owned by Gonville and Caius College, Cambridge. The fields to the north had always drained into the river Gade below, but the canal had been slightly embanked and that drainage way was cut off, rendering the fields too wet to use. The problem was exacerbated by the raising of the levels of the rivers Chess, Gade and Colne, whose interconnecting channels were complicated here by Salter's 'penning' of the flow of the Chess to give a navigable depth in his cut. In 1812 the steward of the college inspected the whole arrangement and required various actions to be taken, not least by Salter but also by the canal company: they were to provide a drainage culvert to the river under the canal.[108] In the same area, the canal complicated the 1805 dispute between the farmer Joseph Bovingdon and the millers John and Joseph Strutt at Batchworth: the former wanted water to irrigate his fields and the latter needed uninterrupted water flow, and the previous rights of both were compromised by the Grand Junction's need to maintain its levels.[109] In 1830 at Kings Langley disturbance to a fishery resulted in a suit in which damages offered by the company of £400, then £600, were overturned by the assessing commissioners and £900 awarded.[110] A claim for damages resulted from a brick maker claiming (falsely) to have permission from the company to dig for clay on Boxmoor and then trespassing on it to load bricks onto a boat; and, separately, an undated note from the Boxmoor trustees sought the restoration of land they had sold to the company in 1809 for clay to repair the canal, it being now worked out, unsightly and dangerous.[111] These are just some examples of the many complaints that kept the clerk, Richard Cowlishaw Sale, alert and reporting frequently to both the general and district committees.

---

108 Gonville and Caius College Archive BUR/XXIX (17), Report from William Custance, steward of the manor of Croxley, to the bursar of the college, August 1812.

109 Gonville and Caius College Archive BUR/XXIX (13), Mr Best's opinion in the case of Strutt v Bovingdon, January 1805.

110 HALS, QS Plan 497/1, record of meeting of commissioners appointed to consider damage to fishery of John Parsley at Kings Langley, 1830; TNA, RAIL 830/44 GJC general committee minutes, 13 November 1828.

111 HALS, D/ELs Q35(8) letter from Harry Grover to GJCCo, 25 August 1820; D/ELs Q35(2) note from trustees of Boxmoor Trust (undated).

Water supply

Ever since Jessop's 1792 report the water supply, especially at Tring, had been of concern to those managing the canal, and we have seen in Chapter 4 the Grand Junction's approach to the problem. Generally, they bought the water mills and either shut them down or leased them out again shorn of their rights to the water. Further measures taken between 1796 and 1838 included building and then increasing reservoirs at Marsworth with a steam engine to pump the water up to the summit; regulating the traffic to reduce lock usage; and even controlling the loading of boats to allow a reduction in the water depth.[112] Three of the company's purchases are directly relevant to canal operations in Hertfordshire, and we will look at them here.

As we have seen, supplies from the rivers Bulbourne and Gade had been contentious issues for the company from the earliest days. This affected in particular the paper mills at Two Waters, Frogmore, Apsley and Nash and, lower down, the cotton mill at Batchworth, where in March 1809 John and Joseph Strutt had offered to sell the Grand Junction their mills, at this time both grinding corn and spinning cotton. The site of the cotton mill in particular, straddling the river Colne, was crucial to the operation of the canal (see Figure 5.7) – the filling of Batchworth Lock had a severe effect on the power produced by the mill wheel if the flow in the river was even a little reduced – and the company's secretary realised that to obviate future disputes (a primary motive of the company, who seem not to have trusted the Strutts) they had also to buy back fifteen acres of Lot Mead just upstream, which they had bought previously as part of the initial land acquisition (see Chapter 4) and then sold to John Strutt as being surplus to their requirements.

After negotiations lasting over a year, the deal was closed in early 1811, the company having offered the very considerable sum of £16,000 but the Strutts having held out for £16,800.[113] John Strutt did not fade away: he and his brother now claimed compensation for historic interference with their water supply from 1797, for which the company agreed to pay £523 16s 9d, and then in November 1811 he applied for a twenty-one-year lease on the mill, with the company to contribute £3,000, on which he offered to pay 7.5 per cent interest, to rebuild the machinery. Perhaps surprisingly, the committee were prepared to discuss this, and in December the rent was

---

112 TNA, RAIL 830/38 GJC upper district committee minutes, 6 September 1796; RAIL 830/35 GJC general committee minutes, 8 March 1827; RAIL 830/37 GJC lower district committee minutes, 1 June 1793; Faulkner, *Grand Junction Canal*, pp. 132–43.

113 Faulkner, *Grand Junction Canal*, p. 119; TNA, RAIL 830/42 GJC general committee minutes, 13 March, 9 October 1810; HALS, GH/323, 514, 525 abstracts of title etc., surrender of Batchworth Mill to GJCCo.

agreed at £910 per year, with £2,000 advanced for the refurbishment of the machinery and £315 for the house. Something then happened that is not recorded, so that in January 1812 it was Henry Fourdrinier who was admitted as tenant on the same terms as had been agreed with Strutt, but for only seven years. The mill was subsequently used to prepare paper pulp, despite the Fourdriniers being already insolvent and about to declare bankruptcy, although they continued to trade. Their tenure did not go well. In April 1816 they asked for more time to pay the rent for Batchworth: the company, noting that the paper trade was 'very dull' at that time, agreed to defer until 1 July, but difficulties persisted.[114]

Meanwhile, in September 1816 the Fourdriniers offered to sell to the company their Frogmore paper mill, powered by the Gade at Apsley. The general committee agreed to progress this, and by mid-1817 they had bought both Frogmore and Two Waters mills. Two Waters, Frogmore and Batchworth mills were then each valued for renting, with the instruction to the select [executive] committee that they were to let them to 'such persons as they shall think proper to rent for seven, fourteen or twenty one years'.[115] Frogmore was quickly taken on by William Nash,[116] and then, on 5 February 1818,

> Mr Fourdrinier having stated that £1,500 had been expended on the mill at Batchworth, and that he was unable to raise any sum of money owing to the shortness of the terms of his lease, being determined at the end of seven years, the Committee ordered that the lease be extended [but only] to fourteen years … .[117]

In August 1818 the Fourdriniers' request for an advance of money on their lease of Batchworth, on which they had already spent a great deal, was refused, and they were told that they could dispose of their lease as they wished. In October 1818 they owed rent of £262 8s 6d, and in February 1819 they needed more alterations. The request for these too was refused, and the arrears were to be collected. In June 1819 they agreed to transfer the lease to Dickinson, who had taken it by 8 July.[118] It was a sad end to the involvement with the Grand Junction of the first truly innovative paper

---

114 TNA, RAIL 830/35 GJC general committee minutes, 11 April 1816; RAIL 830/1 GJC select committee minutes, 20 June, 5 September, 3 October 1816.

115 TNA, RAIL 830/35 GJC general committee minutes, 19 September 1816, 10 July 1817; Pilkington, 'Frogmore and the first Fourdrinier', p. 27; Hands and Davis, *Book of Boxmoor*, p. 49.

116 Finerty, 'Paper mills in Hertfordshire', pp. 425, 426.

117 TNA, RAIL 830/1 GJC select committee minutes, 5 February 1818.

118 TNA, RAIL 830/35 GJC general committee minutes, 8 July 1819.

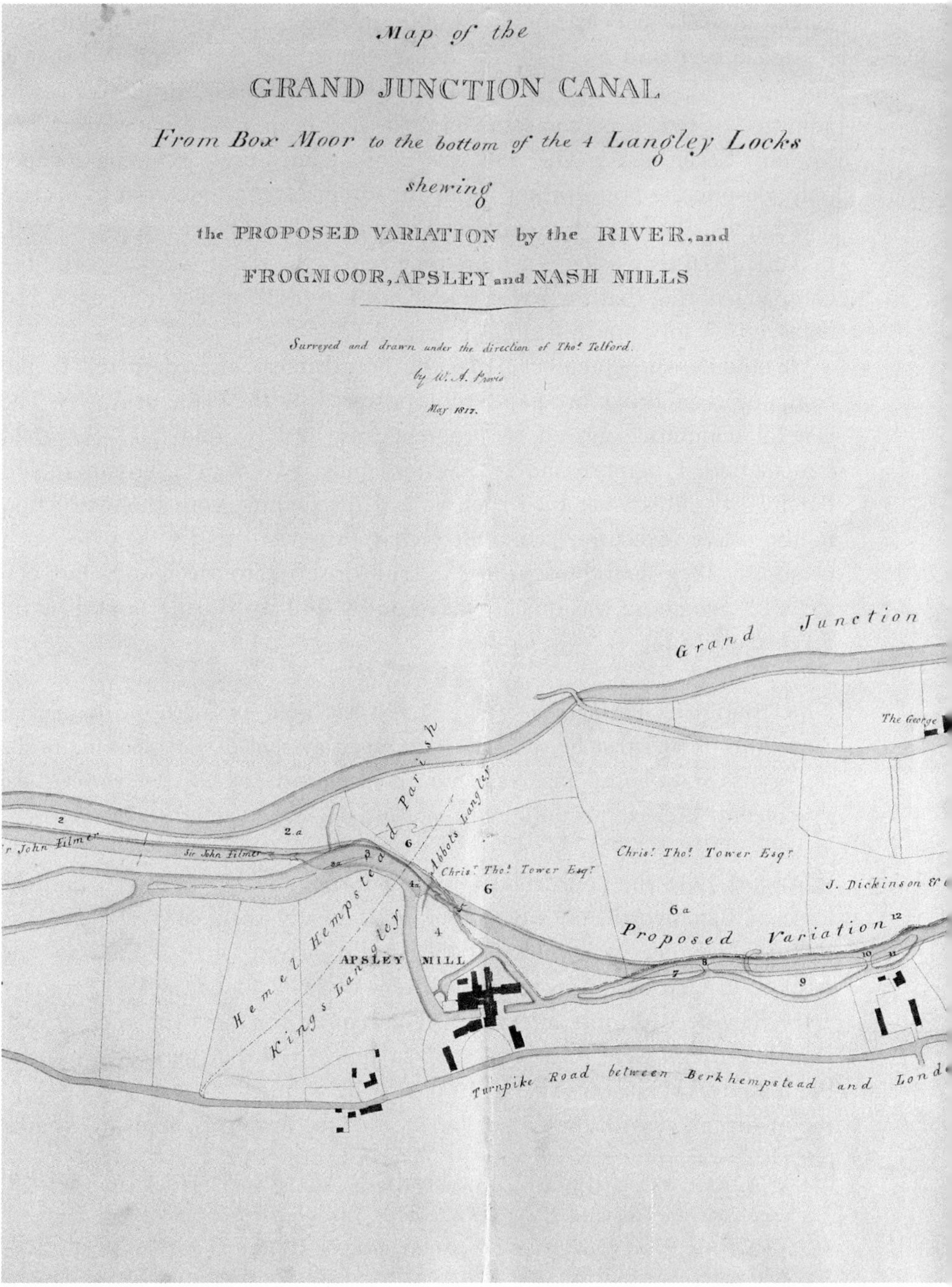

Figure 5.11. The deviation of the Grand Junction Canal past Apsley and Nash Mills, 1818 (parliamentary archive, HL/PO/PB/3/plan22). The original line of the canal is at the top of the plan, and shows the site of the steam pump intended to reduce the loss of water from the river Gade and the paper mills. The way in which the original line bypassed the mills,

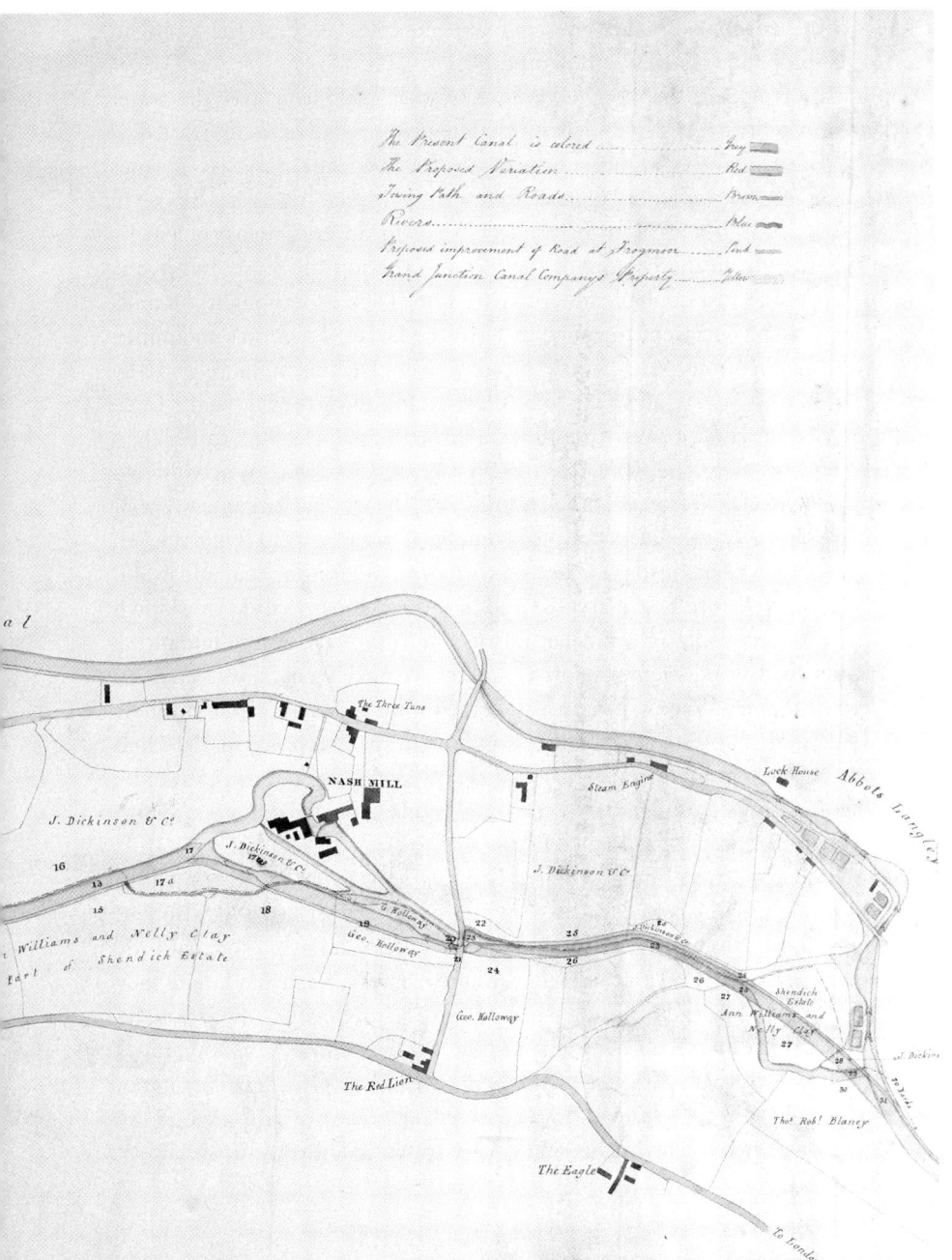

and in which the revised line returned river water to them, is clear. Note that the Sparrows Herne turnpike passing along the bottom of the plan is labelled as being between Berkhamsted and London, giving no indication of a service to the Midlands!

makers, but the episode does illustrate the complex role of the canal in Hertfordshire paper making at this time.

The most prominent dispute, however, was with Dickinson over the water supply to his mills at Apsley and Nash.[119] The dispute had actually started at Apsley before Dickinson's time: the locks on the new canal took river water from above Apsley mill and deposited it below Nash, bypassing both. In 1805 a steam pump had been installed at Nash to address this problem by returning water from the bottom of the locks to the top for reuse, but it was not sufficient. The dispute had gathered pace after Dickinson bought the mills in 1810 and 1811 and went to court. In 1816 the Grand Junction's committee minuted their intention to defend the latest move by Dickinson, but eventually accepted that the canal would have to be diverted to follow the line of the Gade past the mills, so that the river water flowed through the locks into, rather than past, the mill streams. The work was to cost £12,000, and was to occupy two years – and John Dickinson was the contractor.[120] A new parliamentary act of March 1818 allowed the diversion to be completed in early 1820 (Figure 5.11), although only after Dickinson had agreed to accept 100 tons of coal and 1,800 lockfuls of water before 1 January 1819 so that the company could shut down the steam pump early.[121] This put Dickinson's mills directly on the line of the canal rather than being some way off it, and, as we have seen, he was quick to make use of the new line, which greatly helped the expansion of the business in the years that followed. When Dickinson bought his first boats in 1818 and 1819 he based them at Nash, which joined Apsley in using steam power by 1823: his company continued to use the canal to bring in coal and rags, and to deliver paper products, for a further 150 years.[122]

Meanwhile, the Kings Langley miller Thomas Toovey, who had come into the mill through his marriage to the daughter of the owner in 1780, also had a difficult relationship with the canal. Neither he, nor later his son, sold the mill, which lay on the river Gade immediately below Nash Mill, and they continued to exercise their right, enshrined in the Langleybury deviation act of 1794, to draw down the flow of the river when they chose. This sometimes left the canal effectively drained, with boats stranded. On the other hand, in 1817 Toovey himself claimed, and received, damages of £120 when the river level was left too low for his mill owing to water shortage upstream.[123]

---

119 Faulkner, *Grand Junction Canal*, pp. 115–18. Evans, Endless web, pp. 23, 24.
120 Parliamentary Archives HL/PO/PB/3 Plan 22 (Book of Reference and Estimate).
121 TNA, RAIL 830/35 GJC general committee minutes, 8 August 1818; 58 Geo.3 c.16, variation of line past Apsley and Nash Mills.
122 NWA, BW99/6/5/14, GJC gauging register vol. 27.
123 TNA, RAIL 830/35 GJC general committee minutes, 11 December 1817.

Furthermore, when the boats that he used himself (under contract) were impeded he also sought compensation. This continued for many years until in 1849 his son, also Thomas, finally sold the mill and leased it back, which eased the relationship if not the miller's problems. This further illustrates the complex interrelationship between a miller as a user of the river water shared with the canal, the same miller as a customer of the canal as a boat user, and the canal company both supplying service to the canal trader and reluctantly sharing the water with the miller.

From the start the company was prepared to spend a great deal of money to rid itself of troublesome disputes and continued in such a manner for many years. It did not always yield – in 1837 and again in 1840 claims that Boxmoor tenants had suffered loss by Two Waters Mill raising the level of the mill head were resisted, on the basis that the claims were simply unfounded.[124] But generally the company had to accept, as the main controller of water levels, that if things went wrong it had to address them. The local impact of these disputes and their resolution was constantly in the background of the operation of the Hertfordshire mills.

Conclusion
By introducing the first true external influence on the economy of west Hertfordshire, the Grand Junction Canal directly affected the towns along it, which had not previously had long-distance freight transport. The early establishment of wharfs serving each of the towns made available large supplies of coal to industry and to those inhabitants who could afford it and introduced a new range of materials in significant quantities. It permitted the export of both industrial and (to some extent) agricultural products, and it fed the growing demand for goods, mainly in the towns. Raw materials and equipment for industry, including iron for the iron founders, machinery for paper makers and silk throwsters, timber and other materials for building and road surfacing and manure for canal-side farms, could all be brought in more easily.

In these first few years, however, the canal cannot be said to have attracted new industry (although the Tring silk mill was perhaps an exception) or many new businesses except those associated with wharfage and materials dealing. Only one boat builder set up business. In some respects the canal proved a problem: there were several significant and long-lasting disputes between the Grand Junction and other users of the river water on which all depended. But that is not to say that Hertfordshire business people did not benefit from the canal: a number became boat owners and several

---

124 HALS, D/ELs Q35(6), letter from R.C. Sale (GJCCo) to Smith & Grover, 30 April 1837; TNA, RAIL 830/7 GJC select committee minutes, 13 May 1840.

operated both boats and wharfs, while arguably the most significant user was the paper maker John Dickinson, whose business depended to a very large extent on the canal. But neither the silk and cotton thread producers nor most of the other paper makers seem to have used the canal except to bring fuel to the few steam-powered mills – the machinery for which had first come by water.

So how did this leave the area at the end of our study in 1841? The next chapter will examine that.

Chapter 6
West Hertfordshire in 1841

As seen earlier, the Grand Junction Canal provided west Hertfordshire's first high-capacity transport system, and connected it to both London and the industrial Midlands. Although this did not introduce new manufacturing to the area, or affect agriculture much, it did support the development of the existing paper-making industry, and allowed 'consumer commerce' to expand to some degree. But what was the wider effect on the area in the early years of Victoria's reign, as the railway's influence began to be felt? This chapter considers the ways in which the towns and parishes through which the canal passed had developed, and uses the 1841 census, and trade directories and tithe awards from about that time, to draw conclusions about the effects of the canal after forty-five years of operation.

Economic and social changes: the wider picture
Just as Chapter 1 outlined the state of affairs in England as the period of this study opened in the 1790s, so there should be a snapshot of the country in 1841. During the 1830s there had been a number of very significant developments in social, political and economic life, which affected west Hertfordshire to varying degrees. The decade has been described as 'the age of reform', with the 1832 Reform Act, the 1834 Poor Law Amendment Act, the 1835 Municipal Corporations Act, the 1839 Rural Constabularies Act and other legislation creating new national institutions that were highly contested, with protests aimed at government intervention in local affairs.[1] On the other hand, the Tithe Commutation Act of 1836 was more popular, since it modified the ancient tithe system whereby farmers had paid in kind for the upkeep of the Church and its ministers, replacing it with a monetary charge on land assessed on the basis of the prices of wheat, barley and oats. This

---

1   Katrina Navickas, *Protest and the politics of space and place* (Manchester, 2016), p. 130.

was much less contentious with farmers and very relevant to Hertfordshire.[2] Perhaps the most significant, however, was the Poor Law Amendment Act of 1834 ('The New Poor Law').[3] Enacted in the face of rising concern at the unaffordability of the old parish-administered system of poor relief in the home and, in extremis, in the parish workhouse, the New Poor Law deliberately penalised those needing financial help by providing only minimal relief and that, in theory, only in the workhouse, in conditions deliberately made very similar to those of prison. Men and women were separated, young children went with their mothers, and work of various kinds was done inside and occasionally outside the workhouse. The idea was that life in the workhouse had to be clearly less rewarding than any form of work outside it: the system was designed to deter and punish. Whereas 'falling on the parish' under the earlier arrangements was an occasional, indeed necessary, part of life for many people, it was now to be a true last resort.[4] The system did not in fact work as designed, and 'outdoor relief' continued to be widespread: but it was heavily constrained, and despite it life was even harsher for the poor than before.[5] This was to have a significant effect on Hertfordshire as an agricultural county with low wages.

The Reform Act of 1832 was another important feature of the national political landscape.[6] In extending the vote to members of the 'propertied middle class', it excluded non-property owners from the vote, disenfranchising many artisans and other workers and resulting in 18 per cent of the adult male population being able to vote – it had been 24 per cent in 1715, but only 14 per cent in 1831.[7] True, it provided parliamentary seats for the industrial towns, which had previously had none, and formalised the basis on which elections were carried out: but by excluding the unpropertied tradesman it caused tensions between the middle class and the working class, providing one of the motivations for the Chartist movement, which had arisen by 1838. Hertfordshire had always had two county MPs and two each for the boroughs of St Albans and Hertford, and that did not change: but the make-up of the electorate did.

---

2 6 & 7 Will.4, c.71 Tithe Commutation Act, 1836; G.M. Trevelyan, *English social history volume four: the nineteenth century* (Cambridge, 1949; reprinted London, 1963), p. 50; Horn, *Rural world*, pp. 154, 155.

3 4 & 5 Will.4 c.76 Poor Law Amendment Act, 1834 ('The New Poor Law').

4 The workings of the New Poor Law in Hertfordshire are described in detail by Karen Rothery, 'The implementation and administration of the New Poor Law in Hertfordshire, c.1830–1847', PhD thesis (University of Hertfordshire, 2017).

5 Horn, *Rural world*, pp. 119–29; Rothery, 'New Poor Law', pp. 306, 307.

6 2 & 3 Will.4 c.45 The Representation of the People Act [Reform Act], 1832.

7 Daunton, *Progress and poverty*, pp. 481, 482, 500.

Meanwhile, from about 1814 the spread of gas street lighting had resulted in a number of towns getting coal gas-producing works, and as the coal for such works was carried mainly by canal the adoption of gas in Hertfordshire is particularly relevant.[8] So too is the supply of the equipment and of the thousands of yards of iron pipes laid around the towns served; the considerable but often overlooked work required to provide gas lighting deserves mention.

Changes in Hertfordshire

Chapter 5 demonstrated how industries and businesses in west Hertfordshire had developed during the four decades before 1841. Drawing on the 1841 census and the tithe maps and awards made between 1839 and 1844, we now consider briefly two aspects of the economic effects of the canal: the growth of the local population, and the aggregated economic change.

POPULATION GROWTH

In the forty years after 1801 the population of England grew from just over nine million to just under sixteen million, at an average rate of about 1.45 per cent per year. 'High' urban growth nationally at this time is widely accepted as being between 3 per cent and 5 per cent, while 'low' growth was between 0.5 per cent and 1.2 per cent. Towns generally grew by both natural increase among the inhabitants and by migration from the countryside, although London, with its perennially very high mortality, grew at only 1.8 per cent despite attracting continual large-scale migration.[9] In this context, Hertfordshire's small population declined as a proportion of England's (Table 6.1): that is, it grew less quickly than the rest of the country.

The larger the town the greater its attraction, and the Hertfordshire towns, with little industrial employment, exerted only a very weak draw compared with neighbouring London.[10] The population of west Hertfordshire's towns and parishes, as almost everywhere, grew between 1801 and 1841, but the rates of growth show no consistency. In Table 6.2 (which refers to the parishes, rather than the towns themselves), Tring shows the highest overall rate of growth, although there is an anomalous 'blip' there, as we will see below, and Hemel Hempstead's expansion was also relatively high; but the growth of the other parishes was lower.

This does not suggest that there was any special factor affecting the growth of the population in west Hertfordshire. Natural growth was countered by a

---

8 Johnson, *Industrial archaeology*, pp. 86, 87; Clifford Lines, *Companion to the Industrial Revolution* (Oxford, 1990), p. 88.
9 Joyce Ellis, *The Georgian town* (Basingstoke, 2001), p. 35.
10 Ellis, *Georgian town*, p. 31.

Table 6.1. Population of Hertfordshire as percentage of population of England and Wales, 1801–41.

Census year	1801	1811	1821	1831	1841
Population of England (000s)	9,061	10,322	12,106	13,994	15,929
Population of Herts (000s)	97	111	130	143	157
Herts proportion	1.070%	1.075%	1.074%	1.022%	0.986%

Table 6.2. Populations and growth rates of west Hertfordshire parishes (listed north to south), 1801–41.

	1801	1841	Cumulative growth rate 1801–41 p.a.
Herts population	97,577	157,207	1.21%
Tring	1621	4620	2.65%
Aldbury	457	790	1.38%
Puttenham	130	136	0.11%
Wigginton	330	635	1.65%
Northchurch	735	1216	1.27%
Berkhamsted	1690	2979	1.43%
Hemel Hempstead	2722	5901	1.95%
Kings Langley	970	1629	1.30%
Abbots Langley	1205	2115	1.41%
Watford	3530	5989	1.33%
Rickmansworth	2975	5026	1.32%
St Albans	3038	6497	1.94%

steady stream of people moving away, especially to London, as they had always done – in addition, significant numbers were helped by their parishes in the 1830s to emigrate overseas.[11] The western towns of Hertfordshire did grow a little more than parishes elsewhere in the county (Table 6.3), but whatever the causes the towns remained small, as did the county's population.[12]

ECONOMIC CHANGE

The Grand Junction Canal was one of many external factors in an economic model in which the main variable determinant of real wages was the price of food, which in turn drove the demand for goods and so the demand for

---

11 N. Goose, 'Population movement', in Short (ed.), *Historical atlas*, p. 53; Horn, *Rural world*, p. 119.
12 Ellis, *Georgian town*, pp. 26, 27, 40–3. The extent to which Hertfordshire's towns matched the model Georgian market town of the early 1840s is summarised in Appendix A, which draws on the work of Barrie Trinder; Trinder, 'Market town industry', pp. 75–89.

Table 6.3. Populations of west Hertfordshire parishes (north to south), compared with the population of Hertfordshire 1801–41.

Census year	1801		1821		1841		In relation to
Herts population	97,577		132,400		157,207		Herts pop.[1]
Tring	1621	1.66%	3286	2.48%	4620	2.93%	Up
Aldbury	457	0.47%	676	0.51%	790	0.50%	Level
Puttenham	130	0.13%	112	0.08%	136	0.09%	Down
Wigginton	330	0.38%	477	0.36%	635	0.40%	Level
Northchurch	735	0.75%	1028	0.78%	1216	0.77%	Level
Berkhamsted	1690	1.73%	1507	1.14%	2979	1.89%	Up[2]
H. Hempstead	2722	2.79%	3962	2.99%	5901	3.75%	Up
Kings Langley	970	0.99%	1242	0.94%	1629	1.04%	Level
Abbots Langley	1205	1.23%	1733	1.31%	2115	1.35%	Up
Watford	3530	3.62%	4713	3.56%	5989	3.81%	Up
Rickmansworth	2975	3.05%	3940	2.98%	5026	3.20%	Up
St Albans	3038	3.1%	4472	3.4%	6497	4.1%	Up

1 'Up' suggests net immigration, 'Down' net emigration and 'Level' suggests a balance. None of these rates is significant in either direction, however: the parishes generally grew at the same slow rate as the rest of the county, with the towns doing better but not much.

2 The pronounced dip in the population of Berkhamsted in the 1821 census is very unusual, and seems not to have been commented on at all. If the 1821 figures are correct, however, it seems to confirm Birtchnell's observation that the town was in poor shape early in the nineteenth century, despite the arrival of the canal.

labour.[13] As already noted, the canal reduced the cost of fuel, provided a modest increase in employment opportunities and introduced a new route by which rising demand for materials and goods could be met. 'Real wages' certainly increased for many as a consequence, but only for those who already had disposable income. Most people remained isolated from the canal, subject to increasingly marked variations in the price of food, suffering fuel poverty and generally unable to take up the new jobs. Meanwhile, the New Poor Law required children to be put to productive work as soon, and as thoroughly, as they could be, sometimes on the land but often in the silk and paper mills if they lived close enough to them. It is also arguable that structural unemployment in an agricultural county such as Hertfordshire put more able-bodied men into pauperism here than in an industrial one such as Derbyshire.[14] The economic impact of the canal was therefore limited, as the resultant industrial development did not generate sufficient employment to

---

13 For a full discussion of this economic model, see in particular E.A. Wrigley and R.S. Schofield, *The population history of England 1541–1871* (London, 1981), Ch. 11.

14 Rothery, 'New Poor Law', pp. 299, 301.

reach a level that created change. The growth in that part of the population who bought luxury or even non-essential goods was modest, while few of the agrarian poor could afford to buy non-essentials, and the remainder did not buy enough to generate real economic or population growth.

In the 1840s agriculture remained the dominant industry in Hertfordshire: wages were still low compared with London and probably declined in real terms, although the farmers who paid the wages were becoming more prosperous, largely as a result of the London market.[15] The organisation of agriculture as an industry was embryonic: farmers were beginning to come together, with the Royal Agricultural Society forming in 1838, and in 1841 the first association of farmers in Hertfordshire, the Tring Agricultural Society, was formed.[16] But agricultural workers were not to start to unite for another thirty years: they remained at this time wholly dependent on their employer and at the bottom of the economic heap: working in a low-skilled occupation, usually living in rented cottages and at risk of real penury. There was not enough work for everyone all year round, and intense hardship was inevitable.[17] The income of some straw plaiters is often presented in a way that suggests financial comfort, but straw plaiting should not be seen as any sort of panacea. By now labourers' wages were too low to support their families securely, and the addition of a few shillings a week from straw plaiting by wives and children in the winter and spring was essential to allow a family to survive at all.[18] The supply of this cheap labour was enough to delay the introduction of labour-saving machinery – there was no need to save labour – but there was little alternative employment, so the straw plaiters in a family were often instrumental in averting destitution. As the 1830s closed there was a considerable development in social self-help in the form of Friendly Societies being set up, as described in Chapter 2, in all parts of the country, including Hertfordshire, and many of these schemes were aimed at the agricultural sector. But how many labourers could afford to join them? After 1834 families had to live wholly on their income, without much chance of 'relief outdoors' and without the medical care previously available from the parish.[19] Agricultural housing remained generally inadequate, as it was to be for most of the century, and prone to overcrowding, although a rural family might at least have a cottage to themselves without sharing

---

15 Agar, 'The Hertfordshire farmer', pp. 247–56; Wallace, *Children of the labouring poor*, p. 3.
16 Agar, *Behind the plough*, pp. 165, 166.
17 Agar, *Behind the plough*, p. 159.
18 Wallace, *Children of the labouring poor*, pp. 52, 55, 62.
19 Agar, *Behind the plough*, pp. 66, 71, 76, 130–4; Horn, *Rural world*, pp. 124, 125.

with another family.[20] In theory, the growing population added to demand and generated innovation and output, to which the canal contributed: the purchase of manufactured goods by those who could buy increased considerably.[21] But in west Hertfordshire, while the incomes of farmers rose those of their labourers did not. We will see how the towns and parishes along the canal fared in consequence.

The main social–industrial development at this time was arguably the introduction of gas lighting in towns. St Albans, Watford and Hemel Hempstead all had gas works by 1835: but that simple statement conceals a much more complex story. Retorts in which the coal was heated had to be provided and retort houses for them built; pipes had to be brought in and laid through the town; lamp standards had to be procured and set up; then fuel had to be delivered and waste – gas water, tar, coke and ash – removed. How this was done in any given town is unclear: but it is probable that the retorts and pipes came from the Birmingham area, the lamp standards from a local iron founder (perhaps Cranstone of Hemel Hempstead, although he had not then been long in that business) and the coal from the Midlands. This could all have been done by road: but the conveyance of the pipes alone would have required a considerable convoy of waggons, and it would have been much easier for them to come by canal to wharfs at Boxmoor (for St Albans and Hemel Hempstead) or Cashio Bridge (for Watford) and then by a much shorter road journey. Although this is speculation, and more research is needed to confirm this theory for each town's installation, it appears that the canal was necessary to the development of town gas lighting.

Transport and travel
At the end of the 1830s the road system in Hertfordshire had developed under the influence of professional road engineers such as James McAdam, who in the 1820s had become the 'surveyor' for both the Sparrows Herne and the St Albans turnpikes, among many others. Surfacing had been improved, and roads themselves had been straightened and their gradients eased. In parallel with this, waggons had also been improved and light box vans introduced, notably by Pickfords.[22] Fast transport carried a cost, however, and a great deal of traffic was still carried in relatively slow-moving waggons – indeed, although canals had in all areas taken a great deal of the trade, the volume on roads, both local and long distance, had also increased. But a feature of the changed economic pattern was that branches from focal

---

20 Wallace, *Children of the labouring poor*, p. 47.
21 Ward, *Finance*, p. 167.
22 Turnbull, *Traffic and transport*, pp. 66, 67.

points had developed, with the long-distance carriers covering the trunk routes and a large number of local carriers filling the gaps. We saw earlier that the Pickfords' route map (see Figure 5.1) of about 1832 shows the main road – passing through St Albans – as well as the most significant canal-served destinations: Rickmansworth and Berkhamsted were mentioned by name and Watford and Hemel Hempstead were represented by their wharfs at Cashio Bridge and Boxmoor, but Tring was not featured. Delivery by Pickfords to St Albans from Birmingham required canal carriage to one of Watford's or Hemel Hempstead's wharfs, or perhaps to Northampton, then trans-shipment to road vehicle. The Hertfordshire towns listed among the 232 destinations presented on the reverse side of the Pickfords map were limited to St Albans and those along the canal: Tring, Berkhamsted, Hemel Hempstead, Watford and Rickmansworth. Any other destination would have been served by local carrier from one of these places.

All this, of course, was happening under the threat, clearly recognised at the time, from the approaching London and Birmingham Railway (L&BR). The economic effect of the L&BR in Hertfordshire has been covered by others, and is not further considered in detail here.[23] Suffice to say that the Sparrows Herne turnpike trust, having received a briefing delegation from the L&BR in early 1832, joined vigorously in opposition to it, as did the Grand Junction Canal Company.[24] The latter especially were right to be concerned: the progressive opening of the railway from London from July 1837, reaching Birmingham in April 1838, had already caused the canal tolls to be cut from January 1837 in a pre-emptive attempt to keep traffic on the canal. Canal toll revenue began to fall sharply, even though the tonnage carried increased – manufacturing output was growing fast enough to require both rail and canal transport.[25] The L&BR was initially reluctant to carry coal, and indeed its freight traffic grew relatively slowly, partly because the gaps in the system between London and Manchester still had to be filled by waggon or boat.[26] Nonetheless, by the autumn of 1839 Pickfords, having already shut down their 'van' service between London and Birmingham, offered daily rail services from London to Manchester and Liverpool, and although the relationship between Pickfords and the various

---

23 F.R.J. Newman, 'The socio-economic impacts of the coming of the railways to Hertfordshire, Bedfordshire and Buckinghamshire, 1838–1900', PhD thesis (University of Hertfordshire, 2014).

24 HALS, TP4/5 Sparrows Herne turnpike – minutes of meetings of the trustees 1823–1840; Faulkner, *Grand Junction Canal*, p. 154.

25 Faulkner, *Grand Junction Canal*, pp. 156, 157.

26 Turnbull, *Traffic and transport*, p. 114.

railway companies was complex the complete withdrawal of Pickfords from canal carrying was complete in less than another decade.[27] Local canal carriers continued, but by 1841 the monopoly of long-distance high-capacity carriage by water was ending.

The parishes in 1841

Drawing on trade directories, the 1841 census and the tithe awards of 1839–1843, the following section identifies ways in which the parishes had changed during the first forty years of the Grand Junction Canal's operation. As part of the background to this we note in passing that the price of coal seems to have come down from around £3 a ton in about 1810 to between 18s and 24s a ton in 1839, wholesale from six Midlands collieries and without delivery or unloading charges, as recorded by the Grand Junction Canal Company, who purchased it to fire one of its steam engines.[28] This implies a retail price, delivered, of about £2 to £2 10s per ton, which would have represented an increase in the real wage for those who could afford coal at all.

TRING

Tring presents a problem to the researcher because around 15 per cent of the lines of the available census are unreadable and there is no tithe map. The census nonetheless suggests that the single most prominent occupation was straw plaiting, which included children, some as young as six; the numbers of agricultural labourers, general labourers and male and female servants suggest that Tring remained a strongly agrarian parish with characteristics of the typical Georgian market town (Appendix A).[29] By 1841 there were two industries: long-established canvas weaving, as we saw in Chapter 2, and more recent silk throwing in a mill opened in 1824 and now steam powered.[30] A total of 128 people was identified as working in the 'silk factory' and eighty-one worked as weavers, although not all were linked to canvas: one at least was weaving wool. The settlement at Tring Wharf (Figure 6.1), the closest of three wharves near the town, included the wharfinger William Grover, who had bought the wharf in 1810; his son Thomas, operating the windmill next door; a group of seven labourers presumably associated with either wharf or

---

27 Turnbull, *Traffic and transport*, pp. 72, 73, 100–2.
28 TNA, RAIL 830/7 GJC select committee minutes 1839–1841, 13 February 1839. A detailed calculation of the thermal efficiency and so the value for money of each of the types of coal was also recorded.
29 TNA, HO/107/442/5–7 1841 Census – Tring.
30 Austin, *Tring silk mill*, pp. 6–10.

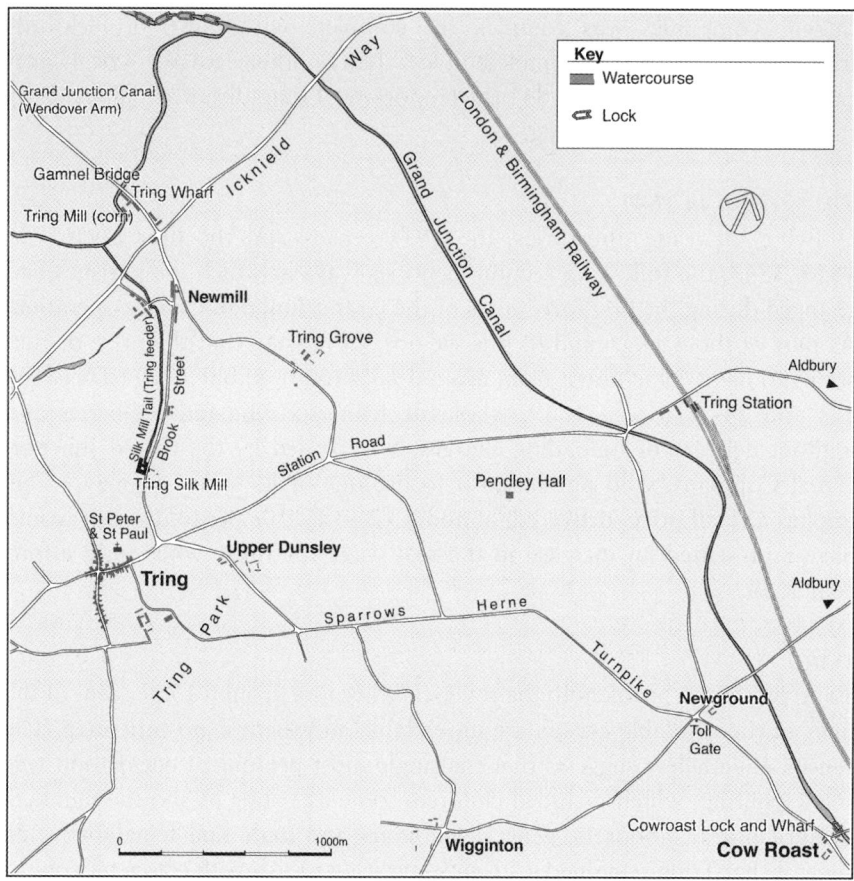

Figure 6.1. Tring and its wharfs, *c.*1839. The distances from Tring Wharf to the town via the silk mill, and from Cowroast Wharf to the town along the turnpike, were not insignificant.

mill; and at least one boatman resident at the wharf. Coal and other heavy or bulky goods for silk mill and town would have come through this wharf. On the other hand, light goods probably came via Thomas Landon's wharf at Cowroast, as advertised in Pigot's *Directory* (1839), or Marsworth, rather than making the time-consuming detour to Tring Wharf.

Agriculture here, on the edge of Aylesbury Vale and the main cattle drove route from south Wales to London, included some pastoral farming, with several graziers and at least one 'dairywoman' listed, but arable predominated. Straw plait remained very strong, although Cobbett had reported the use of imported straw in the 1820s.[31] The hamlets round

---

31   Cobbett, *Rural rides*, vol. 2, p. 207.

Tring, especially the village of Wilstone, remained almost entirely agrarian communities, with even those people without stated occupations closely associated with agricultural labourers and farming families. Pigot's *Directory* described Tring market, on Fridays, as a large one, for straw plait but also 'well supplied with the ordinary articles of consumption': in other words, a retail market was next to the commodity market for straw plait. There were also fairs for cattle and pleasure at Easter and Michaelmas.[32] There was other commerce as well, of course, although no local bank was established until 1836, when Thomas Butcher & Son appeared – possibly the same as was licensed in Northampton in 1801 – and there was still no iron foundry by 1841.[33] Tring did not have a full set of services or a gas works until the 1850s: sanitation came even later.

Tring's cumulative annual population growth rate from 1801 to 1821 was relatively high, at 3.60 per cent, even though the silk mill was not established until 1824. Somewhat surprisingly, the growth rate from 1821 to 1841 was only 1.72 per cent. This suggests that, if the silk mill attracted a new workforce, the resulting growth was balanced by out-migration, although it is not possible to attribute this effect to the canal. The L&BR was already making itself felt in Tring before 1841, and public pressure caused Tring station to be moved from its planned location at Pitstone, two miles north of Tring, to a closer site at Pendley. Near it the brewery owner John Brown built the Harcourt Arms hotel, completed in March 1839, and Station Road followed later that year: Tring was clearly influenced by the railway from an early stage.[34] But it was passenger traffic and related concerns that most affected Tring for some years, while it seems that cattle were being carried as early as 1838, and the canal was not a serious competitor for either.[35] The canal did, however, have one unusual influence on Tring's population: the census counted six miners, evidence of the scope of the tunnelling of the underground chambers and headings associated with the reservoirs then being built and serviced for the Grand Junction Canal.[36]

ALDBURY, PUTTENHAM AND WIGGINTON

Aldbury, Puttenham and Wigginton form a group of agricultural communities close to which the canal passed. Aldbury was not itself served directly by a

---

32 Pigot's *Royal National and Commercial Directory and Topography for the Counties of Essex, Herts and Middlesex* (London, 1839), p. 213.
33 Dawes and Ward Perkins, *Country banks*, p. 593.
34 Petticrew and Austin, *The railway comes to Tring*, pp. 13, 14, 51.
35 Petticrew and Austin, *The railway comes to Tring*, pp. 51–5, 58.
36 Faulkner, *Grand Junction Canal*, pp. 135–8.

Figure 6.2. Lock on the canal, Birkhamsted [*sic*], 1842, by James Wilcox (Hertford Museum, HTFM4180.1.9.28). The canal had been open for about forty-five years by this time. The open setting of the Town Lock (lock 53) reflects the fact that the town is wholly on the ridge to the left, above the marshy valley of the Bulbourne, which had been drained by the canal.

wharf (Appendix C), being some way from the canal as it passed close to Pendley, but there had nonetheless been some effect – not only on the village shops, whose range of wares improved, but also for its builders. For example, the 'Slated Row' of cottages built in the 1820s were roofed in slate brought in by canal to Tring Wharf or to Berkhamsted (Figure 6.2).[37] That aside, Aldbury remained essentially unchanged: an agricultural village of fewer than 800 people dominated by its three estates, with the range of occupations largely unchanged except for the small railway staff at Tring station.[38] Puttenham parish was, and remained, tiny and wholly agricultural. A short length of the Aylesbury Arm of the canal, built slowly between 1811 and 1815, had passed through the parish for twenty-five years by this time, but no canal-

---

37 Davis, *Aldbury*, p. 74.
38 Petticrew and Austin, *The railway comes to Tring*, p. 51; TNA, HO/107/440/1 1841 Census – Aldbury.

related facility was generated by it: every occupation shown in the census enumeration was related to agriculture, and the population had declined as a proportion of Hertfordshire's.[39] No change came as a result of the canal.

The 635 inhabitants of Wigginton, situated on the hill above the canal, were in the main agricultural workers.[40] The Post Office *Directory* shows even in 1848 just two shopkeepers, three publicans or beer retailers and the parish clerk. Most of the men listed in the census were either farmers or their agricultural labourers, and most of the women straw plaiters.[41] Although the wharf and inn next to the top lock at the end of the summit at Cowroast were in the parish, no other part of the canal was: the wharf, in any case, served Tring rather than Wigginton, which seems to have been very little affected by the canal.

BERKHAMSTED AND NORTHCHURCH

From Cowroast the canal passed the 1805 boat horse station at Dudswell mentioned earlier and followed the river Bulbourne into Berkhamsted through the entirely agricultural land of Northchurch.[42] This was a large but sparsely populated parish divided into two parts by Berkhamsted parish; the canal ran through the southern portion of both parts of it. Northchurch had neither industry nor market: in medieval times part of a single, much larger parish before the separation of Berkhamsted town and castle, its village was bordered by the canal and lined the turnpike as an extension of Berkhamsted High Street. Most of its activity and occupations were still agricultural: its tradesmen were routinely included in the *Directories* as if part of Berkhamsted, but were generally those supporting agriculture in the way familiar in such settlements.[43] The canal had already drained the swampy bottom of the Bulbourne valley, and with the canal having absorbed the river the mill head of the Upper Mill came off the canal, although there seems to have been no public comment on the effect of the canal on the mill's stream until much later.[44] Berkhamsted, with a population still fewer than 3,000, had by this time changed as much as any of the towns along the canal, and Figure 6.3 shows the several wharfs serving it.[45] Leaving aside

---

39 TNA, HO/107/442/2 1841 Census – Puttenham.
40 TNA, HO/107/442/9 1841 Census – Wigginton.
41 Post Office, *Directory of Essex, Herts, Kent, Middlesex, Surrey and Sussex* (London, 1848).
42 Hunt, 'A history of Dudswell Mill', pp. 27, 28.
43 TNA, HO/107/440/5 1841 Census – Northchurch.
44 Ken Wallis, 'The River Bulbourne', *The Chronicle*, 5 (2008), pp. 29–35.
45 TNA, HO/107/440/3–4 1841 Census – Berkhamsted; HALS, DSA4/19/2 Berkhamsted tithe map; Pigot's *Directory* (1839), pp. 174–6.

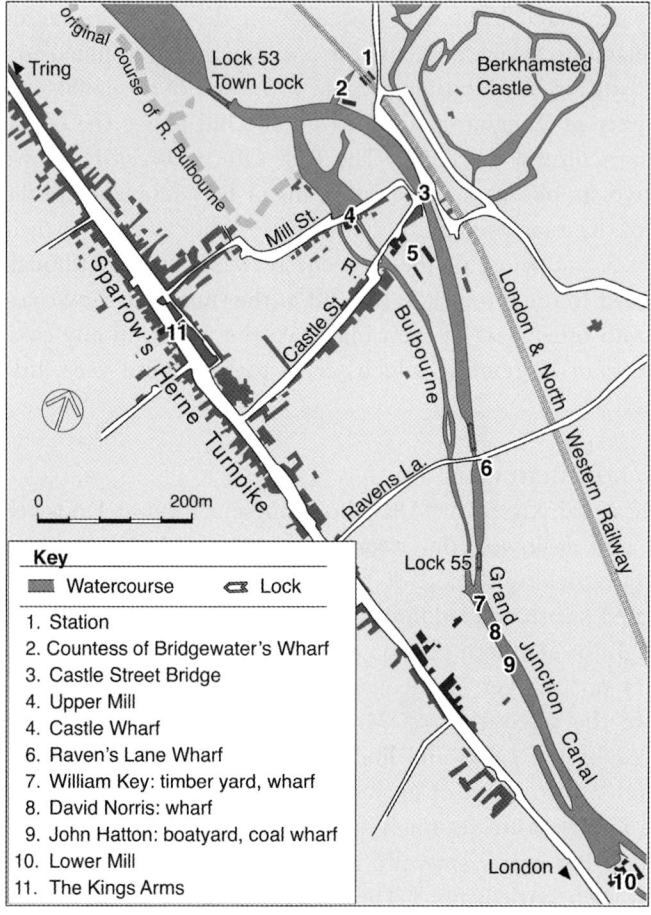

Figure 6.3. Berkhamsted and its wharfs, c.1840.

the private Bridgewater Wharf, the main facility was the large Castle Wharf complex between Castle Street and Raven's Lane Bridges.[46] John Tompkins, the owner, was listed in Pigot's *Directory* (1839) as 'wharfinger and coal dealer' and in the 1841 census as a 'coal merchant'.

Below the lock adjoining the bridge carrying Raven's Lane but, unusually, on the towpath side and in Northchurch parish was the rather smaller Raven's Lane Wharf. The wharfs continued below Lock 55 towards Lower Mill, with William Key and his son as timber merchants and other wharfs dealing in coal near them listed in the trade directory, although not in the tithe award. One of them, that of the boat builder John Hatton, had been established since at least 1823, as we saw in Chapter 5: he operated several

---

46 Faulkner, *Grand Junction Canal*, p. 185; Birtchnell, *Berkhamsted*, p. 82.

boats himself (Appendix B) and, like many boat builders of the time, dealt also in coal and, no doubt, other canal-borne goods, including iron. Hatton later moved up to Castle Wharf, but at this point his wharf seems to have occupied much of the space between Lock 55 and Lower Mill. All these businesses (there were also two iron founders) were important elements of the commerce of any town, especially one served by canal. Neither the prices of canal-imported goods nor how much of Berkhamsted's produce went off to London are clear, but it is certain that the picture drawn by some, with grain and forage, flour and malt going to London in boats that subsequently returned with agricultural manures, was in fact more complex and varied.[47]

Berkhamsted did not, however, have a bank until 1827, when a branch of the Aylesbury business Richford & Co was established immediately after the country bank crisis the year before; a branch of the Tring bank Butcher & Son was listed from 1837.[48] It does not seem that the commercial life of this small town needed, or justified, extensive commercial support, even taking account of canal-related businesses. The entry in Pigot's *Directory* (1839) is telling: it reports the market, held on Saturday, as being 'chiefly for corn, but indifferently attended'. The fairs (Shrove Tuesday, Whit Monday and 12 October) were 'toy and pleasure fairs, but like the market … unimportant'.[49] Although Berkhamsted was by no means 'industrial', cramped and squalid conditions between the High Street and the canal prevailed: prosperity was limited to those in a position to take advantage of the canal rather than accruing to the inhabitants in general.[50] Despite the large increase in the population between 1821 and 1841, this was still a small town, but it had changed under the influence of the canal. It would not, however, have a gas works until 1849.

HEMEL HEMPSTEAD

Leaving Berkhamsted, the canal passed Lower Mill and returned to the eastern part of Northchurch parish, still agrarian and very little affected by the canal, which now approached Hemel Hempstead past Bourne End mill. Hemel Hempstead parish, although the town itself was some distance from the canal, had also benefited considerably from the canal by 1841.[51] The populous areas away from the canal were the High Street, Marlowes, Crouchfield and Leverstock Green, but along the canal lay important

---

47 Scott Hastie, *Berkhamsted* (Kings Langley, 1999), pp. 28, 41, 47; Birtchnell, *Berkhamsted*, pp. 70, 85.
48 Dawes and Ward Perkins, *Country Banks*, p. 45.
49 Pigot's *Directory* (1839), p. 174.
50 Birtchnell, *Berkhamsted*, pp. 15, 66.
51 TNA, HO/107/441/5–8 1841 Census – Hemel Hempstead.

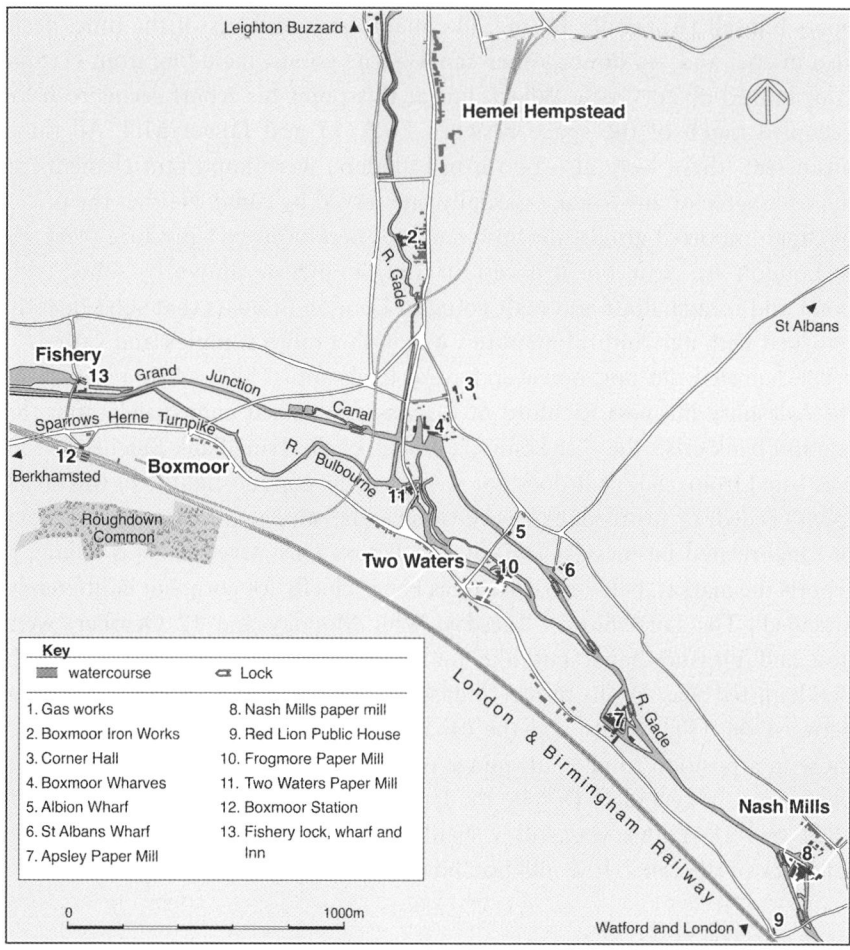

Figure 6.4. Hemel Hempstead, Boxmoor and its wharfs c.1840.

hamlets: Winkwell, Boxmoor, Two Waters, Corner Hall and Frogmore End. Agriculture remained the key contributor to the local economy. Even without counting occupations 'not stated' – but typically female and associated with agricultural labour – we can see that agriculture engaged over a third of the adult inhabitants in farms spread widely across the parish, with a number of tradespeople also working in support of the agrarian sector.

The map of Hemel Hempstead's canal side can fortunately be assembled (Figure 6.4) using earlier and later maps than the largely illegible tithe map. At Winkwell a small wharf and stables had been established around a beer house, and Fishery had a public house, a coal merchant's wharf and several cottages. The main industrial complex was at Two Waters, where the paper mill dominated the approach to the large Boxmoor Wharf area described in Chapter 3. The census and trade directories suggest that the balance of occupations and professions here was more industrial, with Corner Hall, Two Waters and Boxmoor different from the rest of the parish in their occupational make-up. It made the town, with its main market in wheat but with significant straw-plait and general dealing as well, more typical of a Georgian market town than Tring, Rickmansworth or even Berkhamsted, with a strong cadre of 'middle class' and professional families employing both male and female servants.[52] There was a bank here from 1809, when the hay and seed merchant Ebenezer Collett set one up with William Richford and William Treiss, who were both already banking in Aylesbury. They were followed by the Quaker partnership of the solicitor Harry Grover and the draper James Pollard, licensed in 1811 as Grover & Pollard, which became Smith & Whittingstall in 1839.[53] The 1825/6 problems of this and other country banks are well known because of the relationship between Grover and his son-in-law, the paper maker Dickinson.[54]

But the main industry of Hemel Hempstead was paper making, although formally the largest mills lay in adjoining parishes – Apsley in Kings Langley and Nash in Abbots Langley. The industry had been greatly encouraged by the 1837 reduction in excise duty on paper.[55] In 1841 the paper mills at Two Waters and Frogmore, by now owned by the Grand Junction Canal Company and leased out, employed twenty-one identified 'paper makers', while other paper-related trades also appear in the census. Here, however, as in other paper-making parishes, an entire occupational group seems to be missing from the census: the essential (and largely female) paper cutters and rag sorters. The reason is unclear: perhaps these women and children were simply 'not counted', being in casual or part-time employment.[56] This has a significant effect on the 'not stated' component of the census analysis, even though by this time much of the preparation of Dickinson's pulp from rags was being done, largely by women, at Batchworth.[57] One may also surmise that some of the nearly 200 men identified as 'labourer' (as opposed to agricultural labourer) were working at the paper mills as well as in the tannery and on the wharfs and coal yards.

---

52 Trinder, 'Market town industry'; Ellis, *Georgian town*, pp. 52–4; Pigot's *Directory* (1839), pp. 187–90; TNA, HO/107/441/5–8 1841 Census – Hemel Hempstead.
53 Dawes and Ward-Perkins, *Country Banks*, pp. 264, 265.
54 Evans, *Endless web*, pp. 46–50.
55 Evans, *Endless web*, p. 69.
56 Evans, *Endless web*, p. 31; Wallace, *Children of the labouring poor*, pp. 93–100.
57 Evans, *Endless web*, p. 251.

Pigot's *Directory* (1839) lists wharfingers at Fishery, Boxmoor (two), Apsley and Two Waters. The last is significant, as it seems to confirm that Two Waters Mill was connected to the canal. This is supported by the later references in the Grand Junction Chain Book of 1893 to a wooden swing bridge carrying the main line towpath across the river Gade to the mill, which would have been needed only to get boats to the mill and wharf, and to 'Two Waters Mill and Wharfs' in the 1904 directory 'Bradshaws'.[58] Thomas Ebborn's presence at Apsley links Hertfordshire with coal merchants of Coventry through his father, a coal merchant, boat owner and farmer at Sowe near there.[59] For this reason both are included in the listing of boat owners at Appendix B, while the son was in business not only at Apsley but also at Lady Capels' Wharf, Watford (Appendix C).[60] The Pigot's *Directory* (1839) entry for Hemel Hempstead provided very much the same comprehensive list of national canal carriers as it did in 1832 and as shown in Chapter 5, and Hemel Hempstead businesses undoubtedly relied on the canal a great deal.

Hemel Hempstead, then, changed considerably during the forty years after the coming of the canal, and its commercial structures reflected that. Previously it had been a strongly arable parish with an important grain market at its centre, but also with a cattle fair in mid-summer and a large cattle show or market at Easter. It had had two modest water-powered paper mills with two smaller ones nearby, and several flour mills. In the late 1830s the services to the inhabitants were well developed, while arable farming around the town continued, with the important grain market described by Pigot's as 'a superior one for corn' and the fairs still happening as before. But the modest paper mills of the 1790s had now become large, mechanised and important, and the canal was available to the town and its inhabitants though the large wharfs. The census and trade directory show that, while Hemel Hempstead had not become a true industrial town, the canal had significantly enhanced its industry, which included an iron founder and machinery manufacturer (John Cranstone), and from 1834 a gas works, with all the upheaval its building will have caused, managed by the same man. There was a rare agricultural machine maker, coal dealing and a wharf operation, and wire weaving for the paper makers, all in addition to the paper mills themselves.[61]

---

58   NWA, WM/72/58 GJC chain book, 1893; Henry de Salis, *Bradshaw's canals and navigable rivers* (London, 1904; reprinted Oxford, 2012), p. 122.

59   TNA, HO/107/1136/27 1841 Census – Sow (Warks); TNA, RAIL 830/66 GJC treasurer's cash book 1820–1826, 14 July 1820, showing Thomas 'Eburne' (presumably the father) paying tonnage.

60   NWA, BW99/6/5/3, /17, /37 GJC gauging registers vols 3, 30, 49.

61   Pigot's *Directory* (1839), p. 187; Johnson, *Industrial archaeology*, p. 86.

Figure 6.5. Rail bridge over the canal at Kings Langley, *c*.1850 (author's collection). This image was made after the amalgamation of the London and Birmingham Railway into the London and Northwestern Railway in 1848, but the scene had changed not at all since 1836, when the bridge was built. The view is north towards Nash Mills.

KINGS LANGLEY

Leaving Hemel Hempstead, the canal entered Kings Langley parish, passing Dickinson's Apsley Mill, its first and only true industrial feature, and Nash Mills (Abbots Langley parish) – both at this time growing quickly and steam powered – and then the large new railway bridge (Figure 6.5). Kings Langley itself was on a ridge, with the canal and river below, and a small wharf lay below the lock: the census described the wharfinger, John Monk, as a coal merchant (three boatmen and the family of one other were also recorded there, but whether in a boat or not is unclear).[62] The brewery, which had moved from Two Waters to the High Street on the corner with Church Lane in 1826, could have had coal delivered up the hill from the wharf. Thomas Toovey was also using the canal (Chapter 3), but how much for his flour mill and how much for other business is not known.

Generally, however, the canal probably brought goods into Kings Langley rather than providing an outward channel for its produce. The census shows only fifteen people in the parish employed at the paper mill (and some of them may have been at Nash), although as elsewhere the occupational groups

---

62 TNA, HO/107/441/12 1841 Census – Kings Langley; Pigot's *Directory* (1839), pp. 199–200.

'rag sorters and cutters' and 'paper cutters', largely women and children, were not recorded and were probably concealed among the large number (450, which was 50 per cent of the whole) with occupation 'not stated'.[63] Nevertheless, the agricultural character of the parish was not significantly altered by the canal, and the services available in the village do not suggest that it even approached being anything else. Agricultural labourers, with their dependants, were by far the largest occupational group. Although the structure of farming in Kings Langley had been changing for some time, with farms becoming larger and fewer, there was no decrease in the total number of farm workers, while, despite the availability of canal-carried goods, most such items were still made and sold locally.[64] The fact that goods could be brought in did not make them available to the bulk of the inhabitants.

ABBOTS LANGLEY

The same may be said of Abbots Langley, standing above the canal and at a greater distance from it, with a wharf at Hunton Bridge near the flour mill.[65] Nash Mill, just below Apsley, was, as noted, in Abbots Langley parish: rebuilt after fire in 1816, it had been powered by steam since 1823. It was Dickinson's headquarters and the base for both his boat operations and his engineering development.[66] Home Park mill, opened in 1826, also stood on the boundary between Kings Langley and Abbots Langley, along which the canal, following the river, was cut. Hunton Bridge Wharf, close to the Sparrows Herne turnpike, was important to the Abbots Langley economy, and was advertised for sale in September 1835 as 'admirable for conducting a business of consequence in the timber and coal trade'.[67] The village and the parish remained heavily agricultural – agricultural labourers formed the largest single group, with thirty-four farmers employing 250 of them and a number of male and female servants – but the paper mills, Nash and Home Park, with seventy-one workers, were here better represented in the census returns, although only one 'rag sorter' was identified, and very few were women.[68] Again, it seems likely that this group is hidden among those whose occupation was 'not stated'. There was, and was to remain, a strong link

---

63   Evans, *Endless web*, p. 31.
64   Munby, *Kings Langley*, pp. 103, 112, 116.
65   Pigot's *Directory* (1839), pp. 199–200.
66   Evans, *Endless web*, p. 24.
67   Clark, *Abbots Langley then*, p. 213; *The Times*, 19 September 1835.
68   TNA, HO/107/438/1 1841 Census – Abbots Langley. It is, of course, impossible to know whether the enumerator in Abbots Langley was more diligent than his colleagues in recording the paper-making residents or whether more of them lived in the parish.

between Dickinson's and the canal, despite his use of the railway from 1838, when he stated that he delivered paper everywhere to which there was good canal or other water carriage, or by railway: he sent nothing by waggon.[69]

WATFORD

Watford, the largest of the western towns, was served by the canal from two groups of wharfs, as described in Chapter 5 and shown in Figure 5.5. That at Cashio Bridge lay nearly two miles along the Reading and Hatfield turnpike from the crossroads with the Sparrows Herne road at Upper High Street, while the other group, Grove Wharf and Lady Capels' Wharf, was over two miles north along the Sparrows Herne turnpike. Watford had two breweries, the large Rookery silk mill and the paper mill at Hampermill, as well as a new gas works (1834) and George Tidcombe's growing foundry and engineering business; but all these were at or beyond the south end of the High Street, another mile from the turnpike crossroads, which would have inhibited their use of the canal. Francis Conder would later describe Watford immediately before the railway as having a large corn mill, 'a few comfortable houses' at the top of the town, and 'rich millers and farmers, well to do shopkeepers and hard-working cottagers'. He did not remark upon the poverty and squalor of most of the inhabitants.[70] The 1841 census confirms that the alleys and yards that were such a feature of Watford were home to many, and over-crowding was inevitable, while the new Union Workhouse had been built in 1837 a little way out of town.[71]

The census and directories together suggest that Watford provided more comprehensive services than the other towns in this study, although their portrayal of the town still seems incomplete.[72] For example, the census recorded no bankers, and nor did Pigot's *Directory* (1839), although there had been banking activity for some years: the firm of Horwill, Pike & Co briefly operated from 1823 until 1826, when it failed in the country banking crisis. Treiss & Co of St Albans (1810), associated with Collett & Co of Hemel Hempstead (1809), had opened a branch in the town in 1812, and there is no report of its failure, although it may simply have been closed.[73] Muskett's St Albans bank had a branch in Watford briefly between 1835 and

---

69 John Dickinson's evidence to the Parliamentary Commission on the Post Office, 2 March 1838, quoted by Evans, *Endless web*, p. 57.

70 Mary Forsyth, *Watford* (Stroud, 2015) p. 67, quoting F.R. Conder, *The men who built railways* (1868; reprinted London, 1983), pp. 5–9.

71 Forsyth, *Watford*, pp. 69, 81.

72 TNA, HO/107/439/5–8 1841 Census – Watford; Pigot's *Directory* (1839), pp. 217–220.

73 Dawes and Ward-Perkins, *Country banks*, p. 617.

1837. There were several solicitors, such as Thomas Deacon, who represented Gonville & Caius College, Cambridge, as well as the Rickmansworth resident Henry Fotherley Whitfeld, whose widow Deacon subsequently married. The census lists only two 'clerks', however, and a rope maker, an iron founder, a tallow chandler and a tanner appear only in the *Directory*. A population of just under 6,000 included 1,450 adults with no occupation stated and 169 'independent'; of the remainder, agriculture still employed the largest group; the nine women recorded as 'straw plaiters' was probably an underestimate, although straw plaiting was not strong in Watford. Watford's market was described by Pigot's as a 'Chartered market, which is well attended … on Tuesday and another on Saturday is for butcher's meats etc', indicating that there was good trade to be done and that it was mixed. There were also a plate glass maker, at least two wine merchants, a jeweller and a tobacconist, suggesting that the enduring agrarian economy was well sprinkled with residents with disposable income.

Cashio Bridge Wharf (Figure 5.5), owned by Gonville and Caius College, was operated by Watford corn dealer John Cooper, who probably also occupied the Town Wharf in Rickmansworth (see below). At the 'New Wharf' nearby, leased from the earl of Essex by the Grand Junction Company itself, Joseph Rogers was wharfinger and a coal and timber merchant – the census, however, shows him only as the latter, with Warn father and son as the wharfingers.[74] The only other coal dealers were Thomas Ebborn, at Lady Capels' Wharf, and George Howard, who had also been paying 'tonnage' for boats since at least 1820, at Grove Wharf.[75] No coal merchant was listed anywhere else in the town, and it seems likely that there was a considerable amount of coal being sold at these four wharfs, with virtually all Watford's coal still coming by water. It is not clear from the records how many people were employed at the wharfs: none were so identified in the census. Dealing with bulk cargoes such as coal, timber, iron, salt and grain would have required a workforce of perhaps as many as ten in each location, but this is a very small number compared with the number of general labourers (approaching 250) in the parish.

As noted above, the main long-distance canal carriers operated past all these wharfs with considerable carrying capacity, and Ebborn (Ebburn) had strong family links with Warwickshire (Appendix C). The Watford industries they served were certainly locally significant. But silk throwing at Watford did not make much use of the canal, even though there is strong evidence that 'the economic prosperity of Watford was almost entirely dependent upon

---

74   HALS, DSA4/111/2 Watford tithe map; TNA, HO/107/439/8 1841 Census – Watford.
75   TNA, RAIL 830/66 GJC treasurer's cash book 1820–1826, 23 June 1820.

silk manufacture'.⁷⁶ Shute had used steam-powered mills at Chesham and Rickmansworth but not at Watford (Chapter 3). It is possible that the decline of silk throwing in Watford would have been slower had the canal been more accessible, but there is no evidence on which to base that argument. Similarly, there is no evidence of the Hampermill paper mill benefiting from the canal: the census lists only fifty-nine workers there, rather fewer than might be expected, although the Union workhouse inmates may well have been put to work there (as they were at the silk mill) unrecorded. However, a Fourdrinier machine had been built for Hampermill in about 1830 by Tidcombe of Watford (see below), and would probably have required steam for drying by 1841, just as was described in Chapter 5 at Two Waters.⁷⁷ There is no evidence of how the rags and other materials were brought in, but it would be surprising if the coal and at least some of any steam plant did not come by canal to either Cashio Bridge or Rickmansworth wharfs and thence by road. But this is speculation – although Hampermill remained in full production for some time after this, no details of its transport operations are known. The breweries of Dyson and Fearnley Whittingstall, on opposite sides of the lower High Street, could have used the canal in a similarly limited way: coal probably came by canal, as did new barrels, but malt and other ingredients came in by road and beer went out the same way. George Tidcombe's business Tidcombe and Strudwick, building paper-making machinery in the lower High Street for both export and home markets from 1827, was exactly the sort that would take advantage of the canal connection to Birmingham, and it is reasonable to suppose that iron, fuel and some of his equipment came by water from that direction.⁷⁸ The gas works, too, on the river from 1834, would have received its coal by canal and road until it shifted to the railway a few years later.⁷⁹

There was, then, clearly business to be done in serving Watford by the canal, even though it passed two miles from the town with the main manufacturers inconveniently remote from it. As noted, the canal was not so dominant as to generate a large workforce or to require large permanent warehouses (as opposed to sheds) at the wharfs, or for any boat building or repair businesses to be set up. No worker or 'boatman' was recorded in the 1841 census as living near the wharfs. It cannot be said, therefore, that the canal-related activities generated any significant settlement or community at Watford: even by 1841, it had not become a 'canal town'.

---

76 Jennings, 'The silk industry', p. 44.
77 Finerty, 'Paper mills in Hertfordshire', p. 510.
78 Forsyth, *Watford*, p. 73.
79 Williams, *Watford*, p. 73.

RICKMANSWORTH

The development of Rickmansworth's industry, including both paper making and silk throwing, which continued through the 1830s, clearly owed much to the canal.[80] It passed Cashio Bridge wharfs described above and approached Dickinson's Croxley mill, only ten years old and still relatively small but already using the canal to bring in coal and also pulp from Batchworth, and to carry away the paper produced (about eighteen tons a week).[81] At Batchworth Dickinson had leased the long-standing and extensive pulp mill in 1819 and remodelled it in the years to 1830.[82] Although mainly powered by the river Colne, it later also had a steam plant, and the cut to the wharf made in 1819 is shown on the map (Figure 5.7). Other canal-related facilities included 'Matthew Pickford's Cottage and Stables', and the plot next to this was owned by the Grand Junction, as was the side-lock leading to the Chess and Salter's Cut.[83]

Batchworth Bridge Wharf was fifty yards west of Batchworth bridge, which carried the turnpike to London, and other extensive wharfs, with yard and outbuildings, were provided a little further along the canal at Frogmoor by the coal merchant John Laxton, resident near the wharf of which he shared ownership. The census recorded a 'wharfinger' and two labourers also living on Frogmoor Wharf. Town Wharf, cut or at least paid for by Salter in 1805, was now operated by John Cooper of Watford as a public wharf. Another Rickmansworth paper mill was at Mill End (Lewis Munn), which, although some way from the wharfs at Batchworth and water powered, also used coal for steam drying. In 1835 its sale advertisement described 'powerful water paper-mills ... driving six engines and two paper machines, with drying cylinders ... two steam boilers ... blanching and boiling houses'.[84] It was 'contiguous to Rickmansworth and within five miles of the Birmingham railroad', which was not to be operational for another two years: the canal was not mentioned. The census suggests that it employed about forty people: a small but significant local business despite being (one supposes) increasingly overshadowed by the growing might of Dickinson's, although the type of paper being made there is unknown, and it may not have been in direct

---

80   TNA, HO/107/438/20–22 1841 Census – Rickmansworth; Pigot's *Directory* (1839), pp. 203–4.
81   Finerty, 'Paper mills in Hertfordshire', p. 516.
82   Evans, *Endless web*, p. 53.
83   HALS DSA4/80/2 Rickmansworth tithe map. Matthew Pickford himself was by this time out of the firm bearing his name, and we should be cautious of assuming that the stables were in fact related to carrying on the canal, at least by Pickford & Co. See Turnbull, *Traffic and transport*, for the full story.
84   *County Press*, 11 April 1835.

competition with the quality of Dickinson's product.[85] Although the other Rickmansworth paper mills – Solesbridge (also Lewis Munn), Loudwater and Scots Bridge (both Thomas Weedon) have not been considered in detail in this discussion, being largely water powered but with little by way of operational detail, they were an important part of Rickmansworth's paper industry, which employed at least 130 people and should not be forgotten.

Rickmansworth had no iron foundry at this time, and the main manufacturing concern other than the paper mills was the silk mill, set back on the south side of the western end of the High Street (Figure 5.6). This 1806 mill had been rebuilt only in 1830. The necessary coal could have come from any of the three wharfs, and it may be that the mill had been taken on by its proprietor Shute not only because of the availability of labour, as he stated in his evidence to the parliamentary commission, but also to have canal transport for this fuel.[86] As already noted, whether the silk itself was transported by canal is uncertain.

Although Rickmansworth had become a minor manufacturing town, the decline of its market suggests that, overshadowed by Watford, it was not prosperous. The market, held on Saturdays, was described at some length in Pigot's. It was 'exempt from toll, and was for a long period a considerable one; those of Watford and Hemel Hempstead, however, gradually effected its reduction, and at the present day the business transacted at it is by no means important'. Three fairs were still held, two for horses and cattle and one for hiring, but there is no suggestion that these were any more important by this time than the market. Rickmansworth had, however, some provision of banking, although this had not endured to 1841. The bank established by Simeon Howard of Troy Mill in 1808 had lasted only to 1826, and even George Alfred Muskett, resident in Rickmansworth and owner of Batchworth Bridge Wharf, did not have a local branch of his St Albans bank in the late 1830s.[87]

The mill of the Mines Royal Copper Company was close to the southernmost extremity of the parish. Although the mill itself was in Harefield – the canal and river form the boundary between Hertfordshire and Middlesex – it

---

85 We should not read too much into this, however – changing the quality of the paper produced was by this time largely a matter of changing the settings on the machinery (briefing by Mike Stanyon, *Paper Trail*, 6 December 2018).

86 Parliamentary Paper 1834 XX, *Supplementary as to the employment of Children in Factories* Part 11, 25 March 1834 – Answers of Manufacturers to Queries, Western District: Hertfordshire No. 114, Answers of T.R. Shute (quoted by Jennings in 'Ravelled skein'). In fact the 1841 Census records only about twenty people employed there.

87 Dawes and Ward Perkins, *Country banks*, p. 489; David Plaistowe, 'The Plaistowe family in Rickmansworth', *The Rickmansworth Historian*, 7 (1964), pp. 151–4.

owned land on the Rickmansworth side as well as at least three boats, and employed a few people who lived there. It is therefore appropriate to mention it in a Hertfordshire context, although by 1841 increasing use of iron in shipbuilding and the invention of an alternative alloy for sheathing wooden ships had already caused the mill's decline. Below the copper mill the cut to Troy Mill, whose operators, the Howards, had used the canal for flour and corn since 1802, was part of a complex set of watercourses together making up the river Colne in a wide and marshy valley.

None of this local industry based on the canal changed the fundamentally agricultural nature of Rickmansworth town and parish. The census confirms that the majority of the inhabitants were still on the land: the paper mills and silk mill were important, but nowhere near dominant. Under these circumstances the availability of coal and consumer goods at the wharfs and in the shops was of small concern to the agricultural workers, who were scarcely able to take advantage of them. As elsewhere, the canal had an effect in Rickmansworth, but it was not felt by everyone.

ST ALBANS

St Albans is again included here to allow comparison between towns that did and did not have the opportunities offered by the canal. We noted earlier the effects of 'gentrification', especially where that was centred on a family (the Spencers) of national significance; furthermore, its location on 'the great thoroughfare road leading from London to the Midland and Northern counties' gave St Albans a built-in prosperity, with a large number of inns.[88] It had several schools, including a grammar school, a National School and a school for the new Union workhouse, and public buildings, including, from 1832, the town hall, although by the 1830s the abbey was in a ruinous condition.[89] It had had the first gas works in the area, opened in 1826, and also from 1833 a waterworks delivering water from the river, although the extent of the water supply is unclear.[90]

The presence of booksellers and printers, cabinet makers, milliners and dressmakers, music teachers, florists, wallpaper hangers, surgeons, toy dealers and watchmakers all suggest a generally high quality of life in St Albans. One might expect to find a large number of women 'in service' in such a town, and indeed there was a significant skew in the sex ratio: 81 men to 100 women.[91] But in fact the population of about 6,500 in the

---

88 Pigot's *Directory* (1839), pp. 204–8.
89 Freeman, *St Albans*, p. 234.
90 Freeman, *St Albans*, pp. 194, 242; Toms, *St Albans*, p. 144.
91 TNA, HO/107/447/5–9 1841 Census – St Albans; Freeman, *St Albans*, p. 212.

three main parishes shows a very different mix: fewer than 300 'female servants' in comparison with over 900 people, mainly women and girls, employed in straw plaiting.[92] Doubtless, as straw plaiting was a seasonal (winter and spring) occupation, many of these had an additional, often casual occupation. But by 1839 the prosperity of the inns had been greatly reduced by the opening of the L&BR and the almost immediate decline of the coaching traffic. Pigot's *Directory* (1839) recorded that one inn alone had lost the stabling of 250 horses, and that 'letters arrive[d] at the Post Office from the station at Watford'. Although a number of inns and coaching services were advertised in 1839, the number had reduced further by 1841, and the opportunities for employment in them were declining.[93] But freight traffic remained strong: the listing of twelve carriers serving it from London, a distance of twenty-one miles, includes a number of St Albans people identifiable from the 1841 census.[94] Esther Clark (with her son) ran a daily waggon service, so with several vehicles they were in a business of reasonable size. John Garforth ran twice a week, James Humphreys and Abel Chalfont three times: others, not verifiably local, provided less frequent but regular services. So at least three waggons were advertised from London to St Albans every day, and of course they went both ways: from the St Albans listing one can calculate with reasonable confidence that at least nine waggons left the town for London on a Monday, a van on Tuesday, one waggon on Wednesday, Friday and Saturday and five on Thursday. But that was only the start of it: a footnote to the entry says that the town was also served 'by the Liverpool, Manchester and [other] carriers', who were both many and large. The daily Manchester carriers alone included Pickfords (vans), Shipton & Co, Deacon Harrison & Co, Kenworthy & Co, John Jolly, Alexander & Co, Thomas Bache & Co and Robins & Co – very strong 'brands', and almost all of them now offering an integrated service including both canal and railway, as we saw in Chapter 4.[95]

Compare this panoply with the other towns, locally significant but not on a trunk road. In Watford, Mary Ann Boddy ran a daily service from London's Snowhill, a street littered with waggoning and coaching inns, and Hawks another. Otherwise, while three waggons were advertised on Monday, four on Wednesday and four on Saturday, the capacity and the destinations they

---

92 Freeman, *St Albans*, pp. 176–80 describes the straw industry of St Albans in some detail.
93 Jonathan Mein, *The decline of the White Hart, St Albans, in the eighteenth and nineteenth centuries* (St Albans, 2012) <http://stalbanshistory.org/page_id__474.aspx?path=0p2p145p147p>, accessed 22 February 2019; Freeman, *St Albans*, p. 151.
94 TNA, HO/107/447/5–9 1841 Census – St Albans.
95 Pigot's *Directory* (1839), pp. 208, 469–74; Turnbull, *Traffic and transport*, p. 106.

offered were much less than those passing through St Albans. Although Pigot's *Directory* (1839) points out that the Tring and Aylesbury carriers also served Watford, one of them every day, it would have been necessary to move goods to St Albans (or to London) and trans-ship them to longer-range firms if they were consigned further afield. Many of the carriers operating from Aylesbury through Tring to Watford were local to the towns they served. Thomas Rodwell of Aylesbury, William Stevens (using a cart) and John Bunn of Tring, John Chapman of Windsor (running a cart between Windsor and Berkhamsted), John King of Berkhamsted, William Batchelor and William Hughes of Hemel Hempstead, Charles Claridge of Leighton Buzzard, Wootton Clark of Bushey (on the turnpike south-east of Watford) and William Axten and Daniel Darvile of Watford can all be identified and located from the 1841 census. There are few others, nor are any of the major national carriers listed as using this road. Meanwhile, Rickmansworth, off the Sparrows Herne road on the Reading and Hatfield turnpike, had only three services to London, two by local men William Brown and Edward Try, probably managing between them one waggon each weekday, and one twice a week by Darvile of Watford. There were also the Chesham carriers, and presumably services heading between Reading and Hatfield, although because the whole road was a bypass for London this seems not to have been much.[96]

This all suggests that the economy of St Albans was such that the canal was, in fact, largely irrelevant: straw plaiting and hat making, with eighteen straw hat manufacturers listed by Pigot's *Directory* (1839), stood alone, although subject to the vagaries of fashion, as did agriculture. There appears to have been little other manufacturing industry: most of what was needed was brought in, and brought by road. The expected effect of the canal would have been to take some of the industrial through-traffic off the road, but the varied nature of that traffic made St Albans relatively impervious even to that. The town's population grew steadily at a cumulative annual rate of 1.94 per cent (Table 6.2) through the first forty years of the nineteenth century, overtaking Watford to be the largest town on the west side of the county.[97]

The Municipal Corporations Act of 1835 had changed the governance of the borough, but those changes affected the daily lives of the inhabitants very little. It was more important that Woollam's silk mill and a candlewick maker continued to offer employment to some local women and indeed children, but Pigot's *Directory* (1839) notes that by that time even this was

---

96 Pigot's *Directory* (1839) pp. 176–220.
97 But see also the analysis of Freeman, *St Albans*, p. 210, and his Appendix, p. 349, in which factors including the boundary changes of 1835 are addressed.

'not extensive', a remark supported by the census, although there seem to have been as many as 500 in the silk mill in 1815.[98] There were 'several good breweries' in the town, although they too were relatively small.[99] The market was on Saturday, and was 'well supplied with general articles of provision, grain and straw plait'. The banking facilities of St Albans were very much better than those of the other west Hertfordshire towns, and we have seen several examples of St Albans businesses with branches elsewhere. The first bank was that of Joseph and Nathaniel Harris (1800), who in 1810 had sold out to Treiss, whose branches then appeared in Hemel Hempstead and Watford by 1813.[100] The coal merchant Richard Brabant and others set up Brabant & Co in 1804, and they were joined from 1823 by Peter Finch Martineau, a London brewer and sugar refiner who had moved to St Albans. Gape & Aday made a brief appearance between 1815 and about 1820, when it may be that their London agents failed. Then in 1834 the colourful George Alfred Muskett opened his bank in St Albans. Muskett was the owner of a wharf at Rickmansworth, and he certainly had many business interests as well as being briefly one of the St Albans MPs: suffice to say here that there was enough commerce in St Albans in the 1830s to attract men like him to provide this important facilitating service.

St Albans had remained prosperous, important and influential, although small, throughout this period. Dominated by straw plaiting and hat making, its other commerce (in which agriculture played a relatively small part) depended to a very large extent on the main road, and that was now threatened by the L&BR passing a few miles to the west. It seems that the Grand Junction Canal had much less negative and – by facilitating the gas works – probably some positive impact. On the other hand, the failure forty years earlier to provide the St Albans canal meant that St Albans had always had to manage without the direct benefits of water transport: coal and building materials, for example, would have had to come by road from the wharfs at Boxmoor or Watford several miles away. But, on balance, St Albans provides evidence that direct access to a canal was not essential to the economic success of a market town.

Conclusion
By 1841 the canal had given rise to wharfs and related facilities serving Tring, Berkhamsted, Hemel Hempstead, Watford and Rickmansworth. Berkhamsted had developed the only boat-building business, but all these

---

98   Freeman, *St Albans*, p. 181.
99   Whitaker, *Brewers in Hertfordshire*, pp. 189–99.
100 Dawes and Ward Perkins, *Country banks*, pp. 506–8.

towns had extensive wharfs to which coal, timber, building materials, industrial raw materials and manufactured goods were brought and taken away by the many canal carriers, some local, on their way to and from London. The paper maker Dickinson was using the canal in a particularly vigorous way, and his business prospered accordingly. Other paper makers and manufacturers of silk thread, copper sheet and machinery used the canal to varying degrees, although the detail cannot now be demonstrated. But the local population was not sufficiently large to provide a significant market: in general, market-led canal-based business formed round an existing nucleus, but the outlying west Hertfordshire parishes show that where there was nothing in place to be developed the canal passed by without effect.

Hertfordshire remained in 1841 a county whose main products were agricultural, chiefly wheat and plaited straw, whose inhabitants were mostly employed in agricultural occupations, and where wages and standards of living remained low and bread the dietary staple for many.[101] Farmers were unable to use the canal to transform their business, and the canal mainly benefited those in industry or the 'middling sort'. Those who could not afford 'consumer goods' benefited very little, and that group comprised the majority of the inhabitants. As they had done for many years, they left Hertfordshire for a range of reasons, so that there was a relatively low rate of population growth in the county despite the opportunities generated by the canal, which did not change the fundamental nature of the county.[102]

---

101 Agar, *Behind the plough*, pp. 154, 155.
102 Agar, *Behind the plough*, pp. 14–16; Goose, 'Population movement', pp. 53, 54.

Chapter 7
In conclusion

This study originated from a perceived gap in the written histories of both Hertfordshire and the waterways. Neither referred in any detail to the other, but it seemed unlikely that the Grand Junction Canal, a major piece of transport infrastructure, had passed through the county with negligible economic or social impact. But what exactly were those impacts? In this book I have sought to identify the canal's effects on the west side of this small agrarian county. Studies of Hertfordshire tend either to mention the Grand Junction Canal but briefly, or to portray it as bringing the Industrial Revolution to the county, although not to much effect.[1] Accounts of the canal, reasonably enough, do not address Hertfordshire in any depth. The resulting picture is incomplete, and this has been an attempt to fill the gaps.

The preceding chapters have shown that the canal, primarily intended to link London and the industrial Midlands, promised only limited benefits to the inhabitants of Hertfordshire. Landowners on the line of the canal gained a little directly by selling land and some farmers used it for business, although serving agriculture was by its very nature a problem for canals because farmers any distance off its line generally preferred to keep their transport on the road.[2] On the face of it, few of the silk- and cotton-spinning mills, the smaller paper mills or the breweries, even those near the canal, were able to take the commercial opportunities the canal presented. Wharfs in towns and large villages provided local businesses and retailers with a range of raw materials and goods and some with a new way of moving their product to market, but in these first years of the canal's operation only one major industrial development, by the paper maker Dickinson, endured in the area.

---

1 Tony Rook, *A history of Hertfordshire* (London, 1984), p. 81; Johnson, *Industrial archaeology*, p. 140; Faulkner, *The Grand Junction Canal in Hertfordshire*.
2 Wrigley, *The path to sustained growth*, p. 138; Hadfield, *Canals of south and southeast England*, pp. 19–21.

But this top-level view is also incomplete. The major development of machine paper making by the Fourdriniers from 1803 required a new type of manufactured equipment. Considerable amounts of steam-raising plant and its associated pipework, as well as the machines themselves, are very likely to have been transported by canal to Hemel Hempstead from the Midlands and London, and that is in addition to the need to transport the manufactured paper to its market. Iron was made much more readily available to the iron founders who from the 1820s were to become the manufacturing engineers, and to the ironmongers and smiths who served farms as well as road vehicle and carrying businesses. The new silk mill at Tring and those at Rickmansworth and Chesham were steam powered from the early 1830s, and their equipment too was most easily brought by canal. Coal in large quantities was a timely import when firewood and charcoal were becoming increasingly scarce and could not in any case have fuelled the new steam plants. And towards the end of the period the new gas works required not only equipment for making and storing the gas but also yet more piping to deliver it. This too was much more easily delivered by water than by road, and both fuel and waste products required the carrying capacity offered by the canal but not by roads.

It seems nonetheless that, apart from Dickinson and to an extent the Mines Royal copper mill in the far south of the county, industrial operations remained relatively small, with both raw materials (except malt and limestone in the form of chalk) and fuel having to be brought in from a distance and the market for most products lying elsewhere, notably in London. The Rickmansworth cotton spinners continued in business only until late 1810. Whereas the silk-throwing mills in Rickmansworth and Chesham probably used the canal for coal, the large Watford Rookery mill seems to have been wholly independent of the canal, while other smaller throwsters in Watford used mill-horses for power and did not continue in business long into the nineteenth century. Even then, evidence is lacking for the method by which raw silk was brought in and the thrown thread taken away: a road service would have sufficed for its limited volume, although its destinations were usually on connecting canals. It is tempting to infer that the Rickmansworth brewer Salter canalised the Chess in order to serve his brewery, but his cut is more likely to have been a general business investment: none of the other local brewers needed to use the canal to any extent. Local corn millers did not become major industrial producers, at least not until some years later. So significant industrial development in west Hertfordshire did not materialise as a result of the canal's presence.

The canal, providing as it did the first high-capacity long-distance trade route in the area, nonetheless benefited other inhabitants in these early years. The first effect was on employment, with the businesses using the canal providing an increased range of jobs, although not in large numbers. Public wharfs at or near Tring, Berkhamsted, Hemel Hempstead, Kings Langley, Hunton Bridge, Watford and Rickmansworth supported coal, building material and timber merchants as well as providing collection and distribution points for the use of the inhabitants and businesses of those towns and villages. All employed labouring men, and Berkhamsted, Hemel Hempstead, Watford and Rickmansworth changed appreciably as a result of these new businesses. The small parishes without towns, however, generally received very little benefit. Puttenham, Aldbury, Wigginton and Northchurch had been and remained small agricultural settlements: their farmers might have used the canal to some degree, but none of these places attracted new industrial activity. Places that already had a nucleus of industry or commerce around which canal-related activity could coalesce developed, but the others gained very little except perhaps more variety in the village shop.

The Grand Junction Canal affected Hertfordshire in two other ways. The first relates to the cutting of the canal itself between 1794 and 1799. It might have been thought that Hertfordshire's rural economy was particularly vulnerable to losing its labouring workforce to the canal, but in fact that effect was limited. By 1793 much of the digging of the canal and the work of the trades supporting it were being done by experienced professionals, and there is little evidence that labourers left Hertfordshire's fields to join the 'navigators' in any strength. Nor is there any evidence that agricultural labourers' wages increased as a result of the presence of a body of men somewhat better paid – the differential seems to have been at least 6d, perhaps 1s, per day, about 25 or even 50 per cent. No crisis in the gathering of the harvest or in the spring sowings was attributed to the canal cutting in any parish, nor was there much variation in the poor rate or in the support paid out from it, as might have been expected had 'spare labour' suddenly been mopped up for a few years. Hertfordshire farming was affected but little by the cutting of the canal.

The second of these effects has to do with the relationship of the canal company with local people and businesses. Its initial land purchases and approach to damage compensation seem to have been relatively uncontentious, although there were some exceptions and a special case relating to the earls of Essex and of Clarendon. But water supply to mills along the rivers Gade and Colne led to recurring disputes, notably but not only with Dickinson and by no means all won by the Grand Junction Canal Company. Several mills, including large paper mills, had to be bought by the company in order to acquire their water rights, and the main line had later to be moved to accommodate Dickinson's complaint. Field drainage was interrupted in places by the canal's embankment, while water levels at the confluence of Gade and Bulbourne at Two Waters were just one of several issues between the Boxmoor Trustees and the Grand Junction Canal Company. The company was also pursued, although unsuccessfully, by some parishes as a source of extra money to support the poor rates from about 1816, when the end of the Napoleonic Wars caused real hardship in the area.

The Sparrows Herne turnpike, which the canal paralleled for over twenty miles, was affected by the establishment of the canal next to it. A small increase in toll revenue at the start may have resulted from the canal company using the road for its own traffic, and the turnpike's rising costs may have reflected extra wear and tear on the road. After the canal opened, however, toll revenue declined, notably on the southern section around Watford. The turnpike may well have had the benefit of granite road stone brought by boat from Nuneaton on the Coventry canal, but even that was only occasional. But the significant growth of long-distance canal traffic did not result in the collapse of traffic on the turnpike. It seems more likely that the freight traffic on the canal was almost all new and had never been on the turnpike, which had provided a much more local facility for the towns, especially Watford, and villages and continued to do so. Toll revenue remained generally steady for many years, representing a decline in real terms in the volume of trade. By comparison, the traffic on the major London to Manchester and Holyhead route through St Albans some miles to the east continued to grow, and seems to have been relatively little affected by the canal: the railway was to have far more impact on it, but even that was initially largely on passenger traffic, for which the canal was not a serious competitor.

The Grand Junction Canal, therefore, brought benefits to some that were counterbalanced by problems for others, and few of the benefits accrued to the labouring poor. But there is one exception to this general assessment. The provision of coal and reductions in its price had been offered from the start as a benefit to places such as Hertfordshire, whose sea-coal fuel was previously carried from London by cart and was beyond the means of most of the labouring poor, even when supported financially by straw plaiting. The supply of coal at canal wharfs in large quantities made it more accessible and affordable to both inhabitants and tradesmen. The impact of this is impossible to quantify, but it seems unlikely that, before this, the poor had had any fuel other than scrub or fallen wood: the new availability of coal would have made a difference to some, especially in the towns.

Until the mid-1790s the economy of the county had been small in size and relatively self-contained. The low wages of agricultural labourers, supported by those of straw plaiters, had dominated. The post-canal economy of Hertfordshire demonstrated the effect of the canal as a new exogenous influence. The main variable determining real wages had been the price of food, which in turn drove the demand for goods and so the demand for labour. But there was now a new variable – the cost of fuel – along with some increase in employment opportunities and a new route by which rising demand for goods could be met. As a consequence, the overall real wage increased. But this was probably true only for those whose wages gave them disposable income: those whose wages did not reach that level were isolated from the outside influence of the canal and subject to increasingly marked swings in the price of food and to fuel poverty. So although there was an appreciable effect, albeit mainly in towns near to the canal, the overall impact of the canal in Hertfordshire was limited. Industrial development during the first forty years or so of its operation employed relatively few of the inhabitants and did not generate sufficient new employment to result in a general increase in wages. Life for agricultural labourers continued largely unaffected. The canal was not an agent causing widespread economic change, and it did not prevent a steady flow of people moving away from the area.

The wider implication is that industry of only local significance could be sustained using the services of a canal, but even that needed an existing core around which to form. Hertfordshire's experience suggests that small-scale industry not immediately on the canal was able to develop by using local road transport for essential fuel and materials, the cost of which was often reduced by partial canal transport, but the only ones that became large-scale were located directly on the waterway. The presence of minerals was also crucial to real economic growth: where, as in Hertfordshire, there were no minerals except chalk and agriculture was the main industry, benefits were small and growth remained low. Agriculture, needing 'dendritic' transport, was intrinsically unable to use a canal fully, suggesting that waterways predicated solely on agriculture would struggle, as indeed many did. The willingness of a canal-side landowner to provide a wharf was, in any case, a necessary precursor to development. A small local trader could not provide his own, nor could provision be made except near larger centres that provided the necessary volume of trade. Small villages especially were unable to generate their own growth. The consequence was that in communities such as those of this study the Industrial Revolution had little impact: even the presence of a major waterway did not offer many inhabitants any real advantage.

In summary, then, Hertfordshire, whose dominant industry was agriculture, was never expected to benefit from the Grand Junction Canal as it passed to and from London. Indeed, the London market was already accessible to Hertfordshire farmers and small manufacturers. But the canal did have some positive effects. It attracted and helped to prosper a paper maker of true industrial scale; it broadened the range of goods available to people with purchasing power; it improved the availability of raw materials for manufacturing; and it provided a reasonably assured supply of fuel. On the other hand, it generated relatively little employment. Its benefits were mainly indirect – facilitating – rather than direct, although by providing inexpensive, reliable long-distance transport of goods and materials it prepared the way for the much greater impact of the railway.[3] The Grand Junction Canal did not bring the Industrial Revolution to Hertfordshire, but it was by no means simply passing through.

---

3   Newman, 'Socio-economic impacts'.

Appendix A
Market town analysis: west Hertfordshire towns 1790–1840

The consideration of the towns of this study draws on analyses of the *Universal British Directory* for the 1790s, and of Pigot's trade directory for 1839 and the 1841 census.[1] It presents a set of characteristics based on those suggested by Barrie Trinder as indicating a true 'market town', which influenced the area nearby and presented a range of services, including those such as banking, the law, surveying and auctioneering.[2] The leading 'tradesmen' in towns were the butchers, bakers, victuallers, tailors, smiths and shoe makers,[3] but these were not major employers of labour. Trinder suggests that sufficient population size to encompass the various features was important, and here it seems that Tring, Berkhamsted and Rickmansworth, even Hemel Hempstead and Watford, should all fail immediately. But in fact it is clear from Pigot's 1839 directory and the census that they did provide a full range of services, if only to their own inhabitants rather than the wider surrounding area.

The position of each town in the 1790s is summarised in Table A-1. There were some local manufactures. Trinder offers malt as an example, common in every town but only of economic significance when of a scale to be used by brewers elsewhere – as in, for example, east but not west Hertfordshire.[4] The manufacture of goods for more distant markets was important: the trade directories (at this time mainly the *Universal British Directory*) identify the principal manufactures of the main towns, but only Watford, Hemel Hempstead and Berkhamsted are included, which suggests that neither

---

1　Pigot's *Directory* (1839) pp. 174–6, 187–90, 199–200, 203–4, 213–15, 217–20, accessed through www.ancestry.co.uk accessed 9 April 2016; 1841 census TNA, HO/107/442/5–7, HO/107/442/9, HO/107/440/1, HO/107/442/2, HO/107/440/5, HO/107/440/3–4, HO/107/441/5–8, HO/107/441/12, HO/107/438/1, HO/107/439/5–8, HO/107/438/20–22.
2　Trinder, 'Market town industry', pp. 75–89.
3　Ellis, *The Georgian town*, p. 53.
4　Mathias, *Brewing in England*, p. 14; Trinder, 'Market town industry', p. 80.

Tring nor Rickmansworth had regionally significant manufacturing. On the other hand, we know that in Rickmansworth Batchworth Mill was large and productive, and also that there were enough paper mills for it to be the venue for a meeting of the Hertfordshire paper makers in 1796: so it is surprising to find it omitted. Census and directory confirm that in 1839 Tring had silk and canvas, Hemel Hempstead paper, Watford silk and paper, Rickmansworth paper and silk. Berkhamsted alone was not credited with any manufacturing industry, 'wooden ware' having by then declined.

Trinder notes that most towns had banks by 1830, even if only extensions of the financial activities of solicitors, as in Hemel Hempstead, and indeed all the west Hertfordshire towns except Rickmansworth had banks by 1840, and all had had at least one before that.[5] None of the west Hertfordshire towns had a 'resort' function, and none had proper assembly rooms until the 1850s. Trinder refers to the role of wharfs in extending the economic value of a canal to a town, but none of the towns of this study became a 'canal town' (i.e., one providing services to the canal and its traders) except arguably Berkhamsted. They did, however, have in common several features: one or more corn mills (in this area usually water powered, but not necessarily), a market place, some sort of market hall, meeting rooms provided by large inns, maltings, a National school later in the period. The distribution of retailers, dealers, tradesmen and manufacturers (such as engineers) was uneven: the richer the mix, it may be argued, the more prosperous the town, although once again the lack of hard evidence prompts caution. Some features are not universal here: a tannery, a ropewalk, a coachmaker, a common brewer, a gas works, the main-line railway all featured in some but not all of these small towns in the 1830s, while large-scale makers of clothing and furniture were completely absent.

Trinder also observes that 'the presence in a town of an iron foundry' was 'a sign of its virility, and its absence that a community was not prospering'.[6] Tidcombe in Watford from the 1820s and Cranstone in Hemel Hempstead from 1818 were clearly of this sort, although we note that this strongly agricultural county had no significant builder of agricultural machinery. The paper maker Dickinson was by any standards a manufacturer of national importance, and others made paper for distribution beyond the area, but there were no others before 1840.

The role of the canal is of course central to the discussion, and Trinder's model has been modified to take account of it, in particular the wharfs and the businesses and occupations related to them.

---

5 Trinder, 'Market town industry', p. 77; Forsyth, *Watford*, p. 75; L.S. Pressnell, *Country banking in the Industrial Revolution* (Oxford, 1956), pp. 45–56, 344–65; Dawes and Ward Perkins, *Country banks*, pp. 45, 264, 265, 489, 506–8, 593, 617.

6 Trinder, 'Market town industry', p. 81.

Table A-1. Attributes of west Hertfordshire towns in the 1790s.

Feature (1790s)[7]	Tring[8]	Berkhamsted	Hemel Hempstead	Watford	Rickmansworth[9]
Complex central area with varied architecture housing retailers, craft manufacture, professionals	Partial	Partial	Yes	Yes	Partial
Specialist occupations serving local needs:					
Flour milling	Yes	Yes	Yes	Yes	Yes
Tannery	Yes	Yes	Yes	Yes	Yes
Large malting	No	No	Yes	No	Yes
Rope making	No	No	No	No	No
Specialist occupation: straw plait	Yes	Yes	Yes	Yes	Yes
Specialist manufactures for national (distant) markets	Small (Canvas)	No	Yes (Paper)	Yes (Silk thread)	Yes (Paper, cotton thread)
Production of local building materials	Flint	Timber	Bricks	Bricks	Limited – lime, bricks
Wealthy residents and landowners	Yes	Yes	Yes	Yes	Yes
Transport providing freight links to national centres	Turnpike, waggon services	Turnpike, waggon services	Turnpike, waggon services	Turnpike, waggon services	Turnpike, waggon services
Active market serving needs of the area	Partial	Declining	Yes	Yes	Declining
Market town in terms of those of the time?	Limited	Limited	Yes	Yes	Limited

7 *UBD*, vol. II, pp. 278–82 (Berkhamstead), vol. III, pp. 688–704 (Watford), vol. IV, pp. 254–6 (Hemel Hempstead).
8 Tring has a description but no listing.
9 Rickmansworth is not mentioned in the *Directory*. Information is interpolated from Holden's *Directory*, vol. III.

Table A-2. Attributes of west Hertfordshire towns in 1841.

Feature (1841)	Tring	Berkhamsted	Hemel Hempstead	Watford	Rickmansworth
Innovation and organisation in transport					
turnpike (with freight transport facilities)	Yes	Yes	Yes	Yes (two)	Yes (two)
(2) canal wharf in town centre[10]	Close	Yes	Close	Close	Yes
nationally advertised canal destination	No	No	No	No	No
cargo-carrying railway	Not yet	Not yet	Not yet	Not yet	No
Commercial (common) breweries	Yes	Small	Small	Yes (x 2)	Yes
Commercial maltings for distant brewers	No	No	No	No	No
Engineering works (eg from iron foundry)	No	No	Yes	Yes	No
Boat building or repair yard	No	Yes	No	No	No
Canal warehousing	Small	Small	Yes	Small	Small
Water-borne building materials (stone, slate, timber)	Yes	Yes	Yes	Yes	Yes
Regulated market activity – market charter etc	Small	In decline	Yes – mainly wheat	Yes	In decline
Developed facilities:					
market hall	No	Declining	Yes	Yes	Decrepit
(2) assembly rooms	No	No	Yes	Yes	No
boarding schools	No	Yes	No	Yes (1841)	No
legal and financial services (e.g. banks)	Partial	Yes	Yes	Yes	Limited
Printing services	Yes	Yes	Yes	Yes	Yes
Mix of shops, workshops and dwellings	Yes	Yes	Yes	Yes	Yes
Manufacturing industry	Silk	No	Paper, engineering	Silk, paper, engineering	Paper
Specialist manufactures for national (distant) markets	Small (Canvas)	No	Yes (Paper)	Yes (Silk thread)	Yes (Paper, silk thread)
Market town in terms of those of the time?	Limited	Limited	Yes	Yes	Limited

10 The implication was that such a town would justify the building of a dedicated arm. As we have seen, none in this area (except arguably Rickmansworth) did so.

Appendix B
Hertfordshire boat owners and operators 1802–41

This data is drawn from the extant gauging registers of the Grand Junction Canal Company, vols 1–64 (1802–1841).[1] Not all of the sequence is available, and many have no Hertfordshire relevance.

---

1 NWA, BW99/6/5/1–6, 8–34, 122 (gauging registers).

Vol. (year)	Gauging no.	Name or fleet no. (where stated)	Owner/operator	Place of ownership	Builder and year (where known)	Notes
Vol. 1 (1802)	8	No. 1	William Wilkins	Wendover	Mr Hughes, Braunston (1801)	Narrow boat – general cargo between Paddington, Stoke [Bruerne] and Wendover
Vol. 1 (1802)	11	No. 2	William Wilkins	Wendover	Mr Hughes, Braunston (1801)	Narrow boat – general cargo between Paddington, Stoke [Bruerne] and Wendover
Vol. 1 (1802)	30	Tyrringham (No. 2)	John Holladay	Watford	Joseph Piper, Hammersmith (1799)	Barge – hay
Vol. 1 (1802)	31	No. 1	Sir Christopher Baynes Bt	Harefield	Thomas Cotton, Banbury (1799) (for GJCCo)	Narrow boat – lime between Harefield and Paddington
Vol. 1 (1802)	40	William Praed (No. 7)	James Tate	Tring	Joseph Piper, Hammersmith (1801)	Barge – hay to London
Vol. 1 (1802)	48	Watford (No. 1)	John Holladay	Watford (later of Berkhamsted? – see tithe award)	Joseph Piper, Hammersmith (1801)	Barge – coal and timber between Watford, Brentford and Paddington
Vol. 1 (1802)	51	Berkhamstead Castle	William Butler	Berkhamsted	Peacock and Willetts, Berkhamsted (1801)	Barge – hay and coal between Berkhamsted and London
Vol. 1 (1802)	68	Trio (No. 2)	Sir Christopher Baynes Bt	Harefield	Joseph Piper, Hammersmith (1802)	Barge – lime from Harefield to Brentford and Paddington
Vol. 1 (1802)	73	No. 2	John Saunders	Brentford	Mr Ayres, Reading (1801)	Barge – coal from Thames to Berkhamsted and Paddington
Vol. 1 (1802)	77	No. 3	Sir Christopher Baynes Bt	Harefield	Joseph Piper, Hammersmith (1801)	Barge – lime and bricks from Harefield to Paddington
Vol. 1 (1802)	80	Providence (No. 3)	William Wilkins	Wendover	Mr Ayres, Reading (1802)	Barge – hay from Wendover to Thames

HERTFORDSHIRE BOAT OWNERS AND OPERATORS 1802-41

Vol. (year)	Gauging no.	Name or fleet no. (where stated)	Owner/operator	Place of ownership	Builder and year (where known)	Notes
Vol. 1 (1802)	91	Fair Trader	Newman Hatley	Kings Langley	Joseph Piper, Hammersmith (1801)	Sailing barge – corn and flour King's Langley to Thames
Vol. 1 (1802)	92	Thomas (No. 1)	Thomas Coleman	Gray's Inn, London	Mr Warner, Pangbourne (1791)	Barge, coal and dung between Thames and Berkhamsted. Built for West of Windsor, sold to Bentley of Cashiobury and then to Coleman
Vol. 1 (1802)	97	Trojan	Thomas Howard	Troy, Rickmansworth	Joseph Sawyer, Hammersmith (1796)	Wide beam, 45ft long. Rigged for sailing, in foul condition despite being used for corn and flour
Vol. 1 (1802)	98	Earl Temple	James Tate	Tring	Joseph Piper, Hammersmith (1796)	Barge – hay from Tring to river Thames
Vol. 2 (1802)	115	No. 4	Sir Christopher Baynes Bt	Harefield	Nk	Barge – bricks and lime from Harefield to Fenny Stratford and London
Vol. 2 (1802)	119	No. 8	John Hodder	Harefield	Nk	Barge – trade Nk
Vol. 2 (1802)	123	Watford (No. 2)	John Holladay	Watford	Nk	Barge – coal trade
Vol. 2 (1802)	129	No. 1	William Howard	Boxmoor	Mr Warner, Pangbourne (1799)	Barge – trade Nk
Vol. 2 (1802)	133	No. 2	Howard and Sedgwick	Troy, Rickmansworth	Mr Warner, Pangbourne (1802)	Sailing barge – half-decked, presumed for corn and flour
Vol. 2 (1802)	141	No. 2	William Howard	Boxmoor	Hobbs (1796)	Barge – coal and timber to and from the Thames
Vol. 2 (1802)	146	No. 1	Emmott Skidmore	Rickmansworth	Mr Warner, Pangbourne (1795)	Barge – general carrier

Vol. (year)	Gauging no.	Name or fleet no. (where stated)	Owner/operator	Place of ownership	Builder and year (where known)	Notes
Vol. 2 (1802)	153	Delrow	William Stapleton	White Friars	Nk	Barge, in dairy trade. Bought from Mr Perkins of Lady Capel's Wharf
Vol. 2 (1803)	157	George	Thomas Homer	Paddington	Nk	Barge – bought from Mr Ashness of Hemel Hempstead in 1801
Vol. 3 (1804/5)	218	No. 1	Thomas Ebburn	Sow, Warks (on Oxford Canal near Coventry[2]	Shaw, Birmingham (1799)	Narrow boat, to and from Paddington on coal trade. Thomas Ebburn Jr was to become an important figure in Hertfordshire waterways history, and his progress is included
Vol. 3 (1804/5)	279	No. 1	Edward Ellis	Hertford	Best, Hertford (1800)	Barge, timber trade on R Lea to and from Thames
Vol. 9 (1808)	813	No. 1	John How	Berkhamsted	Nk	Barge – trade Nk
Vol. 9 (1808)	852	No. 3	Howard and Son	Berkhamsted	Nk	Narrow boat, coal trade
Vol. 10 (1809)	948	No. 1	William Fantham	Wendover	Nk	Narrow boat, general carrying
Vol. 10 (1809)	963	No. 3	William Haycock	Wendover	Bird, Birmingham	Narrow boat, general carrier. NB: Haycock must have had at least 2 boats listed in vols 4, 5, 6 or 8 (all missing)
Vol. 11 (1810)	1035	No. 4	William Howard	Boxmoor	Nk	Narrow boat, in coal trade
Vol. 12 (1810)	1175	No. 1	Thomas Landon	Cowroast (Northchurch)	Nk	Narrow boat, general carrier

2 <http://www.oldtowns.co.uk/Warwickshire/sow.htm>, accessed 18 January 2016.

Vol. (year)	Gauging no.	Name or fleet no. (where stated)	Owner/operator	Place of ownership	Builder and year (where known)	Notes
Vol. 12 (1810)	1110	No. 4	William Haycock	Wendover	Nk	Narrow boat, in coal trade
1811 (Vol. 14)	1324	No. 1	John Brown	Berkhamsted	Nk	Narrow boat, general carrier
Feb 1817 (Vol. 21)	2005	No. 1	John Beales	Watford	Nk	Narrow boat, trade not stated
Sep 1817 (Vol. 21)	2071	Charlotte (No. 1)	Mines Royal Copper Co	Harefield	Nk	Barge, copper to London
Sep 1823 (Vol. 30)	2951	Nk	Thomas Ebburn (senior)	Sow (Warks)	Nk	Narrow boat, trade not stated (but likely to be coal to London)[3]

3 Thomas Ebburn of Sowe, Coventry (1773–1842), was shown having gauged a boat carrying coal to London in 1804 (Vol. 2), and Thomas Ebbern of Sowe two more in 1823/4, another in 1829 and another (with Lane) in 1832 – there may have been more in the missing registers.

In 1832 Thomas Ebbern of Durrrants Hill Wharf (which the tithe award shows that he later owned, but which was operated by William Robinson) gauged three boats, and another at St Albans Wharf (which he both owned and operated).

The 1841 census shows one Thomas Ebburn at Sowe as a farmer aged sixty-six, and Thomas Ebburn at Watford (Lady Capel's Wharf) a coal merchant aged forty (he also owned a building plot at Two Waters).

Despite the varied spellings it seems likely that they were father and son, both active in the coal trade in the early 1840s, with the son building a prosperous business (complete with landownership) split between Watford and Hemel Hempstead.

Vol. (year)	Gauging no.	Name or fleet no. (where stated)	Owner/operator	Place of ownership	Builder and year (where known)	Notes
Jan 1824 (Vol. 30)	2969	Nk	Thomas Ebburn (senior)	Sow (Warks)	Nk	Narrow boat, trade not stated (but likely to be coal to London)*
Vol. 32 (1823)	3113	Nk	John Hatton	Berkhamsted	Nk	Narrow boats – trade not stated. John Hatton was a boat builder and coal dealer in the 1839 Trade Directory – reasonable to assume that he built as well as operated his own boats
Vol. 32 (1823)	3118	Nk	John Hatton	Berkhamsted	Nk	As above
Vol. 32 (1823)	3119	Nk	John Collins	Berkhamsted	Nk	Narrow boat, trade not stated
Vol. 32 (1823)	3132	Nk	Longman and Co	Nash Mill	Nk	Narrow boat. Longman, the publisher, was the partner of John Dickinson, and this boat will have been part of that business
Vol. 32 (1823)	3188	Nk	William Landon	Aylesbury	Nk	Narrow boat – trade not stated. Likely to be a family connection with Thomas Landon of Cow Roast and Ann Landon of Aylesbury, who later appears as a canal carrier in her own name
Vol. 34 (1825)	3345	Nk	John Johnson	Lady Capel's Wharf	Nk	Narrow boat

HERTFORDSHIRE BOAT OWNERS AND OPERATORS 1802–41

Vol. (year)	Gauging no.	Name or fleet no. (where stated)	Owner/operator	Place of ownership	Builder and year (where known)	Notes
Oct 1828 (Vol. 38)	3747	Nk	John Bunn	Berkhamsted	Nk	Narrow boat. John Bunn described as 'carrier' in 1841 Census, poss link to James Bunn, blacksmith in 1839 Trade Directory or James Bunn lockkeeper
Sep 1829 (Vol. 38)	3784	Nk	John Dickinson	Nash Mill	Nk	Narrow boat, trade not stated but likely to have been taking paper to London and rags back
Mar 1829 (Vol. 40)	3985	Nk	Thomas Ebbern (senior)	Sow, Warks?	Nk	Narrow boat, trade not stated but likely to have been coal*
Vol. 43 (1831)	4226	Charlotte	Mines Royal Copper Co	Harefield	Nk	Barge – trade not stated, but clearly related to the copper business
Vol. 43 (1832)	4254	Nk	John Hatton	Berkhamsted	Nk, but likely to have been himself	Not stated, likely to have been coal
Vol. 43 (1832)	4261	Nk	John Hatton	Berkhamsted	Nk, but likely to have been himself	Not stated, likely to have been coal
Vol. 49 (1832)	4864	Nk	Thomas Ebbern and Lane	Sowe (sic)	Nk	Narrow boat – trade not stated, but likely to have been coal*
Vol. 49 (1832)	4868, 4869, 4870	Nk	Thomas Ebbern (junior)	Durrants Hill Wharf, Hemel Hempstead	Nk	Narrow boats, trade not stated. In the 1843 tithe award Thomas Ebbern* is the owner of this wharf (plot 1117) – see Ch 6
Vol. 49 (1832)	4873	Nk	Ann Landon and Sons	Aylesbury	Nk	Narrow boat

181

Vol. (year)	Gauging no.	Name or fleet no. (where stated)	Owner/operator	Place of ownership	Builder and year (where known)	Notes
Vol. 49 (1832)	4875	Nk	Thomas Ebbern (junior)	St Albans Wharf, Hemel Hempstead	Nk	Narrow boat, trade not stated. This wharf was at Apsley, not part of the Boxmoor wharf complex*
Vol. 49 (1836) (sic)	4886	Nk	Thomas Landon	Aylesbury	Nk	Narrow boat, trade not stated. Likely to have been related to Ann Landon
1841 (Vol. 64)	6315	Nk	John Hatton	Berkhamsted	Nk, but likely to have been himself	Not stated, likely to have been coal
1841 (Vol. 64)	6325		James Hobb	Marsworth	Nk	Not stated
1841 (Vol. 64)	6336	Nk	John Hatton	Berkhamsted	Nk, but likely to have been himself	Not stated, likely to have been coal

Appendix C
Canal-related property in Hertfordshire c.1840

From tithe maps 1838–44 – Hertfordshire parishes (north to south).[1]

Landowner	Year/plot no.	Occupier	Usage
Puttenham			No facilities provided
Tring			There was no tithe award for Tring
Aldbury	1840	DSA4/2/2	No facilities provided
Wigginton	1842	DSA4/73/2	
GJCCo	140	Self	Lock House
Countess of Bridgewater	141	Thomas Landon	House, wharf
Elizabeth Loxley	142	Thomas Landon	Cowroast inn
Northchurch (western)	1840	DSA4/73/2	
Society of Friends	102	James Dell	Garden
James Dell	101	Self	Iron foundry, blacksmith's shop
James Dell	103	Self	House, barn and yards
Pickford and Co	84	Self	Cottage, stables, meadow
James Dell	85a	Thomas Green, John Pocock, William Turton	Beerhouse
James Dell	85	Self	
Countess of Bridgewater	49	Thomas Landon	Cowroast Wharf and yard[2]

1 HALS, DSA4/73/2 (Wigginton), DSA4/2/2 (Aldbury), DSA4/73/2 (Northchurch), DSA4/19/2 (Berkhamsted), DSA4/48/2 (Hemel Hempstead), DSA4/64/2 (King's Langley), DSA4/63/2 (Abbots Langley), DSA4/111/2 (Watford), DSA4/80/2 (Rickmansworth).
2 These plots appear in the tithe apportionments of both Wigginton and Northchurch. There is no explanation for this.

Landowner	Year/ plot no.	Occupier	Usage
Countess of Bridgewater	52	Thomas Landon	Cowroast Inn
GJCCo	82		
GJCCo	82a		The canal
GJCCo	9		Cowroast lock/toll house
Berkhamsted	**1839**	DSA4/19/2	
Duchy of Cornwall	344	Countess of Bridgewater	Wharf and yard
Duchy of Cornwall	342	George Cook	House
John Tompkins	356	Self	(Castle) Wharf and yard
Execrs of Charles Gordon	380, 389	Charles Collens	Meadows
John Dunn	394	William Key	Part of wharf
David Norris	396, 397	Sarah Claridge	Part of wharf
Charles Collins	400	Joseph Goodman and others	Cottages
Berkhamsted School	401	John Hatton	Garden
Berkhamsted School	403	John Hatton	House, yards and wharf
James Hailey	404	John Hatton	Garden
Berkhamsted School	395	William Key, Hannah Picton	House, cottage, timber yard and buildings
Countess of Bridgewater	409, 411	Daniel Norris, Sarah Littleboy	Part of mill head, part of (lower) mill, house
GJCCo	337		the canal
GJCCo	381	Charles Howard	Ravens Lane lock house
GJCCo	339	Thomas Archer	Lock House, lock 53
GJCCo	118	John Allum	Lock 49 (Northchurch) lock house
GJCCo	129	Henry Wimbush	Lock 50 (Bushes) lock house
GJCCo	149	Francis How	Lock 51 lock house
Northchurch (eastern)	**1840**		
David Batchelor	733	Charles Collens	(Ravens Lane) Wharf, house and yard
Countess of Bridgewater	552	Daniel Norris	Part of (Lower) Mill
Countess of Bridgewater	504	Sarah Littleboy	House (Bourne End), mill, etc
James Field	559	Joseph Tents, James Weedon	Smithy?
GJCCo	734	Self	Strip next to Lock 55

CANAL-RELATED PROPERTY IN HERTFORDSHIRE

Landowner	Year/plot no.	Occupier	Usage
GJCCo	558	Self	Lock 55 (top side)
GJCCo	676a	Self	Lock 56
GJCCo	564	Self	The canal
Hemel Hempstead	**1843**	DSA4/48/2	
Corner Hall div			
GJCCo	1035a	Self	Canal from Belswains to Dock
GJCCo	1100	William Hunter	(Frogmore) Mill head and tail from 1038 to parish boundary
GJCCo	1106	William Hunter	Mill house, yard, garden etc.
GJCCo	1111	Thomas Emily	Lock house and garden
GJCCo	1107	William Johnson	Cottage and garden
Rev Christian Borkhardt	1225	Thomas Franklin	Brick kiln Ground
Rev Christian Borkhardt	1225a	Thomas Franklin	Brickfield
Rev Christian Borkhardt	1226	Thomas Franklin	Wood in ditto
William Cole	1055	Joseph Freeman	Beer shop and premises
Thomas Elisha Deacon	1025	Self	House, tannery and premises
Thomas Elisha Deacon	1025a	Self	Buildings and yard
Thomas Elisha Deacon	1031	Self	Farm buildings
Thomas Ebburn	1112	Self	Great Field (arable) (13 acres)
Thomas Ebburn	1113	Self	Cottage, (St Albans) Wharf, dock
Thomas Ebburn	1115	Self	Gravel pit (1 rood)
Thomas Ebburn	1117	William Robinson	Cottage, garden and (Albion) Wharf
Rev Thomas White	1032	William Howard	House and garden
Rev Thomas White	1033	Horatio Hawkins	Yard, wharf, dock, building, house and garden (1 acre)
John Dickinson	1110	Self	Meadows and river by Frogmore End
Two Waters Division			
John Gore	1101	Self, Thomas Turner, empty	Wharf and two cottages
John Dickinson	1096	Self	Meadow at Apsley

Landowner	Year/plot no.	Occupier	Usage
John Dickinson	1097	Self	Stream in ditto
Charles Statham	591	Elizabeth Kinder	Meadow at Two Waters
George Davison	593	Self	Meadow at Two Waters
John Smith	592	Self and Ruth Godwin	Meadow at Two Waters
Thomas Ebburn	1074	Self	Building ground
Field's End division			
Boxmoor Trustees	612	GJCCo	Clay pits
Boxmoor Trustees	1028	Robert Bleakley, William Tipping	Boxmoor Wharf, buildings etc.
GJCCo	1035	Self	Canal and towpath from Billingsgate to Howard's Wharf
GJCCo	57	Thomas Boyle	Lock house and garden
GJCCo	605	John Jeffrey	Lock house and garden
GJCCo	599	Richard Cooper	House, premises and garden
GJCCo	600	John Stevens	House, (Two Waters) mill, premises, garden
GJCCo	601	John Stevens	Mill head and tail from canal to 1041
GJCCo	602	John Stevens	Garden
Elizabeth Field	53	James French	(Winkwell) Wharf and stable
Josiah Hales	627	Self	House, foundry etc.
John Woodstock	628	Self and others	House, mill, 9 cottages and beer house
Town Division			
John Austin	332	Self, James Austin and others	Public house, cottage, wharf, 8 other cottages at the Fishery
Charles Lambert	359	William Hunter and others	Mill cottages and gardens at the Fishery
Gas Light and Coke Company	680	John Cox	Gas House, yard and garden
Sarah Hill	759	Self	Ironmonger's shop and cottage
Henry Hill	358	Henry Norris	Brickyard and wharf
John William Liddon	726	Self	Brewery, malting yard

CANAL-RELATED PROPERTY IN HERTFORDSHIRE

Landowner	Year/plot no.	Occupier	Usage
George Thorp	755	Self	House, warehouse and premises
Henry Campbell White	635	Henry Pedley, William Chambers	House, garden, coal yard
High Street Division			
William Henry Cranstone	1257a	Self	?
Shadrach Godwin	855	Joseph Cranstone	?
Gas Light and Coke Company	680	John Cox	Gas works, garden
Bovingdon	1838		
Henry Campbell White	90, 91	James Holloway	Fishery meadow and river
Hon Granville Dudley Ryder	92, 126	William Rose	Grass meadows
GJCCo	88	Self	Lock house and garden
GJCCo	89	Self	Canal and towpath
Boxmoor	85		Common meadow (tithe free)
King's Langley	1838	DSA4/64/2	
John Dickinson	109	Self	Apsley Mill
John Dickinson	134a	Self	Land and house next to Nash Mill
Thomas Toovey	353, 354	Self	Yard and premises (water mill)
John Monk	583	Self, John Slade, John Price	4 houses, wharf, yard and buildings
Sparrows Herne turnpike	578	Road	Road from turnpike to canal bridge and waterside
GJCCo	115, 134, 345	Self	The canal
GJCCo	565	Self	Lock house and garden, lock 70 (Home Park)
John Andrew Groome	631	Self	Brewery (corner of High Street and road from canal)
Abbots Langley	1841	DSA4/63/2	
Michael Drew	156	George Jaynes	(Hunton Bridge) coal wharf

Landowner	Year/plot no.	Occupier	Usage
John Dickinson	484	Self	Home Park Mill
John Dickinson	1033	Self	Nash Mill
John Dickinson	816	Self	Mansion (Abbots Hill)
John Goodwin	157, 158	George Jaynes	House, premises
John Goodwin	176, 177	John Carpenter	House and premises
John Goodwin	168	William Howard	Hunton Bridge Mill
John Goodwin	178	George Bone	Lock house and garden
GJCCo	173a	Edmund Fearnley Whittingstall	Meadow
GJCCo	183, 682	Self	Plantation, slipe of land
GJCCo	680	Self	Lock house and garden (Lock 69a)
GJCCo	1018	Self	Lock house and garden (Apsley Bottom Lock)
GJCCo	1036	Self	Lock house and garden (Nash Top Lock)
GJCCo	1038	Self	The canal, including Lady Capel's Lock
GJCCo	681, 1016	Self	Gardens
GJCCo	1017b	George Saunders	'Part of Cow Meadow'
Watford	**1844**	DSA4/111/2	
Cloth Workers Company	1628	James Smith	Hampermill paper mill
Earl of Clarendon	1044	James and Frederick Leach	Grove Mill etc.
John Dyson	126	Self	Brewery etc.
Christopher Dalton	200	James White	Water corn mill
Joseph Edmonds	1035	Thomas Ebburn	Lady Capel's Wharf
Earl of Clarendon?	1034	Not attributed	Grove Wharf
Earl of Essex	1020	Self	
Earl of Essex	1079	William Hutchings	Fisherman's lodge and garden
Earl of Essex	1067	Self	Water corn mill
Thomas Rock Shute	1780	Self	Rookery silk mill
GJCCo	1066	Self (tithe free)	Iron bridge lock and house

CANAL-RELATED PROPERTY IN HERTFORDSHIRE

Landowner	Year/ plot no.	Occupier	Usage
GJCCo	1068	Self (tithe free)	Cassiobury Park lock and house
GJCCo	1074	Self (tithe free)	The canal
GJCCo	1095	Self	Arable, slipe
GJCCo	1025	John Willoughby	Cottage and garden (by Grove Mill Lane bridge)
Rickmansworth	*1838*	DSA4/80/2	
GJCCo	1231	Self	Cassio Bridge lock and house
Gonville and Caius College	1237	John Cooper	Cassio Bridge New Wharf, yard and outbuildings
GJCCo	1239	Joseph Rogers	Cottage and garden
GJCCo	1240	Joseph Rogers	Cassio Bridge Wharf
John Dickinson	1244	Self	Garden
John Dickinson	1245–1247	Cottagers	10 cottages
John Dickinson	1253	Self	Common Moor (Croxley) Mill
Gonville and Caius College	1257	George Smith	Chalk quarry
GJCCo	1266a	Self	Lot Mead lock and lock house
Harrow Turnpike Trust	1651	Emma Dyer	Toll Bar
John Dickinson	1655–1657	Self	Batchworth Mill
John Dickinson	1658	Self	Mill house
Matthew Pickford	1630	Self	Stables
GJCCo	1631	Self	Batchworth lock and lock house
GJCCo	1632	Self	Land next to Pickford's stables
GJCCo	1626	Self	Town Wharf lock
George Alfred Muskett	1620, 1621, 1622	John Laxton	Batchworth Bridge Wharf
John Laxton, Christopher Laroche	1618a	John Laxton	Frogmore Wharf
John Laxton	1618	Self	Frogmore Wharf

Landowner	Year/plot no.	Occupier	Usage
Jane Skidmore	1560, 1613, 1614, 1617	John Laxton	Frogmore Wharf
GJCCo	1555	Self	Mill meadow
Joseph Strutt	1047		Half Moon PH
Trustees of Samuel Salter	1469	Letitia Griffith, Joseph Gristwood	2 tenements
Trustees of Samuel Salter	1360, 1360a	John Cooper	Town Wharf and buildings
Trustees of Samuel Salter	1358	John Cooper	Wharf meadow
Trustees of Samuel Salter	1359	John Cooper	Cottage and garden
Trustees of Samuel Salter	1814	William Farnborough	Blacksmith's shop
Trustees of Samuel Salter	1483a, 1484	Joseph Beeson, blacksmith	Blacksmith's yard
Trustees of Samuel Salter	1344	Thomas Fellows, William Capel	Brewhouse
Trustees of Samuel Salter	1342	Thomas Fellows, William Capel	Malting
Trustees of Samuel Salter (Thomas Fellows)	1394	Thomas Fellows, William Capel	Malthouse, timber yard
Thomas Rock Shute	1457	Self	Silk mill
Joseph Skidmore	1458	John Boraston	Silk mill meadow
Mines Royal Co	956, 956a	Self	Meadows
GJCCo	1266	Self	Canal and towpath
GJCCo	1266a	Self	Lot Mead lock house
GJCCo	1603	Self	Stockers lock house
William Wooldridge	1116	Thomas Weedon	Scots Bridge Mill
King's College Cambridge	978	Richard Morton	Troy Cut
King's College Cambridge	969–972	Richard Morton	Troy Farm and mill

Appendix D
Sparrows Herne turnpike: simple financial model, 1786–1806

The revenues of the trust, drawn from the treasurer's journal accounts, in the period before the canal building started are presented at Table D-1.[1]

Examination of the accounts suggests that one problem for the finances of the turnpike throughout the period lay in the steady increase in the bills paid for work done, gravel and stones procured and so on, while another lay in the level of debt. Wages of the toll gate keepers did not increase at all in this whole period – Watford and Ridge Lane gates were taken as a pair and their keepers paid £109 4s a year altogether, while the keepers of the more remote, and less used, New Ground and Veetches gates were paid £27 6s each a year, less by 1806 than a labourer. Labour cost was remitted to some extent by parish compositions (money contributed by parishes, but small sums not included here), but not nearly enough. The burden of interest payments is clear: the loan debt was £6,745 in 1786, and was still £5,455 in 1793. No balance sheet is provided with the six-monthly accounts, so neither the rate of burn of the borrowed capital nor how much capital remained in 1786 are clear: but by 1794 it was being reduced quickly. This continued after work on the canal started (Table D-2): revenue increased somewhat in 1794 and 1796, but outgoings did so more quickly.

Operational losses were high at this time, and were increasing as receipts stayed level and costs continued to rise. This is not evidence that the canal had any direct impact: the trends were established before cutting started, although some canal-construction traffic may be included. But it does suggest that the overall levels of traffic were increasing slowly until the canal opened through Watford in late 1796.

With the canal open throughout, toll receipts decreased further before rising again towards 1806 (Table D-3), during which year the Watford and

---

1   HALS, TP4/28, 29, 30, 31, Sparrows Herne turnpike, treasurer's journal accounts; Bogart, 'Turnpike trusts'.

Ridge Lane gates were farmed out to a contractor. But the outgoings had increased very markedly, and the operational losses were considerable in every year, not helped by continuing high interest payments on loans at 5 per cent or 4.5 per cent. It is possible, but cannot be confirmed, that the drop in tolls was due to the early years of the canal's full operation, but it seems unlikely that the canal was responsible for the continued high outgoings.

Tables D-4 and D-5, with Figures D-1 and D-2, show the disproportionate amount of tolls collected at the different gates, with most coming in the south either side of Watford (Watford and Ridge Lane gates). This continued as the canal was being built and afterwards. The distortion in 1805 was largely due to the fact that Watford and Ridge Lane gates were farmed for the second half of the year, and payment of the fees was made in advance. We do, nonetheless, see a very pronounced drop in the tolls in 1797 as the canal opened from the south, although it recovered somewhat afterwards: the drop was almost entirely due to the Watford and Ridge Lane gates, through which traffic as far north as Berkhamsted had to pass. This confirms that traffic from London was diverted to some alternative – the Grand Junction Canal seems the most likely destination, although the volume of trade due to that diversion is insignificant compared with the total toll revenue of the Grand Junction Canal Company. The small receipts at the northern gates were almost unchanged.

The fact that the Watford gates took the lion's share of the total tends to confirm that most of the traffic on the turnpike was coming from London but not getting much further than Berkhamsted, if that far; and the return traffic was generated largely on the London side of Berkhamsted. The implication is that the Sparrows Herne was not an artery of freight from the Midlands to London: its users were much more local, generally interested in Watford, Hemel Hempstead and Berkhamsted. This suggests that its trade was generally that of those towns: to London wheat, flour and other agricultural produce, paper and some silk and cotton; and returning coal, manures, cotton and silk skein, manufactured goods as well as raw materials. But, as Dan Bogart has shown, up to 50 per cent of the revenue was from passenger traffic, further reducing the contribution made by freight.[2]

It should be pointed out that this analysis of the affairs of the Sparrows Herne turnpike is at variance with some of the findings of Bogart, who has examined in much more detail a very much wider sample of English turnpike trusts. The figures, however, do not appear to support any other conclusion about this particular case.

The situation towards the end of the period, as the railway, strongly opposed by the trustees as the canal never was, began to threaten, led to a

---

2 Bogart, 'Turnpike trusts', p. 499.

deep review of the operation of the turnpike.[3] It confirmed that the financial problems, in particular the need to borrow significant amounts at 4.5 per cent or 5 per cent interest, were deep-rooted. Various measures outside the scope of this study were taken: but it confirms that the role of the canal in the operation of the turnpike was unhelpful, in that it had restricted the growth of freight traffic on the turnpike which might otherwise have developed.

Table D-1. Revenues before cutting of the canal in Hertfordshire, 1786–94.

Year	1786	1787	1788	1789	1790	1791	1792	1793	1794
Toll revenue	£1217.90	£1249.20	£1330.45	£1243.45	£1279.90	£1356.65	£1322.30	£1428.40	£1523.70
Outgoings	£1197.63	£1038.58	£1200.35	£1301.30	£1210.18	£1416.95	£1247.80	£1695.55	£2138.00
Inc interest payments	£455.85	£246.80	£353.80	£257.10	£268.00	£268.55	£279.50	£245.45	£245.60
Loan repayments									
Operating profit/loss	£20.27	£210.62	£130.10	-£57.85	£69.72	-£60.30	£74.50	-£267.15	-£614.30

Table D-2. Revenues during the cutting of the canal, 1794–9.

Year	1794	1795	1796	1797	1798	1799
Toll revenue	£1523.70	£1425.75	£1554.50	£1371.70	£1201.00	£1131.55
Outgoings	£2138.00	£2055.95	£1750.25	£1511.05	£1635.80	£1851.95
Inc interest payments	£245.60	£239.20	£251.70	£246.70	£243.25	£248.40
Loan repayments				£50.00	£50.00	
Operating profit/loss	-£614.30	-£630.20	-£195.75	-£139.35	-£434.80	-£720.40

Table D-3. Revenues with the canal in operation, 1800–6.

Year	1800	1801	1801	1803	1804	1805	1806
Toll revenue	£1094.40	£1111.15	£1182.65	£1249.70	£1341.15	£1476.48	£1601.54
Outgoings	£2186.40	£2320.05	£2234.00	£2202.90	£2325.20	£2416.70	£1252.15
Inc interest payments	£316.25	£316.25	£242.00	£241.00	£252.70	£248.80	£209.70
Loan repayments							
Operating profit/loss	-£1092.00	-£1208.90	-£1051.35	-£953.20	-£984.05	-£940.22	£349.39

---

3   HALS, TP4/13, Sparrows Herne turnpike, minutes 1836–40.

Table D-4. Individual toll gate takings 1786–94.

Tolls	1786	1787	1788	1789	1790	1791	1792	1793	1794
Watford Gate	£543.60	£560.70	£589.50	£538.85	£544.20	£575.75	£562.40	£642.00	£676.00
Ridge Lane	£389.50	£392.40	£426.10	£382.40	£397.20	£434.70	£418.00	£427.40	£467.20
New Ground	£201.80	£211.90	£224.25	£221.80	£227.00	£237.00	£237.40	£247.10	£258.20
Veeches	£83.00	£84.20	£90.60	£100.40	£111.50	£109.20	£104.50	£111.90	£122.30
Total toll revenue	£1,217.90	£1,249.20	£1,330.45	£1,243.45	£1,279.90	£1,365.65	£1,322.30	£1,428.40	£1,523.70

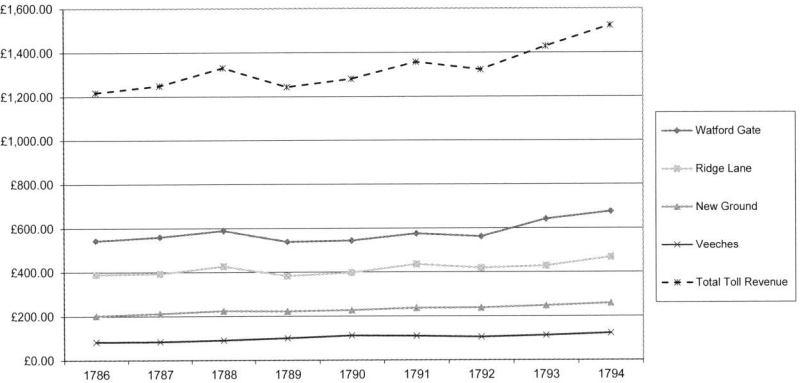

Figure D-1. Individual toll gate takings 1786–94.

Table D-5. Individual toll gate takings 1795–1805.

Tolls	1795	1796	1797	1798	1799	1800	1801	1802	1803	1804	1805
Watford Gate	£632.50	£691.95	£564.95	£453.80	£436.40	£429.00	£421.70	£432.75	£453.70	£509.00	£831.03
Ridge Lane	£406.20	£445.80	£395.80	£334.50	£319.40	£309.95	£327.20	£336.00	£359.90	£383.65	£183.30
New Ground	£254.20	£292.70	£284.65	£299.40	£252.05	£236.95	£250.20	£296.30	£297.80	£308.90	£313.40
Veeches	£132.85	£123.95	£126.30	£113.50	£123.70	£118.50	£112.05	£117.10	£138.30	£139.60	£148.75
Total toll revenue	£1,425.75	£1,554.40	£1,371.70	£1,201.20	£1,131.55	£1,094.40	£1,111.15	£1,182.15	£1,249.70	£1,341.15	£1,476.48

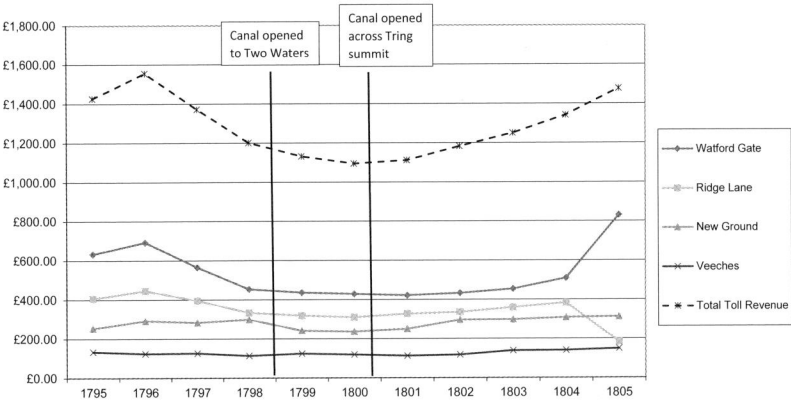

Figure D-2. Individual toll gate takings 1795–1805.

Bibliography

Primary sources
1841 Census Enumerations (www.findmypast.co.uk, accessed 3 April 2016)
HO/107/438/1 Abbots Langley.
HO/107/438/20–22 Rickmansworth.
HO/107/439/5–8 Watford.
HO/107/440/1 Aldbury.
HO/107/440/3–4 Berkhamsted.
HO/107/440/5 Northchurch.
HO/107/441/5–8 Hemel Hempstead.
HO/107/441/12 Kings Langley.
HO/107/442/2 Puttenham.
HO/107/442/5–7 Tring.
HO/107/442/9 Wigginton.
HO/107/447/5–9 St Albans.
HO/107/1136/27 Sow [Warks].

Acts of Parliament (short title)
2 & 3 Ph. & Mary c.8 Highways Act 1555.
5 Eliz.I c.13 Highways Act 1562.
14 Car.2 c.6 Highways Act 1662.
2 Geo.3 c.63 Sparrows Herne turnpike, 1762.
33 Geo.3 c.35 An Act for the Encouragement and Relief of Friendly Societies – 'Poor Act', 1793.
33 Geo.3 c.80 Grand Junction Canal, 1793.
34 Geo.3 c.24 Grand Junction Canal – authorisation of collateral cuts, 1794.
35 Geo.3 c.8 Grand Junction Canal – variation of line through Cashiobury Park, 1795.
35 Geo.3 c.85 St Albans Canal, 1795.
58 Geo.3 c.16 variation of line past Apsley and Nash Mills.
2 & 3 Will.4 c.45 The Representation of the People Act [Reform Act], 1832.

4 & 5 Will.4 c.76 Poor Law Amendment Act, 1834.
6 & 7 Will.4 c.71 Tithe Commutation Act, 1836.

British Library
Baskerfield, Thomas, 'Hertfordshire', Shelfmark Add. MS 9062.
General Reference Collection 713.i.27(2), 'William Jessop, *Report to the Committee of the Subscribers to the Grand Junction Canal*', Northampton, 24 October 1792.
The Gentleman's Magazine, vol. 64.

Centre for Buckinghamshire Studies
Gray and Chaplin Archive GJC/9.

Dacorum Heritage Trust
DAHCT 51.015 receipt for payment (Richard Bard Harcourt), 20 May 1801.

Directories
Holden's *Annual London and County Directory for the Year 1811, Vol. III* (London, 1811; reprinted Norwich, 1996).
Kent's Directory for 1794 (London, 1794)
Pigot's *Royal National and Commercial Directory and Topography for the Counties of Essex, Herts and Middlesex* (London, 1823).
Pigot's *Royal National and Commercial Directory and Topography for the Counties of Essex, Herts and Middlesex* (London, 1832).
Pigot's *Royal National and Commercial Directory and Topography for the Counties of Essex, Herts and Middlesex* (London, 1839).
Post Office, *Directory of Essex, Herts, Kent, Middlesex, Surrey and Sussex* (London, 1848).
Robson's *London Directory and Classification of Trades*, Part IV (Waggons) (London, 1832).
The London Directory for 1798 (London, 1798).
Universal British Directory of Trade, Commerce and Manufacture, vols II–V (London, 1792–98) (Vol V Hathi Trust digital library, https://babel.hathitrust.org/cgi/pt?id=njp.32101072916255;view=1up;seq=188, accessed 1 May 2019).

Gonville and Caius College archives
BUR/XXIX (13) Mr Best's opinion in the case of Strutt v Bovingdon, January 1805.
BUR/XXIX (17) report from William Custance, steward of the manor of Croxley, to the bursar of the college, August 1812.

BIBLIOGRAPHY

Guildhall Library, City of London
Pyne, W.H., *Costume of Great Britain* (London, 1808).

Hertford Museum
HTFM4180.1.9.28, *Lock on the canal, Birkhamsted* (watercolour), by James Wilcox (1842).

Hertfordshire Archives and Local Studies (HALS)
1821 census – abstract of answers and returns.
44209B map, '16 Square Miles round Chorleywood', George Thompson, 1805.
Bryant's *Map of Hertfordshire 1822* – sheet 3 (Hertfordshire Records Society, 2003).
D/Eb 1296 Z1 Inventory of Two Waters Mill.
D/ECp.T11 Indenture (Hatley and Essex vs GJCCo), April 1826.
D/ELs Q35(2) note from trustees of Boxmoor Trust (n.d).
D/ELs Q35(6) Letter from R.C. Sale (GJCCo) to Smith & Grover, 30 April 1837.
D/ELs Q35(8) letter from Harry Grover to GJCCo, 25 Aug 1820.
DE/B1157 B11 Draft agreement between the Master of the Ruislip Workhouse and Thomas Watson of Watford to wind silk in the workhouse, 1792.
DE/Hx/B25 Rules of Hertfordshire Friendly Societies, 1823–1852.
DP/2/8/1 Aldbury vestry minutes 1702–1822.
DP/19/11/2 Berkhamsted overseers' assessments and accounts 1806–1823.
DP/19/11/3 Berkhamsted rate assessments 1831.
DP/19/12/3 Berkhamsted overseers' accounts 1755–1804.
DP/37A/29/1 *Regulations and Prospectus of the Hertfordshire Savings Bank*, 20 March 1816.
DP/47/12/3 Hemel Hempstead overseers' rates and accounts 1791–1804.
DP/47/12/4 Hemel Hempstead overseers' rates 1804–1811.
DP/47/12/13 Hemel Hempstead overseers' accounts 1811–1816.
DP/64/12/4 Kings Langley overseers' accounts 1798–1807.
DP/64/12/6 Kings Langley overseers' accounts 1815–1821.
DP/74/8/1 Northchurch vestry book 1650–1806.
DP/85/8/2 Rickmansworth vestry minutes 1796–1818.
DP/85/8/9 Rickmansworth vestry minutes 1783–1796.
DP/111/8/19 Tring vestry minutes 1782–1815.
DP/111/26/2, Tring enclosure map, 1799.
DP/117/8/2 Watford vestry minutes 1785–1812.
DSA4/2/2 Aldbury tithe map, 1840.

DSA4/19/2 Berkhamsted tithe map, 1838.
DSA4/48/2 Hemel Hempstead tithe map, 1841.
DSA4/63/2 Abbots Langley tithe map, 1839.
DSA4/64/2 Kings Langley tithe map, 1835.
DSA4/73/2 Wigginton tithe map, 1841.
DSA4/80/2 Rickmansworth tithe map, 1839.
DSA4/111/2 Watford tithe map, 1842.
GH/323 abstract of title – endorsements – conveyance from John Strutt and others to William Praed and Charles Harvey, 9 and 10 January 1811.
GH/514 abstract of title ... Batchworth Mill and lands purchased of Messrs Strutt by the Grand Junction Canal Company, 15 May 1811.
GH/525 copy of court roll, surrender by William Strutt, George Benson Strutt and Catherine his wife, and Joseph Strutt ... the company of proprietors of the Grand Junction Canal ... , 26 October 1811.
QS/Misc/2643 Return of Friendly Societies registered with the Clerk of the Peace, 1832.
QSMB Vol. XIII Hertford Easter quarter sessions 1818.
QS Plan 497/1 record of meeting of commissioners appointed to consider damage to fishery of John Parsley at Kings Langley, 1830.
TP4/2–5 Sparrows Herne turnpike, minutes of meetings of the trustees 1772–1840.
TP4/13 Sparrows Herne turnpike, minutes 1836–40.
TP4/28–32 Sparrows Herne turnpike, journal accounts of income and expenditure, 1786–1865.
TP4/93 Sparrows Herne turnpike, draft accounts of tolls collected at each gate, and tables of tolls charged by Sparrows Herne and neighbouring turnpikes 1821–22.
TP5/2 St Albans and South Mimms turnpike, minutes of meetings of trustees 1790–1810.
TP5/3 St Albans and South Mimms turnpike, minutes of meetings of trustees 1810–1827.
TP5/15 St Albans and South Mimms turnpike, treasurer's accounts 1785–1822.

London Metropolitan Archives, City of London
MJ/SP/1804/10/1015 Middlesex quarter sessions, 1804 – appeal of Grand Junction Canal Company against rating assessment by Isleworth parish.
MJ/SP/1810/07/009 Middlesex quarter sessions, 1810 – appeal of Grand Junction Canal Company against rating assessment by Paddington parish.
MS11936/359 Sun Insurance policy 556297, April 1789.
Numbered Illustrations from *Collage*: 321981, 322394, 324191, 23231, 304138.

BIBLIOGRAPHY

The National Archives (TNA)
C101/3295 'Sale of Land at Rickmansworth' in Chancery, July 1828.
MH12/4679 correspondence between T R Shute and Watford Board of Guardians, 1 and 3 November 1835.
MPH 1/451 'Plan of an Estate the Property of Mr Joseph Strutt Situate in the Parish of Rickmansworth in the County of Hertford'.
RAIL 830/1 GJC select committee minutes 1816–1819.
RAIL 830/7 GJC select committee minutes 1839–1841.
RAIL 830/35 GJC general committee minutes 1816–1821.
RAIL 830/37 GJC lower district committee minutes 1793–1797.
RAIL 830/38 GJC upper district committee minutes 1796–1798.
RAIL 830/39 GJC general assembly and general committee minutes 1793–1798.
RAIL 830/42 GJC general committee minutes 1807–1811.
RAIL 830/44 GJC general committee minutes 1828–1858.
RAIL 830/63 GJC treasurer's cash book 1794–1801.
RAIL 830/64 GJC treasurer's cash book 1806–1811.
RAIL 830/66 GJC treasurer's cash book 1820–1826.

National Waterways Archive
BW99/1/2/1 sale agreement.
BW99/5/3 GJCCo *Regulations* 1807.
BW99/6/5/1, /3, /14, /17, /37 GJCCo gauging registers vols 1, 3, 27, 30, 49.
BW99/12/1/7 GJC deposited plan 1792.
WM/72/58 GJC chain book, 1893.

Newspapers
County Press, 11 April 1835 (HALS).
Northampton Mercury, 10 April 1802 (British Newspaper Archive <https://www.britishnewspaperarchive.co.uk>, accessed 16 March 2019).
The Times (digital archive <https://www.gale.com/intl/c/the-times-digital-archive>, accessed 21 May 2015). 4 July 1801, 15 January 1802, 20 May 1802, 10 July 1804, 17 November 1804, 12 December 1804, 5 September 1805, 19 December 1806, 17 June 1815, 19 September 1835.

Parliamentary archives
HL/PO/PB/3/plan4 deposited plan, Cashiobury Park variation.
HL/PO/PB/3/plan22 Map of the Grand Junction Canal from Box Moor to the bottom of the 4 Langley Locks shewing the proposed variation by the river and Frogmoor, Apsley and Nash Mills (Deposited Plans, 1818, A–K).

Secondary sources
Agar, Nigel, *Behind the plough* (Hatfield, 2005).
Agar, Nigel, 'The Hertfordshire farmer in the age of Industrial Revolution', in Doris Jones-Baker (ed.), *Hertfordshire in history* (Hertford, 1991), pp. 247–56.
Albert, W., *The turnpike road system in England 1663–1840* (Cambridge, 1972).
Armstrong, W.A., 'Food, shelter and self-help', in Mingay (ed.), *Agrarian history vol. VI*, pp. 729–54.
Armstrong, W.A. and Huzel, J.P., 'Food, shelter and self-help, the Poor Law and the position of the labourer in rural society', in Mingay (ed.), *Agrarian history vol. VI*, pp. 729–809.
Austin, Wendy, *The Tring silk mill* (Tring, 2014).
Bagwell, Philip, *The transport revolution from 1770* (London, 1974).
Bagwell, Philip and Lyth, Peter, *Transport in Britain* (London, 2002).
Barker, T.C. and Savage, Christopher, *Economic history of transport in Britain* (London, 2012).
Birtchnell, Percy, *A short history of Berkhamsted* (Berkhamsted, 1972).
Blagrove, David, *At the heart of the waterways* (Bugbrooke, 2003).
Blaug, Mark, 'The myth of the Old Poor Law and the making of the New', *The Journal of Economic History*, 23/2 (1963), pp. 151–84.
Bogart, Dan, 'Turnpike trusts and the transportation revolution in 18th-century England', *Explorations in Economic History*, 42/4 (2005), pp. 479–508.
Bogard, Dan, 'The turnpike trusts of England and Wales', in L. Shaw-Taylor, D. Bogart and M. Satchell (eds), *The online historical atlas of transport, urbanization and economic development in England and Wales c.1680–1911* <https://www.campop.geog.cam.ac.uk/research/projects/transport/onlineatlas/>, accessed 1 February 2019.
Borsay, Peter (ed.), *The eighteenth-century town* (London, 1990).
Burton, Anthony, *The canal builders* (Cleobury Mortimer, 1993).
Byrom, Richard, *William Fairbairn: the experimental engineer* (Market Drayton, 2016).
Chambers's *Encyclopaedia vol. III* (London, 1868).
Chambers, J.D. and Mingay, G.E., *The agricultural revolution* (London, 1978).
Chartres, J.A., *Market integration and agricultural output in seventeenth-, eighteenth- and early nineteenth-century England* (Leeds, 1993).
Clark, C.W., *Abbots Langley then* (Cockfosters, 1997).
Clark, Peter (ed.), *The Cambridge urban history of Britain II 1540–1840* (Cambridge, 2000).

Clark, Peter, 'Small towns 1700–1840', in Clark (ed.), *Cambridge urban history of Britain II*, pp. 733–74.
Clarke, M., *The Leeds and Liverpool canal* (Barnoldswick, 2016).
Cobbett, William, *Rural rides*, vol. 2 (London, 1830; reprinted London, 1912).
Collins, E.J.T., 'The agricultural servicing and processing industries', in Mingay (ed.), *Agrarian history vol. VI*, pp. 384–96.
Conder, F.R., *The men who built railways* (1868; reprinted London, 1983).
Cooke, George Alexander, *Topographical and statistical description of the county of Hertford* (London, c.1805–1810).
Cornwall, G., 'The Swan Inn', *The Rickmansworth Historian*, 7 (1964), pp. 127–33.
Cromarty, Dorothy, 'Topography and settlement', in Yaxley (ed.), *History of Hemel Hempstead*, pp. 1–16.
Crompton, G.W., 'Canals and the Industrial Revolution', *Journal of Transport History*, 14/2 (1993), pp. 93–110.
Cussans, J.E., *History of Hertfordshire*, vol. III (Hertford, 1881; reprinted Wakefield, 1972).
Daunton, M.J., *Progress and poverty* (Oxford, 1995).
Davis, Jean, *Aldbury* (Aldbury, 1987).
Dawes, Margaret and Ward Perkins, C.N., *Country banks of England and Wales* (London, 2000).
De Salis, Henry Rodolph, *Bradshaw's canals and navigable rivers* (London, 1904; reprinted Oxford, 2012).
Doggett, N. and Hunn, J., 'The origins and development of medieval Berkhamsted', *Hertfordshire Past and Present*, 18 (1985), pp. 18–36.
Ellis, Joyce, *The Georgian town* (Basingstoke, 2001).
Evans, Joan, *The endless web* (London, 1956).
Faulkner, Alan, *The Grand Junction Canal* (Newton Abbot, 1972).
Faulkner, Alan, *The Grand Junction Canal*, 2nd edn (Rickmansworth, 1993).
Faulkner, Alan, *The Grand Junction Canal in Hertfordshire* (Hatfield, 1993).
Ferguson, Hugh and Chrimes, Mike, *The contractors* (London, 2014).
Finerty, Eric, 'The history of paper mills in Hertfordshire', *The Papermaker and British Paper Trade Journal* (April–June 1957), pt 1 pp. 308–14, 326, pt 2 pp. 422–6, pt 3 pp. 510–18.
Finn, Margot and Smith, Kate, *The East India Company at home, 1757–1857* (London, 2018).
Forsyth, Mary, 'The establishment and development of Watford', in Slater and Goose (eds), *County of small towns*, pp. 276–300.
Forsyth, Mary, *Watford* (Stroud, 2015).
Freeman, Mark, *St Albans: a history* (Lancaster, 2008).
Gerhold, Dorian, *Road transport before the railways* (Cambridge, 1993).

Gladwin, D.D., *The waterways of Britain* (London, 1976).
Goose, N., *Population, economy and structure in Hertfordshire in 1851: St Albans and its region* (Hatfield, 2000).
Goose, N., 'Population, 1801–1901', in David Short (ed.), *Historical atlas*, pp. 56, 57.
Goose, N., 'Urban growth and economic development in early modern Hertfordshire', in Slater and Goose (eds), *County of small towns*, pp. 96–126.
Gourvish, T.V. and Wilson, R.G., *The British brewing industry 1830–1980* (Cambridge, 1994).
Green, Thomas, *On Hertford and its environs 1775*, eds Jean Purkis and Philip Sheail (Hertford, 2016).
Hadfield, Charles, *British canals* (Newton Abbot, 1974).
Hadfield, Charles, *The canal age* (Newton Abbot, 1968).
Hadfield, Charles, *The canals of the East Midlands* (Newton Abbot, 1981).
Hadfield, Charles, *The canals of south and southeast England* (Newton Abbot, 1969).
Hadfield, Charles and Skempton, A.W., *William Jessop, engineer* (Newton Abbot, 1979).
Hands, Roger and Joan, and Davis, Eve, *The book of Boxmoor* (Hemel Hempstead, 1994).
Hanson, Harry, 'Canal travel', *Journal of the Railway and Canal Historical Society*, 25/2 (1979), pp. 70–73.
Hassell, John, *A tour of the Grand Junction Canal* (London, 1819; reprinted London, 1968).
Hastie, Scott, *Berkhamsted* (Kings Langley, 1999).
Hastie, Scott, *Kings Langley* (Kings Langley, 1991).
Hayman, A.W., 'The Bell Inn', *The Rickmansworth Historian* 2 (1961), pp. 19–21.
Haythornthwaite, J.P., *The parish of Kings Langley* (London, 1924).
Higgs, E., *Making sense of the census* (London, 1989).
Hills, Richard L., *Papermaking in Britain 1488–1988* (London, 1988).
Hodskinson, Joseph, *Plain and useful instructions to farmers – or an improved method of management of arable land* (London, 1794).
Horn, Pamela, *Life and labour in rural England* (Basingstoke, 1987).
Horn, Pamela, *The rural world* (London, 1980).
Howarth, David, *Trafalgar* (London, 1969).
Howes, Hugh, *Wind, water and steam* (Hatfield, 2016).
Hunt, J.E., 'A history of Dudswell Mill', *Hertfordshire's Past*, 27 (1989).
Huzel, J.P., 'The labourer and the Poor Law, 1750–1850', in Mingay (ed.), *Agrarian history vol. VI*, pp. 755–809.

Jennings, Sheila, 'The silk industry', in Short (ed.), *Historical atlas*, pp. 96, 97.
Jennings, Sheila, 'A ravelled skein: the silk industry in south west Hertfordshire 1790–1890', PhD thesis (University of Hertfordshire, 2002).
Jennings, Sheila, 'The textile mills at Rickmansworth', *Rickmansworth Historical Society Newsletter*, 52 (2001), pp. 4–7.
Jeppesen, Chris, 'Growing up in a company town – the East India Company presence in south Hertfordshire', in Margot Finn and Kate Smith, *The East India Company at home, 1757–1857* (London, 2018), pp. 251–71.
Johnson, William Branch, *The industrial archaeology of Hertfordshire* (Newton Abbot, 1970).
Jones, E.L., *Agriculture and the Industrial Revolution* (Oxford, 1974).
Langton, John, 'Urban growth and economic change', in Clark (ed.), *Cambridge urban history of Britain II.*, pp. 453–90.
Lansberry, H.C.F., 'The St Albans canal', *Hertfordshire's Past*, 7 (1967), pp. 3–8.
Lines, Clifford, *Companion to the Industrial Revolution* (Oxford, 1990).
Longman, G., *A corner of England's garden* (Bushey, 1977).
Mandl, G.T. (ed.), *300 years of paper* (London, 1985).
Mandl, G.T, 'The case for common sense', in Mandl (ed.), *300 years of paper*, pp. 1–19.
Mathias, Peter, *The brewing industry in England 1760–1830* (Cambridge, 1959).
Mein, Jonathan, *The decline of the White Hart, St Albans, in the eighteenth and nineteenth centuries* (St Albans, 2012), <http://stalbanshistory.org/page_id__474.aspx?path=0p2p145p147p>, accessed 22 February 2019.
Mingay, G.E. (ed.), *The agrarian history of England and Wales, vol. VI, 1750–1850* (Cambridge, 1989).
Mingay, G.E., *Arthur Young and his times* (London, 1975).
Morris, Kate and Merrick, Julia, *St Albans: gentry town* (St Albans, 2014).
Morris, R.J., 'Voluntary societies and British urban élites', in Borsay (ed.), *Eighteenth century town*, pp. 338–66.
Munby, Lionel (ed.), *A history of Kings Langley* (Kings Langley, 1963).
Musson, A.E. and Robinson, Eric, *Science and technology in the Industrial Revolution* (Manchester, 1969).
Navickas, Katrina, *Protest and the politics of space and place* (Manchester, 2016).
Newman, F.R.J., 'The socio-economic impacts of the coming of the railways to Hertfordshire, Bedfordshire and Buckinghamshire, 1838–1900', PhD thesis (University of Hertfordshire, 2014).
Parrott, E.V., 'A survey of the industrial archaeology of Rickmansworth (part 2)', *The Rickmansworth Historian*, 27 (1974), pp. 672–5.

Perren, Richard, 'Markets and marketing', in Mingay (ed.), *Agrarian history vol. VI*, pp. 190–274.
Petticrew, Ian and Austin, Wendy, *The railway comes to Tring* (Tring, 2013).
Petticrew, Ian and Austin, Wendy, *The waterway comes to Tring* (Tring, 2014).
Phillips, John, *A general history of inland navigation, foreign and domestic*, 1st edn (London, 1792).
Phillips, John, *A general history of inland navigation, foreign and domestic*, 5th edn (London, 1805; reprinted Newton Abbot, 1970).
Pilkington, Austin, 'Frogmore and the first Fourdrinier', in *A history of The British Paper Company, 1890–1990* (published privately by The British Paper Company Ltd, 1990), pp. 20–6.
Plaistowe, David, 'The Plaistowe family in Rickmansworth', *The Rickmansworth Historian*, 7 (1964), pp. 151–4.
Plumb, J.H., *England in the eighteenth century* (London, 1968).
Porteous, J. Douglas, *Canal ports* (London, 1977).
Pressnell, L.S., *Country banking in the Industrial Revolution* (Oxford, 1956).
Priestley, Joseph, *Navigable rivers and canals* (London, 1831; reprinted Newton Abbot, 1969).
Reed, Michael, 'The transformation of urban space 1700–1840', in Clark (ed.), *Cambridge urban history of Britain II*, pp. 615–40.
Richards, Sheila, *Tring* (Tring, 1974).
Richardson, Christine, *The waterways revolution* (Hanley Swan, 1992).
Robinson, M. Gwennah and Wrigley, Valentine J., 'Hemel Hempstead in the nineteenth century', in Yaxley (ed.), *History of Hemel Hempstead*, pp. 99–136.
Rook, Tony, *A history of Hertfordshire* (London, 1984).
Rothery, Karen, 'The implementation and administration of the New Poor Law in Hertfordshire, c.1830–1847', PhD thesis (University of Hertfordshire, 2017).
Rowe, Anne and Williamson, Tom, *Hertfordshire: a landscape history* (Hatfield, 2013).
Rowley, Martin, 'British weather from 1700 to 1849' <http://www.pascalbonenfant.com/18c/geography/weather.html>, accessed 21 March 2019.
Sharpe, Pamela, 'Population and society 1700–1840', in Clark (ed.), *Cambridge urban history of Britain II*, pp. 491–528.
Shaw, Solomon, *History of Verulam* (London, 1815).
Sherwood, Jennifer, 'Influences on the growth and development of medieval and early modern Berkhamsted', in Slater and Goose (eds), *County of small towns*, pp. 224–48.
Short, David (ed.), *Historical atlas of Hertfordshire* (Hatfield, 2011).

Shorter, A.H., *Paper mills and paper makers in England 1494–1800* (London, 1957).
Sinclair, David, *The pound – a biography* (London, 2000).
Slater, T., 'Roads, commons and boundaries in the topography of Hertfordshire towns', in Slater and Goose (eds), *County of small towns*, pp. 67–95.
Slater, T. and Goose, N. (eds), *A county of small towns* (Hatfield, 2008).
Slater, Terry and Goose, Nigel, 'Panoramas and microcosms', in Slater and Goose (eds), *County of small towns*, pp. 1–26.
Smiles, Samuel, *Lives of the engineers*, vol. 1 (London, 1862; reprinted Newton Abbot, 1968).
Stanyon, Michael, 'Inventory of Two Waters Mill', *The Quarterly (Journal of the British Association of Paper Historians)*, 61 (2007), pp. 14–18.
Stanyon, Michael, 'Papermaking', in Short (ed.), *Historical atlas*, pp. 80, 81.
Sugden, John, *Nelson: the sword of Albion* (London, 2014).
Sweet, Rosemary, *The English town* (Harlow, 1999).
Toms, Elsie, *The story of St Albans* (St Albans, 1962).
Trevelyan, G.M., *English social history volume three: the eighteenth century* (Cambridge, 1950; reprinted London, 1963).
Trevelyan, G.M., *English social history volume four: the nineteenth century* (Cambridge, 1949; reprinted London, 1963).
Trinder, Barrie, '18th- and 19th-century market town industry: an analytical model', *Industrial Archaeology Review*, 24/2 (2002), pp. 75–89.
Trinder, Barrie, 'Industrialising towns', in Clark (ed.), *Cambridge urban history of Britain II*, pp. 805–36.
Turnbull, Gerard, 'Canals, coal and regional growth during the Industrial Revolution', *Economic History Review*, 2nd ser. 40/4 (1987), pp. 537–60.
Turnbull, Gerard L., 'Pickfords 1750–1920: a study in the development of transportation', PhD thesis (University of Glasgow, 1972).
Turnbull, Gerard L., *Traffic and transport: an economic history of Pickfords* (London, 1979).
Victoria history of the county of Hertfordshire, vol. 4 (London, 1902–1914).
Wallace, Eileen, *Children of the labouring poor* (Hatfield, 2010).
Wallis, Ken, 'The River Bulbourne', *The Chronicle*, 5 (March 2008), pp. 29–37.
Ward, J.R., *The finance of canal building in eighteenth century England* (Oxford, 1974).
Warner, Pat, *Lock keeper's daughter* (Shepperton, 1986).
Whitaker, Allan, *Brewers in Hertfordshire* (Hatfield, 2006).
Williams, Henry, *History of Watford* (London, 1884; reprinted Watford, 1976).

Williamson, Tom, 'Gardens and industry: the landscape of the Gade Valley in the nineteenth century', in Deborah Spring (ed.), *Hertfordshire garden history* (Hatfield, 2012), pp. 121–47.

Wood, Arthur L., 'The bailiwick and the market', in Yaxley (ed.), *History of Hemel Hempstead*, pp. 163–90.

Woodforde, James, *The diary of a country parson*, ed. J. Beresford (Oxford, 1978).

Wrigley, E.A., *The path to sustained growth* (Cambridge, 2016).

Wrigley, E.A., 'Urban growth and agricultural change: England and the Continent in the early modern period', in Borsay (ed.), *The eighteenth-century town*, pp. 39–82.

Wrigley, E.A. and Schofield, R.S., *The population history of England 1541–1871* (London, 1981).

Yaxley, Susan (ed.), *History of Hemel Hempstead* (Hemel Hempstead, 1973).

Young, Arthur, *Annals of agriculture* (London, 1791).

Young, Arthur, *Enquiry into the progressive value of money in England* (London, 1812).

Young, Arthur, *General view of the agriculture of Hertfordshire* (London, 1804; reprinted Newton Abbot, 1971).

Index

References to illustrations, maps and tables are in *italics*. References to footnotes are suffixed 'n'. Main topic references are shown in **bold** text.

Abbots Langley 55, 153, **154**, 183, 187
    land purchases by GJC 73–4
    paper mills 108, 111, 151
    population 44, 138–9
    water mills 85
    wharfs 106
Agriculture 1–3, 6, 11, 69–70
    and the canal 117–21, 149, 165
    in Hertfordshire 32–5, 44, 46, 87–90, 140, 144, 164, 169
    labour market 19, 22–5, 27,
    labourers' work in 19, 22, 25–6, 34–5, 125, 154, 167–8
    types of 5, 26, 32, 140
    women working in 15, 35, 45, 151
Aldbury 28, 40n, 55, 88, **145–6**, 167
    and GJC 75, 88
    population 138–9
Army, the 16, 19, 23, 93
Ashness, Mr, canal carrier and wharfinger 100, 101, 106, 124, 178
Ashridge 28, 47, 55, 101
Assembly rooms 16, 52, 172, 174

Bakers 17, 28, 171
Batchelor & Hughes, road carriers 162
Berkhamsted 2, 40n, **47–9**, 89, 107, 125n, **147–9**, 167
    and Northchurch 54
    banks 149
    boatbuilding 124, 148, 163, 180–2
    breweries 39, 121–2
    canal carrying to and from 98, 123–4, 142, 146
    coach and waggon services 31n, 48, 51, 97, 162
    industry and commerce 100, 113, 116, 119, 151, 172
    population 44, 138–9, 149
    progress of GJC building 75, 77, 79
    turnpike 64, 91–2, 131
    wharfs 106, 113, 124, 167
Bevan, Benjamin, canal engineer 126
Bird, George Ryder & Son, canal carrier 97, 178
Blacksmiths 5–6, 17, 35
Boxmoor 50, 99, 103, 151–2

damage to property by GJC 127, 133, 168
land purchases by GJC 72, 74
wharfs 97, 103, 106, *109*, 141–2, *150*, 163
wharfingers 99, 100–1, 116, 124, 152
Brewing in Hertfordshire 35, **38–40**, 107, **121–3**, 165–6, 171–2
in towns *see entry for each town*
Bridgewater, Duke of 10, 47, 62, 67
Bridgewater, Earl of 19, 106

Canal Mania 23, 60, 65
Carpenters 5, 7, 86, 105
Cashiobury 28, 77, 85, 103–4, 116, 124
Cattle 35, 46, 47, 144–5, 152, 159
Clarendon, Earl of 42, 51, 74, 77, 79, 167
Clark, Esther, road carrier of St Albans 161
Coal 3, 5, 26, 40, **116–17**, 141
and the GJC 61–2, 65, 79, 113, 132, 153
cost 59, 61–2, 116, 143, 168
merchants 99, 101, 124–5, 150, 152–3, 156
Colonies, the 18, 28
Copyhold land 7, 73, 75
Corner Hall (Hemel Hempstead) 50, 74, 150–1, 185
Cotton, spinning of 52–4, 104, 107, 111–14, 128, 165
Cowper, Earl 42
Cranstone, John, iron founder 6, 141, 172
Crowley Hickling & Co, canal carrier 97

Dickinson, John, papermaker
disputes with GJC 132, 167,
paper maker 104, 106, 115, 126, 129, 132, 151, 164, 167
tenant of GJC 111, *114*, 129, 158,
using GJC 111, 124, 134, 155, 158, 164,
Dorrien, Thomas, banker 40, 119

East India Company 7, 8n, 16, 29, 66
Ebbern (aka Ebborn and Ebburn), Thomas, coal merchant of Watford and Hemel Hempstead 97, 125, 152, 156, 178
Ebbern, Thomas William, coal merchant of Sowe, Warks 179, 181
Enclosure, consequences of 5, 8, 24–5, 33–5, 46
Engineering 6, 155, 174
Essex, Earl of 42, 51, 74, 77, 103, 116, 121, 156, 167
Evans, David, silk throwster 113

Farming *see* Agriculture
Fotherley Whitfeld, Henry, lord of the manor of Rickmansworth 74, 105, 156
Fourdrinier, Henry and Sealy, paper makers 50, 103, 108, 110–11, 115, 129, 166
Fourdrinier papermaking machinery 110, 157

Gas lighting 136–7, 141, 145, 149, 155, 157, 160, 163
Gauging of canal boats 101, 109, 119–20

Grand Junction Canal 1, 32–3, 59–60, 65, 79, 107, 117, 142, 148
    business relationships 111, 115, 127–33, 151
    engineering 61, 79
    land purchases 71–5, 84–5
    operation 62, 67, 81–3, 92–3
    wharfs 103, 105, 144, 152, 155, 158
Green, Thomas, musician and poet 21, 43
Grove, the 74, 77, 79, 85, 102, 104, 116, 155–6
Grover, Harry, solicitor 126, 151
Grover, William, wharfinger 100, 143

Harty, William, silk throwster 112
Hatley, Newman, farmer 117, 119, *120*, 121, 124
Hatton, John, boat builder 100, 124, 148–9, 180–2, 184
Hemel Hempstead 28, 43, **49–51**, 55, 106, 125–6, **149–52**
    banks 40, 155, 163
    canal branch 61, 68
    canal carrying services 109, 124, 142
    coach and waggon services 97, 162
    corn market 49
    gas lighting 141
    industry and commerce 6, 125, 166, 172–4
    land purchases by GJC 72–4
    paper mills 36, 50, 108, 111, 151
    population 44, 138–9
    progress of GJC building 75, 79, 90

    relief of the poor 116–17
    straw plait 49
    turnpike 50, 92, 94
    water supplies to canal 85
    wharfs 101, 103, 109, 150, 167
Hertford 21, 43
Higglers 20, 22, 44
Holladay, John, carrier and wharfinger 16n, 100, 103, 124, 176–7
Horseley Iron Works Co 97
Howard, Charles, wharfinger 184
Howard, George, coal dealer, Watford 156
Howard, Simeon, banker, Rickmansworth 159–60
Howard, Thomas, miller 100, 124, 160, 177
Howard, William, wharfinger 101, 103, 177–8, 185

Industrial production
    domestic system 3–4, 18, 34, 49, 107
    factory system 3, 5, 11
    hand crafts 4, 48, 55
    mass production 3–4
Industry 24–5, 27
    control of costs 9, 12
    growth 3–6, 10, 17, 23, 26, 59, 61
    in Herts 34, 35–40, 47–50, 52–3, 107–8, 111–15, 151, 162, 169
Inns 12, 16, 21, 39, 42, 47, 50, 53n, 57–8, 121, 160–1, 172
Iron 5, 35, 40, 98, 106, 110, 137, 166
    foundries 6, 17, 115, 133, 141, 149, 152, 156–7
Ironmongers 6, 166

Jessop, William, GJC engineer 23–4, 61, 69, 75, 77, 82–4, 88

Kay, William, silk throwster 13
Kenworthy & Co, road and canal carrier 97, 161
Kings Langley 39, 54–5, 78, 85, 106, 108, 117, 121–2, **153–4**
    damage to property by GJC 75, 127
    GJC and Poor Rate 125–6,
    land purchases by GJC 74
    paper mills 108, 111, 151
    population 44, 138–9
    progress of GJC building 75, 77, 78,
    water mills 85, 115, 132
    wharfs 100, 106, 119

Labourer 5, 37, 100, 116, 125, 143, 145, 151, 156, 158
    agricultural 42–3, 45, 87, 119, 140–1, 147 *see also* Agriculture, labourers' work in
    canal 24, 85–90, 167
    wages 50, 62, 80, 88, 119, 140–1, 168, 169
Land, value and ownership of 6, 8, 34, 66–7, 71–4, 84, 101, 103, 105, 107, 165
Landon, Ann & Sons, canal carrier 98, 180–1
Landon, Thomas, wharfinger 106, 124, 144, 178, 180, 182–3
Landowners 2, 5–8, 16, 33, 46
    and the canal 66–7, 71–4, 165, 169
    investment by 10, 12
    role in farming 34
    role in local government 18
Lane, John, innkeeper 48
Langleybury tunnel 77, 79, 132
London
    as destination 96–8, 104, 113, 115, 122, 135, 142, 160–2, 169
    migration to 93, 137
    port and metropolis 91–2, 165

Malthus, Rev Thomas 42–3
Malting 3, 5, 33, 38–9, 55, 107, 121, 171, 173
Market
    for agricultural goods 2–4, 19–21, 27, 33, 69, 140
    for agricultural labour 22–3
    for manufactured goods 4, 18, 19, 27, 37–8, 59, 157
Market town 6, 7, 11, 17, 43, **45–54**, 68, **153–63**, 171–4
    decline of 22, 48, 52
McAdam, John, road engineer 141
Mercers 17
Mills 3
    and the canal 11, 84–5, 93, 124, 128–9, 130, 132–3, 167
    cotton 38, 107, *114*
    flour 23, 54–5, 107, 115–16, 128, 132–3, 153, 155
    horse powered 39, 121
    owners 9, 20–1, 107–8, 127, 155
    paper 85, 105, *109*–11, 126, 157–8, 159
    in towns and parishes *see entry for each town*
    silk 37–8, 51–2, 57, 102, 103, 105, 112–13, 143, 145, 155, 162–3, 166
    water 6, 35, 47, 50, 52, 53, 128, 152

INDEX

Millwrights 6
Mines Royal Copper Company 106, 124, 159, 166, 179, 181, 190
Monk, John, coal merchant and wharfinger 153
Moor Park 28, 80, *123*
More Park *see* Moor Park
Munn, Lewis, paper maker 107, 158–9
Muskett, George A., banker and MP 105, 155, 159, 163, 189

Navy, Royal 16, 19, 23, 56
Nelson, Admiral Lord 7, 56
Nicholls, Mrs Sarah, wharfinger 106
Northchurch 54, 73–4, 88, 106n, 148, 167, 183–4
    damage to property by GJC 75
    population 138–9

Pack horses 12, 57
Paper making 23, **36–7**, 54, 107, 108–11, 129
Paumier, Peter, silk throwster 51, 112
Peacock and Willetts, boat builders 123, 176
Peel, Williams and Peel, steam engine builders 113
Pickfords, road and canal carrier 14, 31–2, 57, 96–7, 141–3, 161
Plaistowe, William, wharfinger 105, 109n
Ploughwrights 5
Poor Law 139
Population
    of England 2–4, 15, 17, 136, 171
    growth 2–3, 16, 23, 27, 34, **137–8**
    of west Herts 34, 40, 44, 89, 139–41, 164
    of west Herts towns 17, 44, 117, 138–9 *see also entry for each town*
Proto–industry *see* Industrial production, domestic system
Puttenham 138–9, 145–6, 167

Reading and Hatfield turnpike 32, 53, 103, 155
Rickmansworth 21, 42–3, **52–4**, *104*, **158–60**, 172–4
    agriculture 35, 160
    banks 159
    breweries 39, 121–2, 166
    canal branch 122
    canal carrying services 98–9, 124, 142
    coach and waggon services 31n, 162
    land purchases by GJC 74, 189–90
    market 159
    paper mills 36, 54, 107–8, 111, 159
    population 44, 117, 138–9
    progress of GJC building 75, 79
    relief of the poor 80, 90, 125–6
    silk and cotton mills 37–8, 112–14, 157, 166
    turnpikes 31, 53
    wharfs 100, 103, 105, 114, 156, 158, 163, 167
Road freight transport
    capacity 116–17, 141
    cost 11, 62
    development 10, 95–7, 161–2, 165

in agriculture 68–9, 118–19
in industry 32, 37, 110, 112, 166
Roads 7, 11, 13–14, 90
   importance 10, 20, 57, 141
   in Herts *30*, 31, 62–4, 69
   investment 12, 40, 66, 92
   maintenance 16, 20, 64, 106
Robins Mills & Co, canal carriers 97, 161
Robinson & Co, canal carriers 97
Robinson, William 179n, 185
Rooper, John, farmer 119

Salisbury, Marquess of 42
Sex ratio, in towns and parishes 15, 27, 45–51, 55, 57, 160
Sheep
   manuring by 2, 3, 33, 35, 49
   market for 51, 115
Shipton & Pratt, canal carriers 97
Shoemakers 17
Shute, Thomas Rock, silk throwster 112, 113, 157, 159, 188, 190
Silk, spinning *see* Silk, throwing
Silk, throwing 26, 35, **111–13**, 162–3,
Skidmore, Emmott, wharfinger 100, 105, 177
Skidmore, Joseph 74, 190
Smith, Sir Drummond Bt, estate owner 46, 65, 84
Sparrows Herne turnpike *30*, 31, 55–6, 78, **90–2**, 96, 98, 104, 144
   and the GJC 63, 94, 168,
   and the railway 142
   maintenance 64
   passing through towns 46–7, 50–1, 53
   tolls 32, 62, 64

traffic 97–8
Speenhamland 25–6
Spencer, second Earl (and family), GJC committee member 28, 56, 160
St Albans **56–8**, 136, 141, **160–3**
   banking 41, 57, 155, 163
   breweries 57–8
   canal branch 28, 68, 79
   coach and waggon services 31n, 32, 57, 91, 95–6
   gentrification 30, 56
   industry 107, 112, 114, 163
   population 44, 138–9, 162
   relief of the poor 125n
   silk and cotton mills 37, 112, 114
   straw plait 34n, 107
   turnpikes 31, 32, 57, 62, 64, 142
Steam
   GJC using 83, 116, 128, *130–1*, 132, 143
   power 5–6, 39, 104–5, 108, 113, 132, 153–4, 157, 166
   for drying paper 110, 157–8
Straw plait 4, 23, 48, 57–8, 107, 125n, 140, 143
   sold in markets 34n, 49, 145, 151, 163
Straw plaiting 34, 46, 147, 156, 161, 168
Strutt, John and Joseph, cotton spinners 38, 52, 104, 114, 127–9, 190

Tailors 17, 172
Tate, James 100, 176
Tidcombe, George 6, 155, 157, 172
Tompkins, William and John, wharfingers 101, 148, 184

Tring 9, 28, 35, 40n, **45–6**, 107, 117, 140, **143–5**
   breweries 121–2
   canal carrying services 142, 146
   canal summit *82*
   canal workers 90, 93
   coach and waggon services 31, 51, 97–8, 145, 162
   damage to property by GJC 75
   enclosure act 35, 46
   industry and commerce 112–13, 133, 166, 172–4
   land purchases by GJC 84
   market 43, 145, 172
   turnpike road 31, 91, 94, 106
   population 44, 46, 137, 139, 145–6
   progress of GJC building 77, 79, 88, 90, 93
   relief of the poor 80
   water supplies 72, 76, 83, 128
   wharfs 100, 106, 113, 147, 163, 167
Turnpike roads 16–17, 20, 30–1, 36, 40, 63, 162 *see also* Sparrows Herne Turnpike; Reading and Hatfield Turnpike; St Albans Turnpike *and entries for each town.*
Two Waters 50, 75, 90, 97, 107, 150–2, 168
   paper mill 36, 50, 108, *109*, 110, 128, 129, 133, 152
Verulam, Earl of 42, 79

Watford 28, **51–2**, 74, 141, **155–7**, 173–4
   agriculture 35
   banking 155, 163
   breweries 121–2, 155
   canal branch 61, 68, 79
   canal carrying services 98, 124, 142
   canal diversion 77, 85
   coach and waggon services 31n, 142, 161–2
   coal 62, 116, 125, 152, 156
   industry and commerce 6, 39, 51, 156–7
   market 43, 159
   turnpike roads 31, 51, 64, 91, 168
   paper mills 36, *102*, 155, 157,
   population 44, 54, 138–9
   relief of the poor 80
   silk mills 37–8, 51, 112–13, 156–7, 166
   wharfs 100, *102*, 103–4, 155–6, 163, 167
Watson, Thomas, silk throwster 38, 112
Wheelwrights 5, 35
White, John, wharf owner 103
Whitehouse & Sons, canal carriers 97
Wigginton 55, 88, 138–9, 147, 167
Wilkins and Ashness, wharfingers and boat owners 100–1, 106, 113
Woolams, Mr, silk throwster 112
Worster & Stubbs, canal and road carrier 97

Young, Arthur, agricultural commentator 8, 22, 33–4, 46, 48, 69, 89, 119, 121, 125n
   on canals 60, 67, 117
   on enclosure 33, 46
   on roads 20, 64